CONTESTING CARCERAL LOGIC

Contesting Carceral Logic provides an innovative and cutting-edge analysis of how carceral logic is embedded within contemporary society, emphasizing international perspectives, the harms and critiques of using carceral logic to respond to human wrongdoing, and exploring penal abolition thought.

With chapters from scholars across many disciplines, people in prison, as well as penal abolition activists, the book explores what a future without carceral logic would look like, as well as how such a future is to be developed. The book is also an exploration of penal abolition thought as it is developing in the twenty-first century. Diverse geographical, cultural, identity and experiential frames inform the book's themes of analysing carceral logic as it harms disparate people in disparate places, creating anti-carceral knowledge, exploring case studies pointing to radical alternatives, and to contesting carceral logic from below. Ultimately, *Contesting Carceral Logic* provides the reader with an alternative and critical perspective from which to reflect on carceral logic, the punitive state and the criminalizing systems that almost exclusively dominate across the world. Finally, it raises the questions of how we are to build communities as well as transform our response to human wrongdoing in ways that are not defined by racism/ethnocentrism, class war and heteropatriarchy.

Contesting Carceral Logic will be of great interest to not only scholars and activists, but also provides an introduction to key carceral issues and debates for students of penology, criminology, social policy, geography, politics, philosophy, social work and social history programmes in countries all around the world.

Michael J. Coyle, PhD, is Professor, Department of Political Science and "Criminal" Justice, California State University, Chico. He is the author of *Talking Criminal Justice: Language and the Just Society* (Routledge 2013) and the forthcoming *Seeing Crime: Penal Abolition as the End of Utopian Criminal Justice* (University of California Press).

Mechthild Nagel teaches philosophy and Africana studies and is the Director of the Center for Ethics, Peace, and Social Justice at SUNY Cortland. She co-edited *Prisons and Punishment: Reconsidering Global Penality* (Africa World Press, 2007) and *The End of Prisons: Voices from the Decarceration Movement* (Rodopi, 2013).

Routledge Studies in Penal Abolition and Transformative Justice Series

Michael J. Coyle and David Scott

The *Routledge Studies in Penal Abolition and Transformative Justice* book series provides the leading publishing location for literature that both reflects key abolitionist thought and helps to set the agenda for local and global abolitionist ideas and interventions. It fosters research that works toward the systemic and systematic dismantling of penal structures and processes, and toward social living that is grounded in relationships that consider the needs of all. This international book series seeks contributions from all around the world (east, north, south, and west) that both engages and furthers abolitionist and transformative practice, study, politics and theory. It welcomes work that examines abolition and transformative justice empirically, theoretically, historically, culturally, spatially, or rhetorically, as well as books that are situated within or at the interstices of critiques of ableism, capitalism, hetero-normativity, militarism, patriarchy, state power, racism, settler colonialism, and xenophobia.

Building Abolition: Decarceration and Social Justice
Kelly Struthers Montford and Chloë Taylor

Contesting Carceral Logic
Michael J Coyle and Methchild Nagel

https://www.routledge.com/Routledge-Studies-in-Penal-Abolition-and-Transformative-Justice/book-series/PATJ#:~:text=About%20the%20Series,global%20abolitionist%20ideas%20and%20interventions.

CONTESTING CARCERAL LOGIC

Towards Abolitionist Futures

Edited by
Michael J. Coyle and
Mechthild Nagel

Routledge
Taylor & Francis Group
LONDON AND NEW YORK

First published 2022
by Routledge
2 Park Square, Milton Park, Abingdon, Oxon OX14 4RN

and by Routledge
605 Third Avenue, New York, NY 10158

Routledge is an imprint of the Taylor & Francis Group, an informa business

British Library Cataloguing-in-Publication Data
A catalogue record for this book is available from the British Library

Library of Congress Cataloging-in-Publication Data
A catalog record has been requested for this book

ISBN: 978-0-367-75279-8 (hbk)
ISBN: 978-0-367-75132-6 (pbk)
ISBN: 978-1-003-16181-3 (ebk)

Typeset in Bembo
by codeMantra

This book is dedicated to all those harmed by the carceral state

CONTENTS

List of contributors *xi*
Acknowledgments *xv*
Foreword *xvii*
by Diana Block

Introduction: penal abolitionism as a challenge to carceral logic 1
Michael J. Coyle and Mechthild Nagel

PART I
The harms of carceral logic: people and places **15**

1 Prison provokes people into being more aggressive, hypersexualized, and prone to crime 17
Joseph (Dont'e) Williams

2 If I weren't white I'd be dead 19
Gabriella

3 Reader 20
Emanuel "Eoz"

4 Carceral other and severing of people, place and land: redefining the politics of abolition through an anti-colonial framework 22
Vicki Chartrand and Niko Rougier

5 The lawlessness of law: outlaw nation, settler colonialism, and a possessive investment in whiteness 36
Mechthild Nagel

6 Not behind bars: the rippling of carceral habitus and corrective violence on the family and community life of prison guards 50
S.M. Rodriguez and Brittany Clark

PART II
Creating anti-carceral knowledge **65**

7 Start 67
Emanuel "Eoz"

8 The only advice I got is "Stay out of trouble" 68
David Head

9 Designed to bury you in a mental grave 70
Adrian Outten

10 The courtroom 74
Phillip Johnson

11 Generating abolitionist affect: decarceral feminist methodologies and the closure of Holloway Prison 77
Carly Guest and Rachel Seoighe

12 "There is no justice, there is just us!" Towards a postcolonial feminist critique of policing using the example of racial profiling in Europe 90
Vanessa E. Thompson

13 Against penal humanism: a Foucaudian critique 105
Clécio Lemos

PART III
Case studies pointing to radical alternatives **117**

14 Feet on the ground 119
Emanuel "Eoz"

15 The system is designed for me to fail 120
Douglas Knakmuhs

16 Incarceration as the worst possible treatment for mental illness 125
Richard Sean Gross

17 The rhetoric of dehumanization: Japanese American concentration camps and the US criminalizing system 132
Michael J. Coyle and Stephen T. Young

18 RAP's significance to the formation of the British abolitionist movement 147
Marc Jacobs

19 The struggle over the Ottawa-Carleton Detention Centre: challenging neutralization techniques, fighting state inertia 160
Aaron Doyle, Justin Piché, and Kelsey Sutton

PART IV
Resisting carceral logic **175**

20 Something from here 177
Emanuel "Eoz"

21 Disenthrall 178
Emmanuel X

22 Contesting the collateral damages of imprisonment from below 184
Valeria Vegh Weis and Julieta Sosa

23 Land, race and state: situating the carceral state and the mass imprisonment of Māori in Aotearoa within the settler-colonial landscape 198
Verena Tan

24 Extreme hazards 210
Emanuel "Eoz"

Index *211*

CONTRIBUTORS

Diana Block is a founding and active member of the California Coalition for Women Prisoners, an abolitionist organization. She is the author of a memoir – *Arm the Spirit – A Woman's Journey Underground and Back* (AK Press 2009) and a novel – *Clandestine Occupations- An Imaginary History* (PM Press, 2015).

Vicki Chartrand is Associate Professor in the Sociology Department at Bishop's University, Québec. Her general research interests include penal and carceral politics, modern day colonialism, grassroots justice and collaborative methodologies. She has over 15 years of experience advocating for and with women and children, Indigenous communities and people in prison.

Brittany Clark is a graduate of Hofstra University '20 with a BA in Political Science and minors in Sociology and Criminology. She is the daughter of a former corrections officer and works full-time in the New York construction industry when she is not completing research on the criminal-legal system.

Michael J. Coyle, PhD, is Professor, Department of Political Science and "Criminal" Justice, California State University, Chico. He is the author of *Talking Criminal Justice: Language and the Just Society* (Routledge 2013) and the forthcoming *Seeing Crime: Penal Abolition as the End of Utopian Criminal Justice* (University of California Press).

Aaron Doyle, PhD, is Associate Professor of Sociology at Carleton University and has authored, co-authored or co-edited nine books. Since founding the Criminalization and Punishment Education Project in 2012, his research and teaching have focused on working with communities toward reducing and ultimately ending the use and harms of imprisonment.

Emanuel "Eoz," writer and rapper, is serving a 10-year sentence in Unit 47, San Martin, Jose Leon Suarez, Buenos Aires, Argentina. He describes his leitmotiv as "If you are creative, everything can be transformed, opportunities depend on you, and if you want something you can get it."

Emmanuel X has been incarcerated in Louisiana for ten years and is the author of several published manuscripts. He has written under several pseudonyms. He served a juvenile life sentence during which he spoke in two documentary films about redemption and inspiration for others.

Gabriella lives in the US.

Richard Sean Gross was born in 1966 in York County, Pennsylvania. He is now serving life at Phoenix prison in Montgomery County, PA. He has poetry and an essay online at <https://MinutesBeforeSix.com>. Rich is currently seeking a degree from Villanova University and commutation from the Commonwealth. Direct correspondence to: Rich Gross, FF9878, Box 33028, St. Petersburg, FL, 33733, USA.

Carly Guest is a Senior Lecturer in Sociology at Middlesex University. Her work is concerned with the personal and intimate narratives and memories of political movements, moments and institutions. Carly utilizes creative, narrative methodologies and feminist and critical pedagogies in her research and teaching practice.

David Head is serving a 40-year sentence, having been incarcerated since the age of sixteen in the state of Maryland. He is close to completing an associate degree in business management.

Marc Jacobs is a Senior Lecturer in Criminology at the Institute of Criminal Justice Studies, University of Portsmouth. His pedagogic practice seeks to stimulate students to become critically and politically enlivened while instilling an optimism that they can make a positive impact toward social justice.

Phillip Johnson is in prison.

Douglas Knakmuhs was first institutionalized at the age of 12 and has been incarcerated since the age of 16. He refuses to be a slave for the system and has been sent to solitary for refusing to work.

Clécio Lemos, PhD, in law from PUC-Rio (2018) was visiting scholar at Columbia Law School (2019). He is the author of the book *Foucault e a Justiça pós-penal* and is the Portuguese translator of *White Collar Crime* (Edwin Sutherland). He works as Professor of Law in Brazil.

Mechthild Nagel teaches philosophy and Africana studies and is the Director of the Center for Ethics, Peace, and Social Justice at SUNY Cortland. She co-edited *Prisons and Punishment: Reconsidering Global Penality* (Africa World Press, 2007) and *The End of Prisons: Voices from the Decarceration Movement* (Rodopi, 2013).

Adrian Outten is currently incarcerated at Western Correctional Institution in Cumberland, Maryland. He has been imprisoned for the last 15 years and writes for newsletters. If you would like to correspond with him, write here: Adrian Outten, # 2583871, Western Correctional Institution, 13800 McMullen Hwy SW, Cumberland, MD, 21502, USA.

Justin Piché, PhD, is Associate Professor in the Department of Criminology and Director of the Carceral Studies Research Collective at the University of Ottawa. He is also Co-editor of the *Journal of Prisoners on Prisons* and founding member of the Criminalization and Punishment Education Project.

S.M. Rodriguez is an Assistant Professor of Gender, Rights and Human Rights at the London School of Economics and Political Science. A scholar-activist, they have spent the last decade researching queer transformative justice movement-making throughout the African Diaspora and organizing with the Audre Lorde Project in New York City. They formerly worked to develop Hofstra University's programs in critical criminology and LGBTQ+ studies.

Niko Rougier is Abenaki artist incarcerated in the maximum security penitentiary Donnacona, Québec. Mr. Rougier recently testified at the Commission d'enquête sur les relations entre les Autochtones et certains services publics au Québec to document and provide insight into colonialism in the land now known as Canada.

Rachel Seoighe is a lecturer in criminology at School of Social Policy, Sociology and Social Research, University of Kent. Working from a decolonial, feminist perspective, her research examines agency and memory, state violence, power and resistance. Rachel's research is informed by and contributes to civil society activism.

Julieta Sosa is a lawyer and member of the CTEP (*Center of Workers of the Popular Economy*) and the MTE (*Movement of Excluded Workers*). She was the coordinator of the SEDyF (*Secretary of Former Detainees and Relatives*) and is currently doing grassroots work in the countryside of Argentina.

Kelsey Sutton is an MA student in the Department of Criminology at the University of Ottawa. As a member of the Criminalization and Punishment Education Project she helped create the #NOPE / No Ottawa Prison Expansion infographic series on the history of carceral expansion in the city.

Verena Tan is an East Asian advocate currently based in Naarm (Melbourne), Australia. She was raised in Aotearoa and has worked for several years in criminal and disability law and advocacy for marginalized communities. She is active in abolitionist, decolonial, feminist and anti-racist social justice movements.

Vanessa E. Thompson is a postdoctoral researcher and lecturer at the Department of Social Sciences at Goethe University Frankfurt, Germany. Her research and teaching are focused on critical racism studies, black studies, post- and decolonial feminist theories and methodologies, policing, and abolitionist and transformative justice.

Valeria Vegh Weis teaches criminology at Buenos Aires University and National Quilmes University in Argentina. She is an Alexander von Humboldt Post-Doctoral Researcher at Freie Universität Berlin. She holds a PhD in Law and an LLM in Criminal Law from UBA and an LLM from New York University.

Joseph (Dont'e) Williams is currently serving seven to fourteen years in Pennsylvania's Department of Correction. This is his third incarceration and he now studies the reasons for the system's failure to rehabilitate people.

Stephen T. Young, PhD, is Assistant Professor of Criminal Justice and Criminology at Marshall University. His primary area of research is critical criminology with a focus on the intersections of penal abolition, Appalachian studies, whiteness and anti-capitalist movements.

ACKNOWLEDGMENTS

Michael J. Coyle wishes to thank Anne Seiler, who is a conversation partner and a sounding board for developing ideas as well as an endless source of personal support and intellectual encouragement. He is also deeply conscious of all those, within and without the carceral walls, who have deeply sustained him in his work, that is ultimately done because of, inside of and with others in Greece, the US and elsewhere. He thanks them all: family, friends, colleagues, students and more.

Mechthild Nagel is grateful to her partner Philip R. Otieno. In her abolitionist work, she has been guided by people in prison, especially Tiyo Attallah Salah-El who has joined the ancestors. Mechthild has been supported by family and friends in South Africa, Kenya, Europe and North America. She also acknowledges the financial support from the SUNY Research Foundation.

FOREWORD

Battling Carceral Logic –
With Collective Care and Radical Solidarity
By Diana Block

When the California Coalition for Women Prisoners (CCWP)[1] was founded in 1995, we didn't use the term *carceral logic* to identify the warped criminal-legal policies, the distorted narratives and the punishing mindsets that had led to the exponential growth of the women's prison population which began in 1985 and continues till today. But from the beginning, our work sought to uncover the racist and sexist laws, attitudes and culture that sent women, trans and gender non-conforming (TGNC) people to prison in unprecedented numbers, and the punitive/brutalizing/humiliating conditions that structured people's experiences once they got there.

We started to fight many of these violences on the ground, launching advocacy to challenge abusive health care, sexual humiliation and harassment, rampant racism, homophobia and transphobia, separation from children and family, extreme sentences, perpetual punishment, voicelessness and invisibility. Twenty-five years later, as the movement to abolish the prison industrial complex in all of its forms has grown tremendously, we see how CCWP has been able to undermine carceral logic and win some important battles by building a community of collective care across the walls.

I started working with CCWP during its first six months. I had recently returned from being underground for 13 years. I had been part of a radical anti-imperialist project taken up in solidarity with Black and Puerto Rican liberation forces in the early 1980s. When I returned to the Bay Area at the end of 1995 with my two children, much of my time outside of work and parenting was occupied with prison visits. I visited my husband, Claude Marks, who was a political prisoner at Sheridan prison in Oregon with our two young children, and I visited women comrades who were imprisoned at FCI Dublin in the Bay Area as a result of their political actions against the state. After I attended CCWP's first International Women's Day event in March 1996 where Angela Davis was the keynote speaker, I decided that the fight for incarcerated women, the most marginalized sector of the prison population, was critical for anti-racist feminist organizing. And so I began visiting the Central California Women's Facility (CCWF) in Chowchilla, the largest women's prison in the world.

CCWP was started by women inside CCWF, formerly incarcerated women and activists in the community. When one formerly incarcerated woman, LaTonya, suggested that our acronym – CCWP – could also stand for *Caring Collectively for Women Prisoners*, we embraced the slogan – an organic expression of the type of across-the-walls community we wanted to build. Leaders inside the women's prisons knew from hard experience that caring for each other was both a lifeline and critical form of resistance in an environment where guards and staff constantly used divide and conquer tactics to control and punish the people under their authority.

For me, as well as some of the other founding members of CCWP in the outside community, the concept of collective care was a welcome, inclusive antidote to the harsh, male-dominated political line struggles of the 1960s and 1970s left. We were pushed by our connections with incarcerated and formerly incarcerated women to understand that *collective care* needed to be a core value for political engagement. And consistent visits with people inside were central to building collective care.

In my 2009 memoir, *Arm the Spirit – A Woman's Journey Underground and Back*, I describe the early experience of being part of a CCWP visiting advocacy team:

We organized visiting teams to go into the prisons on a regular basis to meet with women and develop legal advocacy strategies based upon their experiences with the prison system. Every visit was emotional, educational and galvanizing. When a visiting team walked through the multiple locking gates and heard them click shut, when we looked up and realized that we too were encased by miles of barbed wire fences, we got a tiny inkling of what it meant to be cut off from the rest of the world under the daily, arbitrary control of men and women with guns.

Once we were in the visiting room, sitting face-to-face with a woman who had a life sentence, or another who was anticipating her release in just a few months, a small miracle occurred. A spark unlocked our voices. The gates and barbed wire receded for a few hours while we talked about the children they had left behind, the girlfriends they had found in prison, and the dreams and hopes they nurtured for the future. Our conversations usually began with the enormous difficulties of their lives inside, but they branched out to encompass our lives and dreams and hopes as well (Block 2009, pp. 328–329).

Over the years, these visits have been key to contesting the carceral logic that locks up thousands of predominantly Black and Brown women/TGNC people. Torn from their children and communities, isolated and subjected to the disciplinary regimes of prison, our cross-the-walls collaborations have driven the development of CCWP's programs and campaigns to counter inhuman prison conditions and the criminal-legal system as a whole. For us collective care starts with physical, emotional and spiritual support. But it also includes fierce advocacy and organizing on multiple levels to insist on abolition and social/political/personal transformation.

The struggle for basic health care rights in the women's prisons was the specific catalyst for the formation of CCWP. Charisse Shumate, a domestic violence survivor who suffered from sickle cell disease, was the lead plaintiff in a lawsuit against the state of California and the California Department of Corrections, Shumate v. Wilson. The lawsuit demanded multiple changes in the abusive health care system that Charisse and the other plaintiffs had experienced firsthand. Charisse recognized that a lawsuit needed to be complemented by grassroots activism. CCWP was launched to challenge the ways in which Black, Brown and other women were being killed by the lack of basic health care services. The lawsuit was settled in 1997 and some gains were achieved. But most of the grossly negligent conditions continue to this day and have been exacerbated under COVID. CCWP's medical advocacy has consistently battled this lack of health care which callously sucks the life out of incarcerated people.

To provide a space where the women could directly give voice to the range of their experiences, CCWP soon decided to produce a newsletter which we called *The Fire Inside*, a name suggested by another formerly incarcerated woman, Dana. In the very first issue in June 1996, Charisse wrote:

> If we were allowed to have video cameras or tape recorders, the truth could be seen or heard about the junk yard care we receive. . . . Once again, until there is no breath in my body, I will roar the words HELP stop the killing because we are the forgotten ones.
>
> *(Shumate, July 1996)*

And in the sixth issue of *The Fire Inside*, Charisse articulated our philosophy of collective care:

> Now please don't give up. When times get rough, hold your head up ... It is not a "me" thing. It's a "we" thing, and together with the dream [legal] team and the help of CCWP (California Coalition for Women Prisoners) there is a light at the end of the tunnel.
>
> *(Shumate, December 1997)*

By offering an unfiltered record of the brutal conditions inside the women's prisons and the many beautiful forms of solidarity and resistance that are created to challenge those conditions, *The Fire Inside* subverts invisibility and the normalization of invisibility, lynchpins of the carceral system.

CCWP has always prioritized support for survivors of sexual violence. A majority of people in women's prisons have experienced some form of sexual abuse before they are arrested and convicted.[2] Once inside prison, this abuse is regimented through a daily culture of sexual humiliation and bribery as well as specific acts of assault and rape by guards and other staff. As feminists committed to racial and gender justice, we challenged the laws and legal processes that punished women for their acts of self-defense against violence. Our *Free Battered Women* project helped enact legislation (code 1473.5) which made it easier for women/TGNC people to challenge their original conviction. This significant policy win was augmented by teams of volunteer lawyers and legal advocates who have supported survivors in challenging their sentences and going to their parole hearings, resulting in the releases of hundreds of women over the years.

These affirmative programs have indirectly challenged the logic of *carceral feminism* by exposing the harms that the legal and prison systems cause women. We have insisted that carceral solutions cannot provide justice to survivors of sexual violence in a racist, heteropatriarchal society. I had first confronted early forms of *carceral feminism* in the 1970s, long before that term was coined. I was a founding member of San Francisco Women Against Rape (SF WAR) in 1973. Our principles of unity included a strong commitment to racial justice. We pointed to the racist use of the rape charge against Black men as a key form of white supremacist terror and committed ourselves to opposing the racist manipulation of sexual violence to further white supremacy and state control. However, I left the organization as the state's all-out strategy to coopt the anti-rape movement began to chip away at our organizational opposition to police and state determined forms of justice for rape "victims." Over the years, these law and order solutions became dominant within large parts of the anti-violence movement. The equation of justice with arrest, punishment and imprisonment is still widespread in the anti-violence movement and in the society as a whole. Fortunately, SF WAR, unlike many of the other feminist organizations from that period, evolved and is now led by women of color committed to racial justice principles in fighting rape and sexual assault.

The founding of *INCITE! – Women of Color Against Violence* in 2000 challenged the hold which carceral feminism had gained over the anti-violence movement. In 2001 INCITE and Critical Resistance developed a statement, which CCWP contributed to, calling upon social justice movements "to **develop strategies and analysis that address both state AND interpersonal violence, particularly violence against women**."[3] CCWP has tried to center this perspective by bringing our work with incarcerated survivors into the anti-violence movement.

In 2015, CCWP became a founding member of Survived & Punished, a national network whose mission is to end the criminalization of survivors of all forms of sexual and gendered violence. Survived & Punished anchors a vision and practice rooted in abolition and offers a radical alternative to carceral feminism. As stated on their website:

The same system that criminalizes, re-traumatizes and further abuses victims is also the one that the anti-violence movement entrusts and authorizes to protect survivors and create safety. The institutionalization of this racialized "good victim/criminal" dichotomy has left a huge portion of survivors, overwhelmingly Black women, unsupported and unaccounted for by the anti-violence movement.[4]

As the #MeToo movement exploded in 2017, righteously calling out the pervasiveness of sexual harassment and assault at all levels of society, CCWP worked with TGNC people inside the women's prisons to launch a #MeTooBehindBars campaign. The project focused on the invisible and unrecorded sexual violence occurring inside women's prisons on a daily basis. The campaign was catalyzed by a series of attacks on trans and GNC people by correctional officers. These incidents represent a backlash against hard-won legal rights for trans people in prison and the changing cultural norms regarding gender identity. The assaults expose how the carceral logic of prison systems relies on and enforces gender normativity. The #MeTooBehindBars campaign has empowered TGNC and cis women in California prisons to document and resist continued forms of harassment.

Over the past four years, as white supremacy and American nationalism have surged across the US, CCWP has built intentional solidarity with the global struggles of women against the US-led prison industrial complex. The US has exported its model of carcerality worldwide as a means of enforcing colonial and neocolonial control over subjugated populations. In particular, the US and Israel have collaborated on the development of punishment systems that include solitary confinement, torture, sexual violence, surveillance and pre-trial detention as a means of repressing the freedom struggles of entire peoples.

We have brought the experiences of Palestinian women prisoners to the readers of *The Fire Inside,* to illuminate the interconnections between their experiences. Imprisoned Palestinian women have also offered inspiring examples of creative and militant resistance to their conditions of confinement. Through slide shows, pamphlets and workshops we have tried to educate the broader anti-prison movement about the intersections between global structures of oppression and resistance. Learning about and interacting with women's struggles in Mexico, the Philippines, Brazil and Palestine has reinforced our belief that principles of collective care must expand into radical international solidarity in order to counter the global carceral order.

Our commitment to collective care has proven indispensable in the COVID era. We have provided new levels of mutual aid to incarcerated and formerly incarcerated women and TGNC folks. We have increased our regular contact with people inside prison to counter their heightened isolation and to get their reports of unsafe conditions to the public. And we have joined with many other groups to demand mass decarceration, especially for elders and medically vulnerable people, as the only effective means for reducing the risk of infection. But despite the torrent of advocacy, lawsuits and expert medical recommendations, state and Federal officials across the country have shown ruthless disregard for incarcerated lives. In a naked display of carceral logic, most prison releases have been denied to protect "public safety." In reality, the state is protecting the sanctity of a punishment system designed to crush lives and spirits.

During the Black-led uprisings that started in response to George Floyd's murder by Minneapolis police in May 2020, the term abolition has been shouted in the streets, broadcast on network TV, projected on the walls of corporate skyscrapers and painted on sidewalks and storefronts in Minneapolis, Atlanta, Los Angeles, Oakland, Louisville, Rochester and Kenosha. Its popularization signifies rejection of multiple facets of the current political/economic/social system – beyond police, ICE and prisons. At its radical heart, abolition points to the overthrow of racial capitalism and the building of a restructured society which is no longer ruled by white supremacy, gendered violence, carceral logic or capital.

In this insurgent moment, CCWP is honored to be part of a burgeoning movement that is summoning forth an abolitionist future. The struggle continues!

Notes

1 www.womenprisoners.org
2 https://www.aclu.org/other/prison-rape-elimination-act-2003-prea
3 https://incite-national.org/incite-critical-resistance-statement/
4 https://survivedandpunished.org/analysis/

INTRODUCTION

Penal abolitionism as a challenge to carceral logic

Michael J. Coyle and Mechthild Nagel

Introduction

In our era, carceral logic, or the control and punishment mindset that suggests criminalization is the best paradigm to organize human life and to solve social problems besetting the 99% overshadows government thinking and action. The dominance of carceral logic suggests that not only are modern societies indulging in an assumption that has proven false (that threats, punishment and imprisonment broadly work as solutions to social problems), but that in the process they, like a hammer that sees only contexts in which to pummel, have become carceral states that see only contexts in which to punish and imprison. Importantly, the framing and justifying of this carceral logic is one that widely ignores the colonial, racializing and capitalist contexts in which its practices (e.g., policing or imprisonment) were invented.

This book aims to lay out some of the contours of carceral logic and to contest it by highlighting penal abolitionism. *Contesting Carceral Logic: Towards Abolitionist Futures* provides an innovative and cutting-edge analysis of the way in which carceral logic has become embedded within society, and how we might think, feel and act to leave it in the dustbin of historicity. This book is an exploration of the consequences and harms of carceral logic from around the world and from within and without prison walls. As such, it is a valuable tool for students, activists and scholars engaging with critiques of carceral logic and the numerous ways in which it touches our lives.

Carceral logic leaves almost no area of modern life untouched. Primarily it centers a punitive orientation and a control-through-violence framework that belies the ideology, ethics, institutions and practices built to regulate human economies, relations, differences and problems. Almost without exception, the punitive and control orientation of carceral logic governs the dominant thinking about private and social spaces. Typically, responses to fear, poverty, homelessness, social justice struggles, child or adult transgression, the mentally ill, differently abled persons, those crossing the various borders we construct (identity, geographical, etc.) or difference of almost any kind is governed by carceral logic. Even our everyday language is riddled with labels pathologizing and criminalizing, e.g., 'victim vs. offender' that trivializes social problems and wealth distribution, 'illegal immigrant' that trivializes how global predatory capitalism loots and pillages southern economies and communities, 'super predator' that targets and oppresses non-white youth, etc. (Coyle 2013).

While some of this carceral logic results in criminalizing that is formalized in our penal institutions (law, police, courts, prisons and others), some of it remains informal or semi-informal. The less formal expressions of carceral logic are expressed in ideologies, practices and worldviews that are as deeply impactful: child-rearing, education, the ever-expanding reach of surveillance technologies and in general, through all this, what can only be called the dominance of the carceral state through the collateral consequences of criminalization (e.g., impacts on children of the incarcerated, their families and communities, for system-involved persons the loss of access to education, health care, employment and housing, as well as a general dehumanization in the social imagination and the closing of all doors).

In this book we are concerned with the almost complete grasp carceral logic has on what is called the 'criminal justice system', and how it determines the thinking and operation of penal institutions. As the volume title suggests, in *Contesting Carceral Logic: Towards Abolitionist Futures*, we are interested in contesting carceral logic with an abolitionist logic and thus in imagining a different future.

Carceral logic and penal abolition logic

Historically, as well as in modern practice, the carceral logic that has given us what is widely called 'criminal justice' is far more centered on the work of colonialism, white supremacy and racial capitalism than anything else. Though carceral defenders ceaselessly occupy themselves with the penal project's other work, i.e., responding to transgression (what they call 'crime'[1]), the origins of carceral logic are a matter of historical record.

Scholars have recognized carceral logic as a paradigm with roots in colonialism (Agozino 2003; Comack 2012; Dobchuk-Land 2017), white supremacy (Saleh-Hanna 2017), and racial capitalism (Blackmon 2009; Oshinsky 1996; Robinson 1983). Foucault (1977) recognized that the shift from corporal punishment to carceral logic was not a simple change in practice but the building of an entire carceral network that left no corner of society untouched (schools, military, business, social relations or zoos) (see also Nagel and Nocella 2013). This logic is also recognized as crisis ideology (Gilmore 2007), and an organizing principle of social space (Linebaugh 2014), the state (Gilmore and Gilmore 2008) and social policy (Brown and Schept 2017). It is also deeply argued against because of its anachronistic nature (Davis 2003), the human development and justice possibilities it eviscerates (Davis and Rodriguez 2000), and the dystopias it creates (Coyle 2014).

For decades, penal abolitionists have critiqued carceral logic for its role in giving rise to control and punishment regimes, and how these, in turn, have been used to further the colonial, racializing and capitalist agendas of dominant nation states (especially European ones). Penal abolitionists have also rejected penal reform strategies because they have failed to move the needle in any substantial way. In fact, the opposite has happened: the more criminologists and policy makers defend reforming the system, the more it has grown and pushed us to the behemoth prison-industrial complex we have today.

Discourses on carceral logic have not centered on cis women and LGBT lived experiences until very recently. Undoubtedly, the dramatic shift in carceral policies (e.g., determinate sentencing, abolition of 'good time' and 2/3 serving of a sentence, the drug war, increase in natural life sentences for a myriad of 'offenses', and increase of death-qualifying 'offenses') contributed to a need of rethinking carceral logic and how it affects groups of marginalized people. We want to acknowledge the import of BIPOC women's scholarly contributions, who argue against the expansion of the carceral state, including rape crisis centers which have traditionally aligned themselves *with* the state, advocating for more police, greater sanctions against men who harm women, in short, endorsing carceral feminism.

The acceleration of a globalized war on drugs in recent decades has greatly impacted Black and Latina women in the US subjected to lengthy sentences, leading to an explosion of women's prisons. Women are the fastest growing population to be imprisoned, which has had a tremendous impact on their kinship relations; over 80% of women in prison are mothers (Solinger et al. 2010). Queer scholar-activist women of color have been instrumental in advocating law abolitionism (Davis 2005; Mogul, Ritchie, and Whitlock 2011), in providing a global critical lens of women's incarceration (Sudbury Oparah 2005), and in critiquing carceral feminism (INCITE! 2006; Richie 2012; Shenwar and Law 2020). More recently, Liat Ben-Moshe (2020) offers a new abolitionist framework of 'race-ability' by critiquing the framework of racial criminal pathologization *and* the traumatic and disabling effects of incarceration. She critiques disability studies for ignoring racism in policing and detention and she faults penal abolitionists for discounting the centrality of disability in carceral logic (p. 27).

While there are a growing number of articles and a few books which are devoted to these movement politics and even provide a cogent analysis of reform versus abolition, etc., there are many more which obfuscate and offer solutions that do not get at the root of the problems. The discipline of criminology must be challenged for its resistance to penal abolition and for its failure to recognize the importance of a penal abolitionist logic (Schept and Brown 2017). The legal discipline and the related field of philosophy of law are mired in ideal theories of punishment, replete with concepts of individualized responsibility, culpability and calls for proportionate judgment wedded to the rule of law. Such idealization concepts have been contested by critical justice studies scholars, because the profession remains silent on why the same groups of people are sent into total institutions the world over, namely, the dispossessed, racialized, and otherwise socially disconnected from the system's powerful actors. Yet, there are a few legal scholars who are starting to take note of prison abolition and propose a theory of grounded justice (McLeod 2015). Other proposals go astray, as showcased by a recent defense of "retributive abolitionism" (Reznik 2019) or of corporal punishment in lieu of incarceration (Moskos 2011).

In current times, the socio-cultural habit of seeing 'crime' reflects a construction that has produced a theory, a set of practices, and a dominant discourse that collectively is understood as the paradigm of 'criminal justice' (Coyle forthcoming). This paradigm is based on a carceral logic that produces theory, discourse and practices that see only a small proportion of the ubiquity of 'crimes' and 'criminals' (Bohm 1986; Coyle 2018; Hulsman 1997). The logic recognizes only a small percentage of the transgressions humans complete, labels these chosen transgressions 'crimes', and names their actors 'criminals'. In time a gargantuan 'criminal justice' system has been built, and it is recognizable as the penal process through which 'criminals' traverse: from their *conceptualization* within law, to their *surveillance* through police, and finally to their *processing and management* through courts and prisons. Alongside 'criminal justice' institutions have developed intellectual disciplines rationalizing and promoting 'criminal justice' theory (Criminology) and practice (Criminal Justice). This way of seeing, this paradigm, and all the work done in its name, produces an interpretation, or better yet, a line of reasoning that we call *carceral logic* (Calavita and Jenness 2014; Shabazz 2009). The power of this logic is considerable: it overwhelmingly dominates intellectual circles concerned with transgression ('crime'), conservative as well as progressive political ideology, and consequently, public policy. As is everywhere observable (in news media, entertainment formats, public discourse, etc.), 'criminal justice' logic is naturalized (Coyle and Schept 2017).

Against carceral logic stands penal abolitionism which as both theory and action proposes another logic, the realization of which requires the dismantling of the carceral state. *Penal abolition logic* refers to the argument that for a plethora of reasons carceral logic ought to be abandoned. This is not a call for 'reform' to some supposed more successful Nordic punitive system (Barker 2013; Ugelvik and Dullum 2012) or therapeutic justice (Schept 2015). Rather, it is a rejection in the total sense that slavery abolitionists reject the slavery paradigm (Davis 2005; James 2005).

Abolition logic historicizes the carceral as a tool of white supremacy, colonialism, heterosexism, and the numerous forms of heteropatriarchal capitalist hierarchy; it contests that the *raison d'être* of 'criminal justice' is public safety and justice, rejects its assumptions about human beings, and on empirical grounds repudiates the claim that its practices respond to transgressions ('crimes') or promote a society in the interest of all. It argues for the entitlement of communities to define the terms of how they wish to live as long as they fairly, justly and equitably take account of the rights and liberties of all members; contends communities have the prerogative to choose to invest their resources to maintain those terms, maintain community agreements as well as respond to transgression (as long as no such efforts target or oppress some identities or groups over others); and maintains that sociality requires addressing the needs of all, which means designing institutions that interfere with privilege (historic and current). In sum, all these produce an interpretation, or better yet, a logic: the *penal abolition logic.* The power of this logic is strong in reason and evidence, and negligible in manifestation: it is not known (or worse, deeply misunderstood) in academic circles concerned with transgression ('crime'), is considered naïve and utopian by all political ideologies (except in social anarchist and anarcho-pacifist perspectives which are already saddled with these labels), and is consequently not considered seriously in the domain of public policy. As it is rarely observable (in news media, entertainment formats, public discourse, etc.), the absence of penal abolition logic is almost complete (Coyle and Schept 2017).

Penal abolition logic claims that despite the 'criminal justice' rhetoric of 'fighting crime', in practice what we observe is that transgression ('crime') is not being taken seriously (for the following discussion, see Coyle 2018). It would be far more accurate to say that most 'crime' is being ignored. Indeed, the conversation begins and ends with an idealism and a dis-attachment from the realities of human being and community life: that norm breaking behavior ('crime') is the norm, that what we have built (the 'criminal justice system') does not achieve what we claim it does and that we are not addressing the needs of our communities (healing, justice, and the end of white supremacy, heteropatriarchy, colonialism and racial capitalism). Penal abolition is interested in an entirely different conversation, namely, that transgression ('crime') is normative and ubiquitous. From this point of departure, because social living is actually centered on achieving the highest possible embrace of norms, begins a serious inquiry into how communities can best socially organize to respond to transgression. What promotes the adoption of current social norms? How do we as a community develop a flexibility to adapt to shifting social norms? How do we equitably respond to all transgressions ('crimes') regardless of who their actors are? How do we identify and deliver remedial actions needed by all parties involved in transgressions? How do we develop social institutions needed for all the above? How do we complete all the above work without increasing harms? Keeping this transformative justice, abolitionist question-set in mind, the authors in this collection present analyses from diverse social locations.

Voices from people in prison

Our volume centers the voices of people in prison. Eight essayists and one poet in this collection write from inside prisons walls. Their work frames the critique of carceral logic within each of the four parts of the book.

Fyodor Dostoyevsky's famous adage still holds value: "The degree of civilization in a society can be judged by entering its prisons." When catastrophic events happen, such as pandemics or hurricanes, we must urgently ask: "how are people in prison being treated"? In March 2020, during the first height of the COVID-19 virus pandemic, New York's governor Andrew Cuomo announced that people incarcerated in state prisons, paid 16 cents per hour, would be producing hand-sanitizer for New Yorkers. He failed to mention that this captive workforce is prohibited from using the alcohol-based hand-sanitizer (Way 2020). Critics and prisoners' justice organizations responded by demanding that prisoners should be receiving adequate virus protection, a fair wage, and given how closed quarters such as carceral sites function as petri dishes for the virus, people detained in local jails and prisons on technical parole violations should be immediately released. At the time of this writing (fall 2020) this has not happened and carceral sites continue to be hotspots for rampant COVID-19 infections. It is worth noting that these sites are also always potential super-spreaders of the virus in free communities, as prison staff are continuously leaving one space and entering the other.

The chapters from people in prisons vividly discuss the harms of imprisonment and the excesses of carceral logic. Some of them already know first-hand how difficult life on the outside is for people labeled "felons." Many understand the inevitability of recidivism due to the hyper-surveillance they will encounter and the structural violence of the re-entry obstacles course they will face. They are unanimous in their condemnation of solitary confinement, especially, when it is used as a means of first resort for vulnerable persons, who already suffer from anxiety, depression or other disabling mental health issues. Several authors note that they are jailhouse lawyers, but they remain silent on the additional peril of being punished to solitary confinement, a fact that Mumia Abu-Jamal highlights in *Jailhouse Lawyers: Prisoners Defending Prisoners vs. the USA* (2009). By featuring authors condemning the harm of carceral life, this collection breaks with the prison writing tradition that celebrates prison as a place that produces a social good (Lamb 2003; Leder 2000). The people in prison use writing as a tool of resistance against the system that is determined to break their spirit and resilience.

Book synopsis

The book is divided into four parts, each centered on a theme and bringing together voices from the US and others around the world.

Part 1, "The Harms of Carceral Logic: People and Places," is a six-chapter examination of the harms that carceral logic brings to people and places. Like all parts, it begins with several reflections from people already living the carceral nightmare, i.e., people writing from inside the prison setting. In the first reflection, Joseph Dont'e Williams describes how in order to survive his carceral experience he has been propelled toward aggression, hypersexualization and "trouble." In the second, Gabriella writes of an experience of only a few days in a jail and yet, of how deeply traumatic the experience has been in the life following it. Finally, in the third, Eoz muses poetically from Argentina about carceral confinement, skin and paper. The next three chapters of Part 1 examine the carceral setting as an experience of a people, a nation and a profession. Vicki Chartrand and Niko Rougier think through the carceral apparatus and its necessary ties to a colonial logic of dispossession and denaturalization. The chapter brings together two voices: Chartrand, a Canadian abolitionist scholar, and Rougier, an incarcerated, Indigenous man in Canada. Together, these authors reveal the ongoing colonial dynamics of the carceral state and the ways in which it has haunted not only Indigenous ancestors but also the Indigenous people alive today. Next, Mechthild Nagel argues that settler-colonialism and a possessive investment in whiteness produced the ideology of abstract, rights-bearing subjectivity cloaked in a race-neutral rule of law disguising effectively the making of an outlaw nation. Finally, S.M. Rodriguez and Brittany Clark examine how the worst of carceral impacts fall not only on those sentenced to it by the criminalizing system but also to those whose poverty, general lack of access to broader opportunities, or experiences with structural racism/ethnocentrism and classism have relegated them to the violence-worker profession of the carceral state. Their examination of the impact the prison guard profession has on such guards' families and communities demonstrates how carceral logic damages all those that come into contact with it.

Part 2, "Creating Anti-Carceral Knowledge," is a seven-chapter examination of how anti-carceral knowledge is produced. The first four chapters are, again, from inside voices. Eoz poetically reflects from Argentina on carceral identity. David Head testifies how the defining element of carceral logic is frequently the absence of any operating logic. Next, Adrian Outten further elucidates the illogic of the carceral state by drawing out a lifetime of interactions that defy reasonable explanation and more appropriately resemble what he calls a "mental grave." Finally, Phillip Johnson describes the carceral setting of the courtroom in a way the reader has likely never considered before, leaving one with a Kafkaesque sense of horror about this setting and how little it has to do with even the most obscene sense of justice. Three uncommonly encountered analyses complete Part 2. First, Carly Guest and Rachel Seoighe deconstruct the carceral setting from a most unusual angle: the closure of a British prison. Using a reflexive, feminist methodology, these authors propose that an emotional engagement, what they call an "abolitionist affect," is required to properly deconstruct carceral logic and can contribute to the intellectual and political project of abolitionism. Second, Vanessa Thompson offers another feminist critique of policing, using the example of racial profiling in continental Europe (Germany, France and Switzerland). She examines not only the theory of policing but the witness statements of racialized Others as they are profiled and resist the police state. Finally, Clécio Lemos engages in a Foucauldian critique of penal humanism. He argues that, despite any Quaker/humanitarian origins the carceral state claims, the knowledge-power of carceral regimes today has long departed from any "truth" about human beings, communities and state actions.

In Part 3, "Case Studies Pointing to Radical Alternatives," the reader will encounter case studies pointing toward alternatives to carceral logic. Three chapters from the inside launch this section. With another poem Eoz asks us to imagine a different present. Douglas Knakmuhs, as a 38-year-old who has been incarcerated since the age of 16, imagines how instead of being placed in a system "designed for me to fail" he could have received the medical services a boy in his position needed and could have had a very different future than the one he finds himself in now. Richard Sean Gross further drives home this point in his chapter titled "Incarceration as the Worst Possible Treatment for Mental Illness." The dystopian conveyer-belt violence Gross describes – instead of mental health treatment – will leave the reader pondering what exactly carceral logic aims to accomplish. Three chapters by abolitionist scholars complete Part 3. In the first, Michael J. Coyle and Stephen T. Young pursue the similitudes of two carceral logic enterprises: the Japanese Americans concentration camps of World War II and the modern US criminalizing system. The authors demonstrate how the state's rhetorical construction of both Japanese Americans and Criminalized Americans is arranged in an underlying logic that depends on the frames of war, protection (from simulated danger, threat and fear) and supposed aid. Second, Marc Jacobs gives an account of the significance of Radical Alternatives to Prison, an abolitionist movement in Britain in the 1970s, which provides abolitionist activists and intellectuals of today an important lineage. Finally, Aaron Doyle, Justin Piché and Kelsey Sutton deconstruct how a new, Canadian "rehabilitation" prison, instead of challenging the failures of carceral logic, became notorious for not only repeating them but also for its inhumane conditions. The authors analyze how activists' efforts to oppose the reproduction of carceral logic in what was supposed to be a space of recovery were opposed by the carceral state with neutralization techniques and persistent rhetoric that thwarted change.

Lastly, in Part 4, "Resisting Carceral Logic," a series of chapters invite the reader to consider what resisting carceral logic looks like. In the first two chapters, Eoz and Emmanuel X share more about the shape of carceral logic from the perspective of those whom it targets. Many of those writing from prison note the impact of imprisonment on their families; notably, X shows how difficult it is for mothers to parent their children who are thousands of miles away. Next, scholar-activist Valeria Veigh Weis and grassroots activist Julieta Sosa explore an Argentinian initiative aimed at overcoming one of the hardest, collateral consequences of punishment: unemployment. The chapter exposes the importance of contesting carceral logic by engaging in emancipatory politics and praxis within the specificities of the southern socio-economic context. Then, Verena Tan's chapter returns us to the settler-colonial landscape and its use of mass imprisonment of Māori persons in Aotearoa/New Zealand. This chapter examines how the prison industrial complex and the carceral state are embedded within settler-colonialism, heteropatriarchy and global imperialism's ongoing project of colonial expansion. Finally, the volume closes with a two-line poem from Eoz that captures much of the voice and content of carceral logic.

Concluding thoughts on abolitionist futures

At the time of this writing, news media and prisoners' justice activists around the world are referring to US prison sentences (and elsewhere) as death sentences. The COVID-19 virus pandemic affords prison critics (and gerontologists) a chance to review whose life is sacred and who will not be treatable/treated. The US Justice Department has ordered the release of high-profile prisoners (a special attorney to US President Donald Trump, celebrities caught in a college-admissions scandal, etc.) months or even a year ahead of their scheduled parole. Others who are not socially connected to the powerful do not even get as much as test kits nor access to personal protective equipment. As a result, thousands of prisoners and detained people will be condemned to perish from the disease, and, in the words of Nigerian penal abolitionist Uju Agomoh (2000), will be described as having died "from natural causes."

The pandemic has disproportionately affected Black and Latinx communities and their kin inside prisons. By June 2020 the COVID-19 case rate for people in prison is 5.5 times higher than that of those in free society and their mortality rate is three times higher (Saloner et al. 2020). Instead of thinking of their death as "unfortunate" or a "natural cause," should we not at least be spreading the counter-hegemonic knowledge that such punishment kills prematurely (Gilmore 2007)? A protest movement that focuses on antiracist public health policies in conjunction with a sustained critique against policing brings new energy into the decarceration and prison reform movements with campaigns of "free our elders," "release the youth" and emptying jails of persons there on remand who are too poor to pay bail, fines, etc.

Remarkably, since May 2020 we have heard cries for police abolition and sustained calls for defunding the police in the US. Specifically, the city of Minneapolis may be a focal point of abolitionist practice in terms of the future of policing and community reparations. Activists burned down the police precinct building which was associated with the four men who murdered George Floyd. Instead of rebuilding this carceral fortress, activists envision the emergence of a community center replete with garden plots for its residents. Many remember that a community center was razed to the ground to make room for a police building complex.[2] As Minneapolis grapples with restructuring and perhaps reducing the size of its police presence, it should heed well the lessons of the much-touted Camden, NJ policing remodeling effort. As Brendan McQuade (2020) points out, in Camden, this model of putting police departments in receivership and "defunding" them did little to change the occupation mentality of police workers. In fact, advanced surveillance technologies now assist Camden's police workers to increase their reach over the city, where "e-carceration" is the new face of "decarceration." The city has faced neoliberal austerity cuts and intensified neighborhood watch sentinels, who enlist for free to report to the police. While Operation TIPS under GW Bush's administration was cancelled under popular protest, Camden's citizens now willingly contribute "domestic intelligence" under the guise of strengthening community police partnerships.

Fortunately, across US cities, BIPOC activists reject the Camden model and draw attention to a critical genealogy of policing, rooted in slave patrols and slave catching. Popular media has also contributed to a soul-searching review of the invention of policing, which goes beyond the reformist call for ending police brutality or the racist/classist application of policing work, noting its terrorist beginnings as posse comitatus in 1702 in South Carolina (Lepore 2020). The rallying cries of Black Lives Matter and the battle chant of "No justice, no peace, no racist police" have gone global. To date, we note that there are mass protests across Brazil against police murder of Black bodies, as there are across Trinidad and Tobago, reckoning with legacies of enslavement and colonialism (Mendes-Franco 2020; Phillips 2020).

At the grassroots level abolitionist practices already abound everywhere. Within the US, organizations such as Critical Resistance, Audre Lorde Project, Philly Stands UP! and generationFIVE led by gender queer and gender nonconforming persons of color fight the criminal legal system in their communities and advocate transformative justice through community accountability praxis (Dixon and Piepzna-Samarasinha 2020). Across the Global South, and in Indigenous communities, activists and scholars are reckoning with the legacy of imperialist warfare and colonial subjugation, occurring centuries prior the advent of the modern penitentiary in 1790 Philadelphia, Pennsylvania.

It is time to do what lived experience and research show is necessary: abolish carceral logic. It is time to shape public opinion and public policy with what we know to be true: that all prison sentences, remand and detention practices in their myriad carceral structures are race and class (and all too often death) sentences. From here, as Coyle and Young argue in this book, it follows that people in prison, their families and all those profoundly impacted by the ruin that the carceral state and criminalizing system has rained on them are owed reparations.

Notes

1 We use the word *transgression* and not 'crime' because the latter is oxymoronic and illogical: while few are convicted of 'crimes' almost all are guilty of transgressions (see Hulsman 1986 and for a more recent accounting, Coyle 2018).
2 Thanks to Susan Buechler for this historical note.

References

Abu-Jamal, M. 2009. *Jailhouse Lawyers: Prisoners Defending Prisoners vs. the USA*. San Francisco, CA: City Lights.

Agomoh, U. 2000. *Plenary Talk*. Toronto: ICOPA.Agozino, B. 2003. *Counter-Colonial Criminology: A Critique of Imperialist Reason*. London: Pluto Press.

Barker, V. 2013. "Nordic Exceptionalism Revisited: Explaining the Paradox of a Janus-faced Penal Regime." *Theoretical Criminology* 17(1): 5–25.

Ben-Moshe, L. 2020. *Decarcerating Disability: Deinstitutionalization and Prison Abolition*. Minneapolis: University of Minnesota Press.

Blackmon, D.A. 2009. *Slavery by Another Name: The Re-enslavement of Black Americans from the Civil War to World War II*. New York: First Anchor Books.

Bohm, R.M. 1986. "Crime, Criminal and Crime Control Policy Myths." *Justice Quarterly* 3(2): 193–214.

Brown, M. and J. Schept. 2017. "New Abolition, Criminology and a Critical Carceral Studies." *Punishment & Society* 19(4): 440–462.

Calavita, K. and V. Jenness. 2014. *Appealing to Justice: Prisoner Grievances, Rights, and Carceral Logic*. Berkeley: University of California Press.

Comack, E. 2012. *Racialized Policing: Aboriginal People's Encounters with the Police*. Winnipeg: Fernwood Books Ltd.

Coyle, M.J. 2013. *Talking Criminal Justice: Language and the Just Society*. London: Routledge.

Coyle, M.J. 2014. "How Prisons Became Dystopias of Color and Poverty: Prison Abolition Lessons from the War on Drugs." In S. Bowman (Ed.), *Color Behind Bars* (pp. 435–450). Santa Barbara, CA: ABC-CLIO.

Coyle, M.J. 2018. "Transgression and Standard Theories: Contributions toward Penal Abolition." *Critical Criminology* 26: 325–339.

Coyle, M.J. Forthcoming. *Seeing Crime: Penal Abolition as the End of Utopian Criminal Justice*. Berkeley: University of California Press.

Coyle, M.J. and J. Schept. 2017. "Penal Abolition and the State: Colonial, Racial and Gender Violences." *Contemporary Justice Review* 20(4): 399–403.

Davis, A.Y. 2003. *Are Prisons Obsolete?* New York: Seven Stories Press.

Davis, A.Y. 2005. *Abolition Democracy: Beyond Empire, Prisons and Torture*. New York: Seven Stories Press.

Davis, A.Y. and D. Rodriguez. 2000. "The Challenge of Prison Abolition: A Conversation." *Social Justice* 27(3): 212–218.

Dixon, E. and L.L. Piepzna-Samarasinha. 2020. *Beyond Survival: Strategies and Stories from the Transformative Justice Movement*. Chico, CA: AK Press.

Dobchuk-Land, B. 2017. "Resisting 'Progressive' Carceral Expansion: Lessons for Abolitionists from Anti-Colonial Resistance." *Contemporary Justice Review* 20(4): 404–418.

Foucault, M. 1977. *Discipline and Punish: The Birth of the Prison*. New York: Pantheon Books.

Gilmore, R.W. 2007. *Golden Gulag: Prisons, Surplus, Crisis, and Opposition in Globalizing California*. Berkeley: University of California Press.

Gilmore, R.W. and C. Gilmore. 2008. "Restating the Obvious." In M. Sorkin (Ed.), *Indefensible Space: The Architecture of the National Insecurity State* (pp. 141–162). New York: Routledge.

Hulsman, L. 1986. "Critical Criminology and the Concept of Crime." *Contemporary Crises* 10(1): 63–80.

Hulsman, L. 1997. "Themes and Concepts in an Abolitionist Approach to Criminal Justice." Retrieved 10/2016 from: http://hulsmanfoundation.org/wp-content/uploads/2014/07/abolitionistapproach.pdf

INCITE! 2006. *The Color of Violence: The INCITE! Anthology*. Boston, MA: South End Press.

James, J. 2005. *The New Abolitionists: (Neo)slave Narratives and Contemporary Prison Writings*. Albany: SUNY Press.

Lamb, W. and The Women of York Correctional Institution. 2003. *Couldn't Keep It to Myself: Testimonies from Our Imprisoned Sisters*. New York: Harper.

Leder, D. with C. Baxter, W. Brown, T. Chatman-Bey, J. Cowan, M. Green, G. Huffman, H.B. Johnson Jr., O. Johnson, A. Jones III, M. Medley, "Q", D. Thompson, S.

Tillett, and J. Woodland. 2000. *The Soul Knows No Bars. Inmates Reflect on Life, Death, and Hope.* Lanham, MD: Rowman & Littlefield.
Lepore, J. 7.20.2020. "The Long Blue Line: The Invention of Police." *The New Yorker.*
Linebaugh, P. 2014. *Stop, Thief! The Commons, Enclosures, and Resistance.* Oakland, CA: PM Press.
McLeod, A. 2015. Prison Abolition and Grounded Justice. *UCLA Law Review* 62: 1156–1239.
McQuade, B. 7.4.2020. "The 'Camden Model' Is Not a Model: It's an Obstacle to Real Change." *Jacobin Magazine.* Retrieved 9/11/20 from: https://jacobinmag.com/2020/07/camden-new-jersey-police-reform-surveillance
Mendes-Franco, J. 7.10.2020. "Authorities' Response to Social Unrest in Trinidad & Tobago Raises Debate about Police Power and Public Trust." *Global Voices.* Retrieved 8/12/20 from: https://globalvoices.org/2020/07/10/authorities-response-to-social-unrest-in-trinidad-tobago-raises-debate-about-police-power-and-public-trust/?utm_source=Global+Voices&utm_campaign=d0f109aaf2-Daily_Digest_COPY_01&utm_medium=email&utm_term=0_633e82444a-d0f109aaf2-290199921&ct=t(Daily_Digest_COPY_01)
Mogul, J., Ritchie, A. and Whitlock K. 2011. *Queer (In)Justice: The Criminalization of LGBT People in the United States.* New York: Penguin Random House.
Moskos, P. 2011. *In Defense of Flogging.* New York: Basic Books.
Nagel, M. and A. Nocella (eds.). 2013. *The End of Prisons: Reflections from the Decarceration Movement.* Amsterdam: Rodopi.
Oshinsky, D.M. 1996. *Worse Than Slavery: Parchman Farm and the Ordeal of Jim Crow Justice.* New York: Free Press.
Phillips, T. 2020. "Black lives Shattered: Outrage as Boy, 14, Is Brazil Police's Latest Victim." *The Guardian.* Retrieved 8/12/20 from: https://www.theguardian.com/world/2020/jun/03/brazil-black-lives-police-teenager.
Reznik, R. 2019. "Retributive Abolitionism." *Berkeley Journal of Criminal Law,* 24(2): 123–194.
Richie, B. 2012. *Arrested Justice: Black Women, Violence, and America's Prison Nation.* New York: New York University Press.
Robinson, C.J. 1983. *Black Marxism: The Making of the Black Radical Tradition.* London: Zed Press.
Saleh-Hanna, V. 2017. "An Abolitionist Theory on Crime: Ending the Abusive Relationship with Racist-Imperialist-Patriarchy [R.I.P.]. *Contemporary Justice Review* 20(4): 419–441.
Saloner, B., K. Parish, J. Ward, G. DiLaura, and S. Dolovich. 2020. "COVID-19 Cases and Deaths in Federal and State Prisons." *JAMA,* 324(6): 602–603.
Schept, J. 2015. *Progressive Punishment: Job Loss, Jail Growth, and the Neoliberal Logic of Carceral Expansion.* New York: New York University Press.
Shabazz, R. 2009. "'So High You Can't Get Over It, So Low You Can't Get Under It': Carceral Spatiality and Black Masculinities in the United States and South Africa." *Souls* 11(3): 276–294.
Shenwar, M. and V. Law. 2020. *Prison by Any Other Name: The Harmful Consequences of Popular Reforms.* New York: The New Press.
Solinger, R., P. Johnson, M. Raimon, T. Reynolds, and R. Tapia (eds.). 2010. *Interrupted Life: Experiences of Incarcerated Women in the United States.* Berkeley: University of California Press.

Sudbury Oparah, J. (ed.). 2005. Global Lockdown: Race, Gender, and the Prison-Industrial Complex. New York: Routledge.

Ugelvik, T. and J. Dullum (eds.). 2012. *Penal Exceptionalism? Nordic Prison Policy and Practice*. London: Routledge.

Way, K. 3.25.2020. "Cuomo's Prison Workers Say They're Not Actually Making Hand Sanitizer." *Vice*. Retrieved 8/13/20 from: https://www.vice.com/en_us/article/5dma4k/cuomos-prison-workers-say-theyre-not-actually-making-hand-sanitizer

PART I

The harms of carceral logic

People and places

1

PRISON PROVOKES PEOPLE INTO BEING MORE AGGRESSIVE, HYPERSEXUALIZED, AND PRONE TO CRIME

Joseph (Dont'e) Williams

The prison system is ineffectual and should be abolished. It should be abolished, from my experience, because it only serves to make people worse. I say this because jail has only led me to become more aggressive, hypersexualized, and more inclined to commit crime.

When I went to prison for the first time it was for burglary. I had left home at 17 and found the world to be more difficult than I imagined. I started stealing primarily for food and clothes which put me on a path which eventually led me to jail.

Once incarcerated I witnessed young men fighting and stabbing each other over telephones, cookies, and dirty looks. I suppose there was violence in the community I lived before I came to jail but at least on the street there were homes I could retreat to for respite. In prison, especially in the "dorms" I was housed in for most of my time there were no breaks from the program. It took a while before I could even use the phone without any difficulties, but I never complained because I saw plenty of people who were not allowed to use the phone at all. In many prisons, in order to overcome such conflicts, one has to impose their will or associate with others from the past.

The same methodology also holds true if one desires not to be robbed or extorted for a variety of things, up to and including sex. Upon my realization of these intimidating facts and my understanding that I was far from the most assertive person, I started to work out furiously and attempted to alter my personality. As a result, I have found that jail has altered the way I treat and speak to everyone that I come in contact with, including my family. I am quicker to take offense to things and act in a way which lets people know that I am not to be taken advantage of, which they often try to do in jail but, far less often in the community.

Another way the prison system has altered the way I interact with the community is by hypersexualizing me. When imprisoned I was stopped from having normal interactions with women for years. I was not allowed to work beside, to have flirtatious with, or even have platonic conversations with women. The face-to-face interactions I did have with females were forced dictatorial relationships, i.e., prison guards or work supervisors. The encounters only served to inspire spite and resentment toward women. The only agreeable reflection of the opposite sex that I had was on television which often projects women in a placated and misleading manner. The years of being force-fed a warped perception of women are coupled with an overwhelming need to overcompensate for years of state sanctioned sexual abuse at the hands of men telling me to get naked, lift my balls, and spread my cheeks. Although, I understand that these searches are designed to curb the flow of contraband within a prison and that not all of the men enjoyed looking at me naked, there is no amount of explanation able to alleviate the pain these experiences cause. For this reason, many men, including myself, have attempted to scrub horrific and unexplainable memories from our minds with an exaggerated number of sexual conquests.

The prison system has also helped to make me and many like me more prone to commit crime after our release. This heightened criminality, although conceived elsewhere, was incubated and brought to terms within the cold corridors of the penal system. When I entered prison, I entered as a young man who had committed a few crimes but, once there, I found that was not descriptive enough. I was labeled by my charge and thrust into its correlating category. "What are you in for?" I quickly learned was not an innocent question, but an opportunity to introduce myself and an introduction of how I would be treated by others. I was put around people who had already accepted their labels and schooled by these people on how to "better" do my class of crime. Once released I would try to live a normal life, but I quickly discovered that convicts were not the only ones who label me by my conviction. I was often denied opportunities and offered skepticism when trying to advance. Although difficult, I always manage to find employment and some semblance of regularity. Life however, is irregular and obstacles at times present themselves. When these obstacles did arrive, I would remember or, be reminded of my history. I would never make the best decisions or even experiment with a different type of crime because, I had been told time and time again that I was a burglar. I sometimes would try to ask for help when I found myself in precarious positions. I was not however, exactly sure what my problem was so, my questions were always lacking. Consequently, also lacking were the answers I received. It was not until being incarcerated for a third time that I decided to investigate the reasons I kept committing crimes and coming back to jail even though, I did not want to. Following my investigation, I discovered that the reasons were routed within the prison system itself. While the prison has been advertised as the solution to all our society's problems, it actually emotionally and psychologically provokes people into being more aggressive, hypersexualized, and prone to commit more crime. The prison system is therefore ineffective and should be abolished.

2

IF I WEREN'T WHITE I'D BE DEAD

Gabriella

I was arrested and went through severe opioid withdrawal during three days in jail. It was one of the most traumatic experiences in my life, as I was kept in handcuffs behind my back (despite the fact that my costochondritis illness meant that my breathing was severely compromised and the pain was OFF ANY CHART KNOWN TO HUMANKIND) and ankle shackles (that were too tight to go around my extremely swollen ankles such that they cut deep gashes in each Achilles tendon – and I'm immuno-compromised due to my steroid medications) for most of that time. It took two days before they took me to the hospital, and then another to finally see a judge. I was arrested for trying to steal toothpaste and fragrance-free soap and deodorant at a Whole Foods Market. And this maltreatment was WITH my white privilege. Without my white privilege I too would have ended up dead on Rikers Island. They never took me to Rikers, and they waived my bail, and they gave me such a sweetheart deal that left me with NO criminal record. If I weren't white, I would NOT have gotten those benefits and I'd be dead.

It took me six months to heal, physically, from the experience, and I'll never FULLY HEAL psychologically. I still suffer terribly from olfactory hallucinations. When I get upset, I smell the jailhouse smell, even food smells like the jail to me at times, and then I am unable to eat anything at all. I have been judged very harshly by several people who were once close to me; extremely painful losses. I'm telling you because I know that truth-telling helps me eliminate shame, and because it is a very powerful illustration of white privilege. Too many people think white privilege means not getting arrested, but white privilege means SURVIVING getting arrested! I feel guilt and shame about the privileges I experience that Black and Brown people do not. I do think that gender-conforming privilege is something I don't get, and though it's impossible to estimate accurately, I do believe that some of my maltreatment was from gender non-conformity-related bigotry. But still. I know firsthand why so many people die in jail!

3

READER

Emanuel "Eoz"

Like every day, he walks a walk, gets views, experiences fragrances

aromas and accepting that not everything is pink, he also feels the putrid smell of a city that he ignores and (they) ignore.

With barriers in all kinds of places, between prejudices and past condemnations of error, between blacks and whites, between walls and bars, between a yes and a no, even so,

he has his mind, a book and an imaginary escape. Fantastic and cautious for some.

That escape begins on an empty sheet, curious to find answers to his routine.

Assimilating, it was something that appealed to him.

Starting with the prolog, settling into discomfort, he continues another journey, in which, moving away from all the saddening surroundings, he reads smiles, and feels them his, reads landscapes, and sits out there, reads feelings, and makes them his.

This not so nice looking book, with not so many sheets, and earth color, makes him understand that the essential is not the superficiality, and with that new knowledge he is ready to apply it to the interactions with his surroundings, to involve all in what he sees and to avoid rejecting arguments different from his own.

"Not everything is pink", he said, and then, smiling and closing for today that book already written, he added "that the grey of others does not ruin your color".

And with the light off, looking at the ceiling and ready to continue navigating in imagined sheets, he says goodbye to the day with a sigh that follows the feeling of the hours lived with open eyes.

Awake, and once already sanitized, he carries out his work, carrying the wall that society – unfortunately – made him build, angry faced, not forgetting where he temporarily lives, he lets out little laughs to his loved ones and shares some other words while looking for his early release, he only hopes for physical freedom, and if it doesn't come today, he knows what he has.

Another temporary escape in his confinement.

4

CARCERAL OTHER AND SEVERING OF PEOPLE, PLACE AND LAND

Redefining the politics of abolition through an anti-colonial framework

Vicki Chartrand and Niko Rougier

Introduction

> You can't apologize, for genocide
> To the ones who are dead inside
> Your sincerity is a joke, – We're hungry homeless in jail and broke
> (Turcotte, Forthcoming, *Original Savages Part III*)

The carceral logic and techniques that proliferate our social world are an endemic feature of modernity. Emerging with modern colonial logic of the 17th and 18th centuries, the carceral was developed as a denaturalizing[1] apparatus that severed connections of people, place and land. From a trajectory of reserves, residential schools, child welfare, inner city poverty traps, youth detention and prisons in the land now known as Canada, the carceral continues to remove people from their lands, culture, communities, supports, families and homes. In the 21st century, modern colonialism's dispossession, segregation and assimilation practices continue to haunt the nation-state.

In this chapter, we think through the carceral apparatus as it is tied to a colonial logic of dispossession and denaturalization, used to sever connections and the implications this has for Indigenous people in Canadian prisons today. Given this, we also consider alternative or inclusive justices advanced within the politics of an anti-colonial abolition. First, we establish the links between colonialism and the carceral by tracing settler colonial and carceral logic and practices in the land now known as Canada. Second, using a situated political knowledge from various incarcerated Indigenous men across Canada, including the author Niko Rougier, we highlight the ongoing colonizing practices of the carceral. Finally, we consider alternative justices as embedded in abolitionist politics and argue that, given the centrality of colonialism in current carceral arrangements, abolition must be grounded in anti-colonial approaches that center Indigenous knowledge and ways of being. Overall, by exposing the pervasive and fluid character of colonialism, we seek to challenge a habituated and normalized colonial violence and offer different possibilities for thinking outside of carceral controls. In this way, we not only want to illuminate the colonizing tendencies of carceral systems, but rethink the perpetual machinery invested in the *carceral other*.

As part of an anti-colonial approach, this work is the result of deep collaborations that privilege Indigenous experience and wisdom. First, this chapter is based on both authors' testimony at the *Public Inquiry Commission on relation between Indigenous Peoples and certain public services in Quebec: listening reconciliation and progress*, Val d'Or QC, 9 April 2018. The inquiry was established in response to media accounts of sexualized police violence against Indigenous women in Val d'Or, Quebec.[2] Second, this work is built on the situated knowledge of incarceration of one of the authors, Niko Rougier, an Abenaki artist who has been incarcerated for more than 26 years, in addition to being subject to many other facets of the carceral apparatus, including child apprehension, foster care and adoption. Finally, this work also draws from six other incarcerated Indigenous writers who, through an initiative with the Centre for Justice Exchange,[3] submitted parliamentary briefs to the House of Commons Standing Committee on Public Safety and National Security's 2018 study on Indigenous people in the correctional system (see McKay, 2018).[4] The public testimonies of the two authors and the parliamentary briefs reflect a means to mobilize and politicize a situated knowledge and shape public and political discussion. By drawing from these sources, the authors do not seek to simply consult or 'give voice', but to locate penal and carceral knowledge with the expertise of Indigenous people in prison and mobilize change.

Through such a situated approach, this work is cultivated in and advances Indigenous knowledge and ways of being. This is particularly significant given that the prison is a carceral space that has long been used as a way to destroy the culture, traditions and knowledge of the original inhabitants. As we further discuss below, given this history and activity of the carceral, grounding knowledge and action in Indigenous tradition and knowledge is an important framework for developing alternative justices such as those advanced in abolitionist struggles. This is not only important for those in prison or for Indigenous self-determination, but for all of us as we struggle against carceral tropes and technologies that continue to shape our modes of thinking and ways of being. I'm not your *carceral other*.

Colonial modernity

The formation of the world today has deep and widespread roots in a European colonial logic. Emerging with modernity, European colonization pervaded more than three quarters of the world's land mass by the mid-20th century (Loomba, 1998, p. 15). Foundational to this modern form of colonialism was not only the extraction of goods and resources, but a restructuring of economies, governance and cultures advanced through the logic of imperialism, racism and heteropatriarchy (Quijano, 2005). With these advances of modernity, colonial logic instituted and naturalized these interlocking structures of patriarchal, white supremist and imperial dominance, to which a criminalizing system of justice has long been tied (Saleh-Hanna, 2017). Today, entire populations continue to be incarcerated, immobilized, displaced and assimilated in the name of civility and progress. As Rodríguez (2016, p. 146) notes, the "systemic logic and power formations of white supremacy, racist state violence, bodily disintegration and racial chattel logic are articulated throughout the carceral system in the form of modern logic". As we outline below, modern colonialism was legitimated through an entire framework that elevated the colonized through the separation and subordination of populations, projected and contained as an 'other'.

In Canada, carceral projects were fundamental to colonizing the people and land and establishing the nation-state. This was achieved by imposing British laws, policing the original land custodians and establishing a legal code throughout the country. To ensure the proliferation of settler society, Indigenous knowledge, governance and ways of being were targeted for destruction at every level. In line with carceral logic, this occurred through segregation such as reserves, assimilation projects such as residential schools, and banning Indigenous ceremonies and tradition. At its inception, the penitentiary was part of a system that was initially reserved for a white settler population, while Indigenous people were exclusively managed by the Indian Agent; although all part of the same carceral network (Chartrand, 2019). Residential schools in Canada, for instance, were adopted from the Mettray penal colony in France (Woolford, Forthcoming). In Mettray, one could find the functions of the family unit, the army, the workforce, the school, spirituality and the judiciary (Foucault, 1977, p. 293). Segregated from white settlers, the carceral operated at every facet in the lives of the original custodians, with residential schools acting as an all-encompassing apparatus of dispossession from people, place and land.

Epistemic orderings embedded in White European supremacy are central to modern colonial logic. McKittrick (2011, p. 949), for example, points out that a slave economy "normalized black dispossession, white supremacy and other colonial-racial geographies, while naturalizing the racist underpinnings of land exploitation as accumulation and emancipation". Through claims of white superiority, the eradication, segregation, enslavement and reformation of entire populations across the globe was made possible. In Canada, the 'Indian industry' was not so much used to exploit labor or material goods, but provided physical and psychic life that established white settler dominance and control over people and resources (see Said, 1995). This economy of supremacy neutralized intricate Indigenous relations to people, place and land – the roots of life. The violence of racism, imperialism and patriarchy currently experienced by Indigenous people is not the effects of a colonial past, but central to modern operations and logic today.

Denaturalizing people, place and land

Today, the colonial relationship has not ended. Historically, this relationship was reflected in the practices of enslavement, reserves, assimilation and genocide. Today, it is a part of a colonial pattern found in citizenship and immigrations laws (Thobani, 2007), sterilization practices (Stote, 2012), child welfare apprehensions (Blackstock, 2007) and imprisonment – all carceral institutions and techniques that continue to intervene in the lives of targeted populations and disrupt connections to people, place and land.

Where Indigenous people were initially governed through reserves and residential schools, in the post-war era of welfare and reform, Canada silently ushered in the penitentiary as the new carceral control. From the inception of the penitentiary in 1835 up until 1960, the rates of Indigenous incarceration remained low from 1 to 2%. In the 1960s, while formal segregation and assimilation laws were receding, the prison took over in the colonizing of Indigenous people (Chartrand, 2019). In 1965, the federal Indigenous incarceration rate jumped to 11% and increased 1–3% every year to its current rate of 28% (Office of the Correctional Investigator, 2018). This is an increase that continues today, despite a decrease in the overall federal prison population since 2012 (Correctional Service Canada, 2018). Indigenous people in prison are also more often contained to higher security classifications, segregation placements, maximum security and forced interventions (Auditor General of Canada, 2016). Fewer Indigenous people in prison are granted full parole and, if they are granted some form of release, it is often later in their sentence. This is further evidenced in Seth's (2018) brief where he outlines how the system continued to work against him at every level and prioritized his containment.

> Upon my second release to the CRF [Community Residential Facility], I started the Welding course, 5 days a week, 8 hours a day, for 16 weeks, attending PATH employment, seeing my son whenever my mother was available to drive from Dunnville to Hamilton, and I was trying to setup a mechanic course from Mohawk college. I was doing everything CSC [Correctional Service Canada] expects from guys released from prison. … My parole was eventually revoked for a urinalysis positive for THC, even though I did obtain a prescription for use of medical marijuana.

On a continuum of carceral containment, the prison continues as the preferred and 'natural' space in what has been a long series of carceral interventions for Indigenous people. Throughout colonization, Indigeneity continues to be passed from one carceral institution to another and another and another.

Throughout his testimony, Rougier (2018) often discussed how he was repeatedly exposed to colonial systems similar to residential schools prior to his incarceration. This exposure included being part of the Indigenous child apprehensions known as the 60s scoop; a series of policies enacted by Canadian provincial child welfare authorities starting in the mid-1950s when thousands of Indigenous children were taken from their homes and families and placed in foster homes or adopted out to white families (Dart, 2019). (Dart, 2019). Rougier was taken from his Abenaki mother, placed into the foster care system and subsequently adopted into a white military family. As experienced by many, the children lost their names, their languages and a connection to their heritage and experienced many varieties and forms of abuse. The 60s scoop, like the countless other colonizing practices experienced by Indigenous people, is reflective of the multiple functions of the Mettray penal colony noted above, whereby interventions and displacements occur in all aspects of life. Just as how black people in the US were forcibly displaced and tied to the plantation economy and subsequently the penal industrial complex McKittrick, 2011, p. 948), Indigenous people, like their ancestors before them, are similarly circulated in a perpetual state of dislocation and dispossession over generations through shifting carceral modalities.

Dislocated into child welfare, youth detention and inner-city service traps where rates of violence, poverty and suicide are high (Culhane, 2003), the prison is only part of a long string of carceral spaces that continue to contain and sever Indigenous connections from people, place and land. Catcheway (2018) notes this with his own experiences of ongoing dispossession "Our mother went back to Manitoba, abandoning us. Shortly after, our father was killed in the downtown eastside. You can perhaps imagine how long I've been in the system". Those who are Indigenous to the land signify bodies that can be displaced, segregated, enslaved, experimented on, assimilated, immobilized, modified, saved, rehabilitated and even eliminated. As Rougier (2018, pp. 62–63, *translated from French*) testified, "Completely denaturalized of our birth as a human being; torn from our culture, its origins, its roots, its land then becoming a permanent product for correctional services or other systems". This dispossession severs the vital relations Indigenous people establish with the land, with others and with themselves.

The severing and destruction of ties and connections is a central component of colonial practice and is intensified in the microsites of the prison. Historically, traditional Indigenous culture was banned in prison; a legislative practice that was officially abandoned by the Canadian government beginning in the 1950s, but retained within the prison until the 1980s. It was through the birth of Native Brother and Sisterhoods in the prisons and their struggle to practice their ceremonies and traditions that shifted penal practice and policies (see Adema, 2012).

As expressed by all the authors, culture and tradition are important to retain a sense of self in relation to who one is and where one belongs. "As a Residential School Survivor, I find that all of the First Nations teachings which we receive through our Elders are extremely important and essential components to our Healing Journeys" (Delorme, 2018). For many, given this ongoing colonizing, it is within the prison that they experience any aspect their culture for the first time. Using the carceral system as a means to introduce Indigenous culture, however, ensures it remains invested in Western and white articulation for assimilation, now coined 'rehabilitation' or 'programming'.

> We also find it extremely insulting when Upper Management tells the Elders how they must run ceremonies. When the Elder tries to tell them about proper protocol he is told that he must do it the way CSC wants or they will find someone else to conduct the ceremonies.
>
> *(Jamieson, 2018)*

> The most destructive of these initiatives within the federal prison system is CSC's Pathways program (CD 702-1) that, from my perspective, must be seen as the next phase in Canada's Residential school program and cultural genocide of its Indigenous people.
>
> *(Hachey, 2018)*

Today, as the authors point out, Indigenous culture and ceremony are appropriated by the institution, bartered as a commodity and privilege, or fully denied. In is not a coincidence that many incarcerated Indigenous people only experience ceremony and tradition in a controlled prison environment for the first time. This is reflective of an ongoing colonial logic and strategic relations that continue to control and leverage what can be practiced and cultivated by Indigenous people.

> The [Native Brotherhood] has become a complete failure in its capacity to provide the Indigenous population with a sense of brotherhood and family. Indigenous cultures are highly orientated towards family and community and this was the whole reason this group was created.
>
> *(Johnny, 2018)*

> Aboriginal people in prison and their supporters have been (politely) asking Corrections to accept traditional teachings on their own, as credible resources for (rehabilitating) its people.
>
> *(Jamieson, 2018)*

Rougier (2018) points out that the prison is artificial; synthetic – "there are no stories, no songs, no connecting with nature". This artificial environment is also reflective of a colonial logic that is designed in the image of white modern civility that proliferated carceral institutions to separate and segregate families, communities and many other connections to each other and oneself. A carceral modernity from which Indigenous people ostensibly cannot 'recover from' or 'keep up with' and other fictions of a system designed to deny connections and sovereignty.

The incarceration of Indigenous people cannot be set apart from their colonization and the forms of carcerality invested in their dispossession and segregation. It is a part of a long string of ongoing denaturalized settings. This kind of separation of people from land and relations denies an ability to connect and create in ways that are germane to Indigenous traditions and ways of being

(Kermoal and Altamirano-Jiménez, 2016). As revealed in this chapter, a situated knowledge exposes these colonial patterns of the carceral or what Art Solomon (1994, p. 81) describes as the "abomination" of the prison; an abomination that continues to "disrupt the naturalness of who we are".

Anti-colonial abolition

The carceral has deep roots in colonial conquest that recapitulate entire populations into its folds over and over. These colonial formations, although not necessarily homogenous or totalizing, reproduce and reaffirm the hierarchies and tropes of white supremacy, racism, hetero-patriarchy and the many more *carceral others* established through modern colonialism's advances. As a heterogeneous ensemble invested in the ordering of human life, colonialism is reproduced, redefined and renegotiated over time and place (Stoler, 1997, p. 433). Abolition, to be equally creative and fluid, must account for these deep colonial roots and denaturalizing relations of the carceral apparatus.

Abolition has long history of targeting a number of repressive and exploitive institutions and practices such as slavery and the death penalty (Mathiesen, 2008). Today, abolition has expanded to many spaces of dispossession and violence from border control (Bhandar, 2008), community control (Chapman, Carey and Ben-Moshe, 2014) and prison to school pipeline (Meiners and Winn, 2010). Abolition has also been advanced on many anti-violence, anti-racist and anti-heteropatriarchy fronts (see Coyle and Schept, 2017 inter alia). While much of the abolition scholarship from an anti-colonial framework has emerged from the US (e.g., Davis, 1998; Rodríguez, 2019; Saleh-Hanna, 2017), it is only a growing area in Canada (Chartrand, 2019; Dobchuk-Land, 2017; Nichols, 2014; Palacios, 2016), despite more than 150 years of colonial settlement. Australian scholars Blagg and Anthony (2018, pp. 259–260) argue that while abolition is an important pursuit, it can only be made meaningful from decolonizing processes. As we further discuss below, an anti-colonial abolition considers how carceral violence and control is linked to a colonial logic including liberation politics, how colonialism continues to be reproduced throughout carceral arrangements that are experienced by many colonized people across the globe, and how to move away from its structures through grassroots activities and movements, particularly exemplified by Indigenous traditions.

Saidiya Hartman (1997), in her seminal text *Scenes of Subjection*, underlines how liberation discourses of enslaved black peoples in the US would draw on white witnessing of spectacles of violence as the only vehicle for black emancipation – "the humanity of the enslaved and the violence of the institution can only be brought into view by extreme examples of incineration and dismemberment or by placing white bodies at risk". The author's work highlights the violent nature of not only colonialism, but also a liberation politics that requires some form of white intervention on behalf of the carceral other's suffering; diminishing any of their own claims to personhood. This longstanding white savior trope has been reflected in many abolition movements, including that of slavery in the US. As argued by Rodríguez (2016, p. 149)

> the assumptive objects/targets of white academic knowledge-making – the racially enslaved and their descendants, civilly socially dead, militarily displaced, colonially eviscerated, and genocide-vulnerable – are understood to be intellectually diseased with the toxin of external determination

The violence in this approach is the failure to contest the underlying colonial relationship "where Black carcerality and White power are morphed and intertwined into a singularizing and complex organism out of which European colonialism and its children, racial genocide and chattel slavery were born" (Saleh-Hanna, 2015, para. 42). As Leah Gazan, a Wood Mountain Lakota Nation political activist points out, interventions are advanced by those with colonial titles and privileges on behalf of the carceral other, who remain unheard or invisible (Chartrand et al., 2016, p. 251). Such liberatory politics, particularly those that require more urgent action such as solitary confinement, forced interventions and high-risk designations, nonetheless continue to reinforce the colonial relations and hierarchies in a carceral system designed to colonize difference. An anti-colonial abolition must challenge the roots of the colonial relationships of liberations politics, as well as the colonial character of the carceral.

In her book *Golden Gulag* (2007, p. 242), Ruth Gilmore points out that the growth of anti-prison groups comes from an awareness that the "prison is not a building 'over there' but a set of relationships that undermine rather than stabilize everyday lives everywhere". This fundamental observation that the carceral apparatus both severs and inscribes relations is central to anti-colonial abolition that prioritizes relations and where a liberation politics is mutually conditioning. In other words, as quoted by Australian Indigenous activist Lila Watson, "If you have come here to help me, you are wasting your time. But if you have come here because your liberation is bound to mine, then let us work together". An anti-colonial abolition recognizes how a patriarchal, white supremist, and imperialist framework has colonized us all and must seek to subvert and disrupt the colonial relations, as something that is mutually beneficial and not part of the white savior trope.

In recognizing the significance of relations in liberation politics, Gilmore (2007, p. 27) further explores the idea of the "power of motherhood" where every person in prison is someone's child. In describing the anti-carceral work of the group Mothers Reclaiming Our Children (Mothers ROC), she highlights the strength of relations in their justice struggles. "In the process of cooperative self-help, the mothers transformed their caregiving or reproductive labor into activism, which then expanded into the greater project to reclaim all children, regardless of race, age, residence, or alleged crime" (Gilmore, 20007, p. 183). This anti-carceral organizing emerges from the profound relations of motherhood that (re)connect people to each other, which is at the heart of many Indigenous traditions and an anti-carceral abolition.

> To the Aboriginal people, family is considered a very sacred and spiritual part of any Healing Journey. Family and community are both part of the sacred circle that helps to define who we are as a people. Everyone knows about the damages that the Residential School system caused when it interfered with that sacred circle. Is this what CSC [Correctional Service Canada] wants to have as part of its own legacy?
>
> *(Delorme, 2018)*

In visiting Gilmore's work, McKittrick (2011, pp. 95–99) further points out that the 'labor' of these women and the love for their children creates a "relational and connective life-force" in the face of gendered and racial violence that "underwrites the making of prison life"; a connective life-force that also underwrites the denaturalizing processes of the carceral.

As expressed by many of the Indigenous authors in their briefs, despite the spiritual appropriation and programing of the prison system, they still sought to connect with their traditions in their own way; found their roots in whatever form that could take; and established connections with themselves and spirit.

> I spent five (5) years of my life in the high security corridors. … [still] devoted to all kinds of spiritualities; the true things of the earth, like making a fire, sitting down, sharing among others, indigenous ceremony, but also a lot of the exercise of physical and mental health and hygiene.
>
> *(Rougier, 2018, pp. 66–68, translated from French)*

In returning to the traditions, just like the Mothers ROC, an Indigenous approach within the prison offers a relational and connective life-force that runs against the currents of colonial segregation, dispossession and denaturalizing in its ways of (re)connecting people, place and land. Indigenous epistemologies and knowledge diversely recognize the sacred connections to all living and non-living beings, strong kin connections, and the equal importance of all those relations (see Simpson, 2000). In its relational connections, Indigenous traditions instinctively swim against the colonizing currents of hierarchies, white supremacy, patriarchy, imperialism and the denaturalized spaces of the carceral. An anti-colonial abolition, that recognizes how carcerality impacts us all, does not centralize institutions or the 'wearing down' strategies traditionally seen in abolition; nor does it centralize the white colonial hierarchies and titles that intervene on behalf of the 'carceral other', although these can be a part of its exercise; rather, at the heart of its work, are the constellations of relations, economies of support and mutual well-being, as found in many Indigenous traditions. This is clearly articulated in the situated knowledge of those Indigenous peoples of this chapter and the many more who continue in the struggle to bring back their traditions and teachings, reconnect with themselves and each other and to return their people home (Monture-Angus, 1999). As Rougier (2018, p. 8, *translated from French*) testified,

> It is always important to find your roots, no matter who or what kind of person you are. I believe that the roots, is to know who we are, where we come from, and who our parents are, these are vital connections.

An anti-colonial approach to abolition goes beyond a colonial and 'oppositional logic' to a relational logic; a relational connective life force that sees the carceral operations and their investment in severing and altering relational patterns. Healing, ceremonies, sweats, fasts, feasts, drumming, walks and other Indigenous connections of kith and kin, along with decarceration strategies, offer a relational knowledge outside of this primary colonizing logic of the carceral. Patricia Monture-Angus (1999), Mohawk legal scholar, termed this as "relational justices" – an understanding of justice as relational, including colonial and penal relations and the ways in which individuals can reclaim justice based on traditional Indigenous justices (see also Craft, 2016) as a way to reconnect with oneself and others.

While abolitionists have developed many important in roads, it has focused much of its energy on 'resistance' or oppositional logics that foster difference, separation and hierarchies similar to that of the carceral. These divides often fail to support a relational and connective life force. Anishinaabe-Métis legal scholar, Aimee Craft (2016), holds that Indigenous people have long held relationship-driven legal orders that take all aspects of life into account. For example, Anishinaabe spiritual, natural, customary and human legal structures are connected and must be considered in decisions related to water and land. Justice, in this sense, does not concern itself with revenge, just deserts, rehabilitation or any other modern capital principles; but the impacts acts have on relationships to all sentient life, water and land. Accountability then must address those harms. While it is outside of the purview of this chapter to discuss Indigenous legal traditions, the United Nations Declaration on the Rights of Indigenous Peoples (UNDRIP) recognizes these Indigenous legal traditions and that Indigenous people have distinctive spiritual relationships with lands and waters, and that they have the right to maintain those relationships and custodianship of them. Its implementation in the land known as Canada would be a part of establishing important forms of accountability at many levels and outside of a simple 'criminal' justice framework. Embedded in grassroots Indigenous traditions, an anti-colonial abolition is founded in more enduring ancestral relations and practices that have always existed outside of and antithetical to colonial and carceral logic.

Conclusion

With colonialism a central feature of our current carceral systems, the displacement, dispossession and disposing of entire populations targeted as inferior to

White Western civility is a central logic of the modern world today. Captured by these carceral spaces and imaginaries, the carceral is not only punitive and restrictive, but also shapes and habituates all of us to narrow understandings of incarcerated persons, ourselves and our relations with each other and ourselves. By tracing the carceral's relation to colonial practices, in this chapter, we wanted to expose the denaturalizing tendencies of the carceral and reveal the ongoing colonial facets at play, including in our own liberation politics. We use a situated knowledge of incarcerated Indigenous men to interrogate these hidden colonial relations that continue today. We further considered how Indigenous traditions based on relations and a collective life force are important to (re)connect us to people, place and land (see also Dei, 2005) and how an anti-colonial abolition can be antithetical to the carceral. In this way, abolition is informed not only on the deeply problematic and endemic ways the colonialism is bound to its configurations, but also how to persist, subvert and resist carceral landscapes through Indigenous strength and resource. Where colonialism continues to haunt the nation-state, so do the people and ancestors of its many carceral violences. The accounts in this chapter provide an entry into new understandings and approaches in a politics of abolition; one that reframes a discussion of justice as relational and that challenges a more subtle carceral logic, including those of our own – I'm not your *carceral other.*

Notes

1 Denaturalized here does not suggest an a priori or natural order, but that carceral systems remove people from their original order into foreign and artificial institutions.
2 On October 22, 2015, Radio Canada broadcasted the documentary on the televised series *Enquête* "Abus de la SQ: les femmes brisent le silence", which uncovered the specific stories of different forms of sexual abuse by Sûreté du Québec officers on Indigenous women in Val-d'Or (Ici radio-Canada, 2015).
3 The Centre for Justice Exchange, at Bishop's University Québec, is a collective of academics, students and individuals who seek to share and create more inclusive understandings and practices of justice and accountability in Canada.
4 In addition to these brief submissions being publicly available, the authors of the briefs also agreed individually to using their public submissions for future publications with the author Vicki Chartrand.

References

Adema, S. (2012) '"Our destiny is not negotiable": Native Brotherhoods and decolonization in Ontario's federal prisons, 1970–1982', *Left History: An Interdisciplinary Journal of Historical Inquiry and Debate*, vol. 16, no. 2, pp. 37–54.

Auditor General of Canada. (2016) *Reports of the Auditor General of Canada: Report 3 Preparing Indigenous Offenders for Release – Correctional Service Canada*. Ottawa, Office of the Auditor General of Canada.

Bhandar, D. (2008) 'Resistance, detainment, asylum: The onto-political limits of border crossing in North America', in Cowen, D. and Gilbert, E. (eds) *War, Citizenship, Territory*, New York, Routledge, pp. 281–302.

Blackstock, C. (2007) 'Residential schools: Did they really close or just morph into child welfare', *Indigenous Law Journal*, vol. 6, pp. 71–78.

Blagg, H. and Anthony, T. (2018) "Stone walls do not a prison make': Bare bife and the carceral archipelago in colonial and postcolonial societies', in Stanley, E. (ed) *Human Rights and Incarceration*, Switzerland, Palgrave Macmillan, pp. 257–283.

Catcheway, L. (2018) 'Parliamentary Brief to the Standing Committee on Public Safety and National Security', *Indigenous People in the Federal Correctional System: Report of the Standing Committee on Public Safety and National Security*, 42nd Parliament, 1st Session, Ottawa, House of Commons Canada. Available at https://www.ourcommons.ca/Committees/en/SECU/StudyActivity?studyActivityId=9736176 (Accessed 27 August 2019).

Chapman, C. Carey, A. and Ben-Moshe, L. (2014) 'Reconsidering confinement: Interlocking locations and logic of incarceration', in Ben-Moshe, L., Chapman, C. and Carey, A. (eds) *Disability Incarcerated: Imprisonment and Disability in the United States and Canada*, New York, Palgrave Macmillan, pp. 3–24.

Chartrand, V. (2019) 'Unsettled times: Indigenous incarceration and the links between colonialism and the penitentiary in Canada', *Canadian Journal of Criminology and Criminal Justice*, vol. 61, no. 30, pp. 67–89.

Chartrand, V., Abraham, M., Gazan, L., James, C., Osborne, O. and Richard, C. (2016) 'Visualizing grassroots justice: Missing and murdered indigenous women', in Lavell-Harvard, D.M. and J. Brant, J. (eds) *Forever Loved: Exposing the Hidden Crisis of Missing and Murdered Indigenous Women and Girls in Canada*, Bradford, Demeter Press, pp. 255–266.

Correctional Service Canada (2018) *Data Warehouse at 2012–2013 Year-End & 2017–2018 Mid-Year*, Ottawa, Correctional Service Canada.

Coyle, M. and Schept, J. (2017) 'Penal abolition and the state: Colonial, racial, and gender violences', *Contemporary Justice Review*, vol. 20, no. 4, pp. 399–403.

Craft, A. (2016) 'Giving and receiving life from Anishinaabe nibi inaakonigewin (our water law) research', in Thorpe, J., Rutherford, S. and Sandberg, L.A. (eds) *Methodological Challenges in Nature-Culture and Environmental History Research*, London, Routledge, pp. 125–139.

Culhane, D. (2003) 'Their spirits live within us: Aboriginal women in downtown eastside Vancouver emerging into visibility', *American Indian Quarterly*, vol. 27, no. 3/4, pp. 593–606.

Dart, C. (2019) 'Birth of a family: The 60s scoop explained', *CBC-TV*, 24 June. Available at https://www.cbc.ca/cbcdocspov/features/the-sixties-scoop-explained (Accessed 27 August 2019).

Davis, A. Y. (1998) 'Political prisoners, prisons, and black liberation', in James, J.A. (ed) *Angela Y. Davis Reader*. Malden, Blackwell Publishers, pp. 39–52.

Dei, G.J.S. (2005) 'Critical issues in anti-racist research methodologies: An introduction', *Counterpoints*, vol. 252, pp. 1–27.

Delorme, J. (2018) 'Parliamentary Brief to the Standing Committee on Public Safety and National Security', *Indigenous People in the Federal Correctional System: Report of the Standing Committee on Public Safety and National Security*, 42nd Parliament, 1st Session, Ottawa, House of Commons Canada. Available at https://www.ourcommons.ca/Committees/en/SECU/StudyActivity?studyActivityId=9736176 (Accessed 27 August 2019).

Dobchuk-Land, B. (2017) 'Resisting 'progressive' carceral expansion: Lessons for abolitionists from anti-colonial resistance', *Contemporary Justice Review*, vol. 20, no. 4, pp. 404–418.

Foucault, M (1977) *Discipline and Punish: The Birth of the Prison*, New York, Pantheon Books.

Gilmore, R.W. (2007) *Golden Gulag: Prisons, Surplus, Crisis, and Opposition in Globalizing California*, Stanford, University of California Press.

Hachey, P. (2018) 'Parliamentary Brief to the Standing Committee on Public Safety and National Security', *Indigenous People in the Federal Correctional System: Report of the Standing Committee on Public Safety and National Security*, 42nd Parliament, 1st Session, Ottawa, House of Commons Canada. Available at https://www.ourcommons.ca/Committees/en/SECU/StudyActivity?studyActivityId=9736.176 (Accessed 27 August 2019).

Hartman, Saidiya V. (1997) *Scenes of Subjection: Terror, Slavery, and Self-making in Nineteenth-Century America*, New York, Oxford University Press.

Ici radio-Canada (2015) 'bus de la SQ: les femmes brisent le silence', *Enquête*, 22 October. Available at https://ici.radio-canada.ca/tele/enquete/2015-2016/episodes/360817/femmes-autochtones-surete-du-quebec-sq (Accessed 27 August 2019).

Jamieson, C. (2018) 'Parliamentary Brief to the Standing Committee on Public Safety and National Security', *Indigenous People in the Federal Correctional System: Report of the Standing Committee on Public Safety and National Security*, 42nd Parliament, 1st Session, Ottawa, House of Commons Canada. Available at https://www.ourcommons.ca/Committees/en/SECU/StudyActivity?studyActivityId=9736176 (Accessed 27 August 2019).

Johnny, I. (2018) 'Parliamentary Brief to the Standing Committee on Public Safety and National Security', *Indigenous People in the Federal Correctional System: Report of the Standing Committee on Public Safety and National Security*, 42nd Parliament, 1st Session, Ottawa, House of Commons Canada. Available at https://www.ourcommons.ca/Committees/en/SECU/StudyActivity?studyActivityId=9736176 (Accessed 27 August 2019).

Kermoal, N. and Altamirano-Jiménez, I. (2016) 'Introduction: Indigenous women and knowledge', in Kermoal, N. and Altamirano-Jiménez, I. (eds) *Living on the Land: Indigenous Women's Understanding of Place*, Edmonton, Athabasca University Press, pp. –17.

Loomba, A. (1998) *Colonialism-Postcolonialism*. London: Routledge.

Mathiesen, T. (2008) 'Response: The abolitionist stance', *Journal of Prisoners on Prisons*, vol. 17, no. 2, pp. 58–63.

McKay, J. (2018) *Indigenous People in the Federal Correctional System: Report of the Standing Committee on Public Safety and National Security*, 42nd Parliament, 1st Session, Ottawa, House of Commons Canada.

McKittrick, K. (2011) 'On plantations, prisons, and a black sense of place', *Social & Cultural Geography*, vol. 12, no. 8, pp. 947–963.

Meiners, E.R. and Winn, M.T. (2010) 'Resisting the school to prison pipeline: The practice to build abolition democracies', *Race Ethnicity and Education*, vol. 13, no. 3, pp. 271–276.

Monture-Angus, P. (1999) 'Considering colonialism and oppression: Aboriginal women, justice and the "theory of decolonization"', *Native Studies Review*, vol. 12, no.1, pp. 63–94.

Nichols, R. (2014) 'The colonialism of incarceration', *Radical Philosophy Review*, vol. 17, no. 22, pp. 435–455.

Office of the Correctional Investigator (2018) *Annual Report of the Office of the Correctional Investigator 2017–2018*, Ottawa, Office of the Correctional Investigator Canada.

Palacios, L. (2016) 'Challenging convictions: Indigenous and black race-radical feminists theorizing the carceral state and abolitionist praxis in the United States and Canada', *Meridians*, vol. 15, no. 1, pp. 137–165.

Quijano, A. (2005) 'The challenge of the "Indigenous movement" in Latin America', *Socialism and Democracy*, vol. 19, no. 3, pp. 55–78.

Rodríguez, D. (2016) 'Disrupted Foucault: Los Angeles' coalition against police abuse (CAPA) and the obsolescence of white academic raciality', in Zurn, P. and Dilts, A. (eds) *Active Intolerance*, New York, Palgrave Macmillan, pp. 145–168.

Rodríguez, D. (2019) 'Abolition as praxis of human being: A foreword,' *Harvard Law Review*, vol. 132, pp. 1575–1612.

Rougier, N. (2018) 'Public testimony Nicolas Kurt Rougier témoin citoyen', *Public Inquiry Commission on Relation between Indigenous Peoples and Certain Public Services in Quebec: Listening Reconciliation and progress*, Val d'Or QC, 9 April. Available at https://bit.ly/2x2CHgm (Accessed 27 August 2019).

Said, E. W. (1995) *Orientalism*, London, Penguin.

Saleh-Hanna, V. (2015) 'Black feminist hauntology: Rememory the ghosts of abolition?', *Champ penal/Penal Field*, vol. XII, pp. 1–33.

Saleh-Hanna, V. (2017) 'An abolitionist theory on crime: Ending the abusive relationship with Racist-Imperialist-Patriarchy [RIP]', *Contemporary Justice Review*, vol. 20, no. 4, pp. 419–441.

Seth, L. (2018) 'Parliamentary Brief to the Standing Committee on Public Safety and National Security', *Indigenous People in the Federal Correctional System: Report of the Standing Committee on Public Safety and National Security*, 42nd Parliament, 1st Session, Ottawa, House of Commons Canada. Available at https://www.ourcommons.ca/Committees/en/SECU/StudyActivity?studyActivityId=9736176 (Accessed 27 August 2019).

Simpson, L. (2000) 'Anishinaabe ways of knowing', in Oakes, J., Riew, R. Koolage, S. Simpson, L. and Schuster, N. (eds) *Aboriginal Health, Identity and Resources*, Winnipeg, Manitoba, Native Studies Press, pp. 165–185.

Solomon, A. (1994) *Eating Bitterness: A Vision beyond the Prison Walls*, Toronto, NC Press.

Stoler, A.L. (1997) 'Racial histories and their regimes of truth', *Political Power and Social Theory*, vol. 11, no. 1, pp. 183–206.

Stote, K. (2012) 'The coercive sterilization of Aboriginal women in Canada', *American Indian Culture and Research Journal*, vol. 36, no. 3, 117–150.

Thobani, S. (2007) *Exalted Subjects: Studies in the Making of Race and Nation in Canada*, Toronto, University of Toronto Press.

Turcotte, N. (Forthcoming) 'Original savages: Part III', in Chartrand, V. and Savarese, J. (eds) *Unsettling Colonialism in the Canadian Criminal Justice System: A Reader*, Edmonton, Athabasca University Press.

Woolford, A. (Forthcoming) 'The destruction of families: Canadian Indian residential schools and the refamilization of Indigenous children', in Chartrand, V. and Savarese, J. (eds) *Unsettling Colonialism in the Canadian Criminal Justice System: A Reader*, Edmonton, Athabasca University Press.

5

THE LAWLESSNESS OF LAW

Outlaw nation, settler colonialism, and a possessive investment in whiteness

Mechthild Nagel[1]

The year 1619 is important, as it marks the arrival of 20 African women and men in the North American territory, now known as the United States. I argue that it marks the beginning of an outlaw nation. Chased, chained, traded, and forced into a death march in Angola, these African human beings were then kidnapped from the Portuguese slavers' ship only to end up on the shores of the British colony against their will. The pirates traded in the Africans in exchange for food, marking the violent advent of chattel slavery. Over the next 400 years, slave codes, black codes, convict lease, and Jim Crow, and other targeted disenfranchisement policies, laws, and statutes, have been carefully designed to accomplish two goals: (1) to protect the white polity in the United States from a population that has been systematically denied rights that white citizens enjoy (and demand) from their state institutions; and (2) to shield the white polity from accountability for the individual and social harms white people through the political-legal process caused to Black and Indigenous populations. In this chapter, I critique the state's legal reasoning as fundamentally Hobbesian and Manichean. This means that the state defends sovereign immunity reserved for white property owners (who claimed stolen territory) and, in turn, practices legal subjugation of racialized subjects, especially those of African descent. Ultimately, such ideology critique is meant to showcase that an investment in legal protection for subjugated people is futile; specifically, the concept of an abstract rights-bearing individual is a ruse and that the belief of the race-neutral rule of law has been used to buttress white supremacist practices.

My analysis acknowledges the insights of scholars (in this book) who have critiqued the settler colonial criminalizing system that has targeted Indigenous peoples the world over. In addition, the system is characterized as racist, imperialist, and heteropatriarchal (cf. Saleh-Hanna, 2017). Building on Viviane Saleh-Hanna's analysis, I want to draw the line between the law which circumscribes the procedural system for those deemed citizens (white, colonial, straight cis men) and what I label as an outlaw criminal legal system which is reserved for subjects residing beyond the pale: subjugated, racialized as Other, disposable, Indigenous peoples, in other words, those who live beyond the protection of the law. According to the English law, an outlaw is someone who willfully does not submit to the rule of law, someone who engages in acts of treason and sedition (Bellamy, 1973). I turn to historiographies of the United States which give us histories 'from below' (e.g., Zinn, 1980; Davis, 1983; Takaki, 2008 Miller, 1995; Dunbar-Ortiz, 2014).

Importantly, I argue that it is the state itself that is devoted to strategic lawlessness, designating certain groups to live 'beyond the pale' (Nagel, 2014). They are rendered disposable, caught up in the vagaries of capitalist exploitation, racism, colonialism, and empire-building. Thus the project of outlaw nation-building is defined as a set of contradictory practices which are designed to ensnare a racialized and impoverished Other. The outlaw nation-state decrees by law that the caste of disposable people be thrown into a permanent status of insecurity and vulnerability, condemning them to a life beyond the pale, unworthy of protection or rights-bearing privileges. The outlaw state is not bound by universal principles of morality.

In the final analysis, we are dealing with a paradox: a law that is committed to supporting lawlessness. This is the definitive characteristic of the *outlaw nation-state*: the use of statutory law, legal precedent and discretionary legal procedures that keeps people of African descent 'in their proper place'—their right to life is strictly determined by those who formulate contract theory and decide who is worthy of receiving contracts. Black people are not even permitted second-class citizenship; they are the denizens of a republic that continues to wage war on Black lives and livelihood. Their chattel slave and subject status continues through the invisible and invincible dragnet of surveillance, occupation, and finally submission to the white supremacist, capitalist police state of the colonizer. My social justice abolitionist reasoning draws on the brilliant insights of those who have been subject to the 'laws' of a captive nation, hunted down by the state and its charges. From David Walker to Ida B. Wells-Barnett, Assata Shakur and Angela Y Davis, marooned intellectuals serve as way-showers for abolition democracy.

Outlaw Origins of Nation-Building

In 1845, Stand Watie, a member of the Cherokee nation, describes poignantly that the white man's conquest is imperial and genocidal.

> If there was a crime … it was more your crime than ours. … You abolished our government, annihilated our laws, suppressed our authorities, took away our lands, turned us out of our houses, denied us the rights of men, made us outcasts and outlaws in our own land, plunging us at the same

> time into an abyss of moral degradation which was hurling our people to swift destruction.
>
> *(Stand Watie, cited in Miller, 1995, p. 344)*

Stand Watie's analysis points out the legal contortionism inherent in the imperial project: the colonial settlers (a polite descriptor for English invaders committed to outlawry) are the real outlaws, deny the harm of their behaviors and place their behaviors within the law while victimizing and harming the colonized whom the settlers deem the 'outlaws'. Genocidal practices are part and parcel of the nation-building project.

Radical historians note that the US republic is founded upon genocide (of Indigenous peoples[2]) and slavery (of African peoples). What is forgotten in this sober account is that both peoples faced both evils. It is forgotten that Indigenous human beings were not only enslaved on their own territory on both coasts but they were transported to the Caribbean islands by the slavers. It is also forgotten that peoples of Africa not only lost their lives in the Middle Passage but that the conditions of enslavement meet criteria of the UN genocide convention. Mainstream historians defend the Enlightenment ideals of liberty and equality as overriding progressive principles of the US republic's social contract. Some try to complicate it somewhat, as told by Matthew Desmond in the celebrated (and controversial) "1619 Project" of the *New York Times*:

> What made the cotton economy boom in the United States, … , was our nation's unflinching willingness to use violence on nonwhite people and to exert its will on seemingly endless supplies of land and labor. Given the choice between modernity and barbarism, prosperity and poverty, lawfulness and cruelty, democracy and totalitarianism, America chose all of the above.
>
> *(Desmond, 2019)*

I argue that the founders of the US republic above all chose *lawlessness* for their new outlaw national project. It is a well-disguised endeavor. The criminal logic of enslaving human beings and their descendants in perpetuity was based on the enduring ideological claim that the plantation served as a civilizing mission for human beings of African descent. To be effective and quell unrest outlaw economic policies were buttressed by a theological promise: through pious submission, enslaved humans would earn salvation.

However, there were protest voices 'from below'. As early as 1635, a leader of the Patuxent Nation wrote a pointed letter to settler colonial occupiers protesting their imposition of English law on all Indians accused of taking the lives of English persons. He argued that "since that you are here strangers, and come into our Countrey, you should rather conform yourselves to the Customes of our Countrey, [than] impose yours upon us" (Unnamed Patuxent leader, cited in Miller, 1995, p. 121). A certain Captain John Odber had been killed in retaliation for his murder of a Wiccomiss woman. Indian people knew very well that a white captain would never face any colonial court of law for crimes committed against them. Two scenarios showcase the impossibility of imposing Indigenous legal standards. (1) If a member of an Indian nation retaliated, the English simply proclaimed total warfare on the nation, killing most and enslaving all survivors. (2) If Indian people did not resist colonial transgressions and violence, the English declared that they were savages who did not have a system of punishments. In the case of Odber, what started as an interpersonal conflict and personal harm ended up in harming the entire community: by 1669, the extermination of the Wiccomiss was assured. They were "hunted down in swamps and mires, and sold as slaves in Barbados. Jubilantly, the English report their total annihilation" on the shores of the territory, now known as Maryland (Miller, 1995, p. 120).

Sovereign immunity—*The king can do no wrong.* Such is the elegant outlaw language of English common law; its logic is extended to settler colonial commoners who not only trespass on 'foreign' soil, but also commit genocidal crimes against 'foreign' peoples, dubbed 'natives'. Colonial 'law' was ever so exacting even when a trifle offense occurred such as theft of a single silver cup in 1585. Such 'property crime' lead to the torching of an entire Indian village and the villagers had to seek refuge with neighboring peoples (Zinn, 1980, p. 12). Indian generosity toward starving strangers was taken for granted by the English. The invaders' own grand theft, clearcutting, and massive dispossession could literally not be seen as major transgression (and barbarism). Here it is helpful to study Hobbes' *Leviathan.* It seems to serve as a blue print for settler colonial outlawry. Sovereign power is granted by (a) 'natural force' (i.e., by waging wars against hostile peoples) or (b) a social contract, where men qua subjects submit voluntarily to the sovereign. Governing by force describes a "commonwealth by *acquisition*", whereas peaceful consent is called a "commonwealth by *institution*" (Hobbes, emphasis in original, 1651/1982, Chapter 17, p. 228). Hobbes gives us a hypothetical case:

> [I]nto what place soever a man shall come, if he do anything contrary to that law, it is a Crime. If a man come from the *Indies* hither, and perswade men here to receive a new Religion, or teach them anything that tendeth to disobedience of the Laws of this Country, though he be never so well perswaded of the truth of what he teacheth, he commits a Crime, and may be justly punished for the same, [...] because he does that which he would not approve in another [...].
>
> *(Ibid., Chapter 27, p. 338)*

Hobbes seems to make a moral case for respecting sovereign customs while using the principle of reciprocity. Applied to the case of the Patuxent leader's petition, the English colonials should have submitted to the Wiccomiss' sovereign legal system. For failing to do so, it is the English who exemplify outlaw behavior. However, Hobbes does not really think of Indigenous peoples as sovereign nations. Legitimating a commonwealth by acquisition means that the Wiccomiss are not legally entitled to the land and must submit to English Common Law.

Long before social contract theory found its way into the Declaration of Independence, outlaw ideology was firmly rooted in Hobbes' ideas of commonwealth and dominion. *The Leviathan* serves as a blueprint and stern warning: those who are endowed with inalienable rights such as legal and civic personhood may give their consent to be governed and included into the (white) brotherhood. In its US contract version, it brings civilizing measures such as the rule of law, free and equal treatment under the law, habeas corpus, and the right to a trial of a jury of one's peers. These are to be 'controls' on the sovereign's power, but they are used to solidify power over those controlled in the mythology of law. In other words, a commonwealth that keeps all in awe, by balancing rights and security. However, there are indeed those, who Hobbes believes are not endowed with such precious inalienable rights. What shall be done to them? In no uncertain terms, he decrees that they simply be conquered—their lives can even be sacrificed in order to preserve law-and-order for those who are rightful participants in the social contract. This is how Manichean outlaw ideology creeps into a text defending a social/civic contract. Why is such conquest legitimate? Hobbes justifies it because these "savages" (sic) do not consent to the social contract. Later contractarian philosophers have more subtle ways of expressing their racism and imperialism, but the point is made. As Charles Mills (1997) argues, the social contract is a racial contract, and philosopher John Locke provided the necessary legitimation: Indians had merely a natural right, but not a "civil right" to the land. Thus, Governor Winthrop was able to expropriate Indian nations living in the Massachusetts Bay Colony. I argue that Winthrop used outlaw logic to declare their land a legal vacuum. With a stroke of genius, they were landless, because natural rights do not have legal standing (Zinn, 1980, p. 13). The social contract was also used to legitimize a plutocracy—personal wealth dictates that laws are only legitimate when they serve and protect the interest of the white male elites, and the legal punitive, i.e., criminalizing law binds the 'unruly' masses by force. (The elites, by contrast, enjoy sovereign immunity in the event they do harm to others, not socially connected to them.)

Much has been made of the Doctrine of Discovery and the fiction of *terra nullius*—the idea that colonialization is justifiable when land does not belong to anyone. Of course, the Americas were already occupied by peoples having diverse justice systems. I suggest an additional focus on the claim of sovereign immunity is needed to legitimate the nullification of Indigenous legal practices. Outlaw colonials with blessings of their religious leaders impose colonial law on subjects who do not consent (especially Indigenous and Black subjects). Witness the kingdom of Hawai'i which lost its sovereign status when the queen was overthrown and jailed by US military forces in the 19th century. Apologies were made under the Clinton administrations but no mention of reparations accompanied that symbolic gesture. (And Puerto Rico and other islands are still considered 'dominions', or captive nations, of the US empire.) Today, sovereign immunity is legally invoked in order to deny claims by torture victims of CIA agents, military and private mercenaries, who operate in (secret) prisons the world over (e.g., Abu Ghraib prison in Iraq).

To summarize, the US republic is founded on multiple layers of outlaw violence—the embodiment of a well-disguised 'legal' hegemonic apparatus.

A Freed from the empire in the east (England), it pursued its own empire building in the West (Zinn, 1980, p. 85). Territorial expansion meant elimination of peoples by any means necessary, including systematic genocide such as the Cherokee Nation's death march, known as Trail of Tears, and brutal containment into 'reservations'. Furthermore, genocidal practices included forced 'assimilation' of Indian children into a 'boarding school' system that led to hundreds of children's premature death and intergenerational trauma. The outlaw state has violated and continues to dismiss Indigenous nations to self-determination and right to peaceful co-existence. Treaties were supposed to preserve such mutually agreed principles. Every single treaty between the government and Indian nations was systematically broken through various devious practices by one side—the agents representing the settler colonial nation-state (Miller, 1995).

B The US government built on the British colonial legal instruments justifying and expanding enslavement of human beings. The US government stands alone in the world defending chattel slavery for adjudication purposes.

C The US government maintains an obstinate belief in the "possessive investment in whiteness" (Lipsitz, 2006), which means that whites and their families benefit in cumulative ways while Black people are systematically disadvantaged, oppressed and punished.[3] Marc Mauer (2000) of the Sentencing Project estimates that during the height of the war on drugs 80 percent of adolescent whites received probation while 80 percent of young Black people were sentenced to prison terms. The benefits of whiteness carry structural, enduring life-affirming advantages. Anti-Black racism, by contrast, leads to "premature death" Gilmore (2007).

Applying the logic of sovereign immunity to the white imaginary gives us a special insight into the performativity of lawlessness. When whites turn their hatred toward the racialized Other, they enjoy immunity from prosecution for instigating racist pogroms, coordinating lynchings, violently boycotting desegregation. While others have analyzed the violence of the law, I focus on the violence of lawlessness—the systematic lack of federal, state, local enforcement of constitutional law, statutes, and ordinances. Sovereign immunity is of course hegemonic ideology, giving outlaws the irresistible pleasure of never having to say 'sorry'. For the (white) hegemonic, Manichean nation-building logic to succeed, it needs diversionary fear-mongering strategies by inventing Black criminality, the myth of Black superpredators. Imprisonment then becomes the right and proper tool of white supremacist carceral logic and law (enforcement) inflicted on those who will never become white (enough).

The remainder of this chapter is focused on state-sanctioned violence: the law's support for chattel slavery and its legacy, the criminal legal system since 1865, the date of the supposed abolition of slavery.

Enslavement codes and the battle cry for dignity

Numerous appellate courts in slave states had to deal with the following paradox: judges ruled that enslaved humans were considered personal (movable) property and incapable of making rational decisions. Enslavers offered them the choice of staying enslaved or moving to another state to be freed. A Virginia decision, *Bailey v. Poindexter* (1858), opposed such offer because the enslaved "have no civil or social rights". Furthermore, giving enslaved persons a choice was "an effort to accomplish a legal impossibility" (Kennington, 2019, p. 234). Alabama judges considered enslaved persons as humans endowed with intelligence and could therefore be found "capable of committing crimes". But they are "in respect of all civil rights and relations, not persons, but things" and could not possibly make choices regarding their civil status, i.e., choosing freedom (Kennington, p. 235). Enforcement of slave codes meant that rebellious people who committed crimes of insurrection, large and small offenses, on the plantation, faced the full weight of the law. Yet, slavers who punished excessively never faced legal consequences. Over six decades, some 800 people filed freedom suits across Southern states. Fairly uniformly, antebellum judges considered them chattel, not humans or the courts prized upholding the rule of (slave) law higher than moral values (Kennington, passim). Kelly Kennington's analysis also shows that judges supported slavery, even when enslaved human beings were granted manumission and material inheritance by the slavers. In that case, the law was ignored due to judges' fears of a free Black populace (pp. 233–34).

The formal strategy of appealing to the courts for freedom was one avenue that was usually unsuccessful. From a maroon's perspective, the struggle for liberation by other means was more practical, if not, more dangerous. In his autobiography, Frederick Douglass (1855) shares what precipitated his decision to run away. He describes one epic fight with a notorious enslaver Edward Covey, "as though we stood as equals before the law. The very color of the man was forgotten" (Douglass, 1855). Covey never punished him again and did not report Douglass to "authorities". Douglass (1855) speculates that Covey was too ashamed to admit to other whites that a 16-year-old teenager fought back—and "won".

Radical abolitionist David Walker, a businessman from Boston, fought in another way with his incendiary manifesto for all Black people. His *Appeal to the Colored Citizens of the World* (1830) was deemed so dangerous that anybody caught with the tract would be severely punished; for Black people—swift execution. Walker's manifesto rallies Black people to commit a concerted insurrection against the institution of slavery (David Walker Memorial Project, n.d.).

It represents a first-rate indictment of the 'Christian' nation-state's outlaw ideology. Walker addresses fellow brothers as citizens, even though the nation-state has only treated him and others as subjects. He died under suspicious circumstances. Georgia's governor had promised a reward of $10,000 for his capture. Walker, born free, was not entitled to free speech (guaranteed by the First Amendment), and his manifesto was seditious, dangerous literature: "The crackdown against the *Appeal* was swift and harsh. Authorities also passed new and stricter laws against anti-slavery material and against slave education" (David Walker Memorial Project, n.d.). Black abolitionist groups took on the US republic's promises of liberty, representation, and free speech to demand liberation from all shackles. This is best exemplified in Frederick Douglass' speech: "What to the Slave is the fourth of July?" (in Foner, 1999) and its ideology critique and prose are indebted to David Walker's appeal.

I argue that outlaw behavior of the slavers' empire starts in 1619 before the legal codification of enslaving Africans and their descendants. The arrival of Africans in Virginia was an event unlike the transports of indentured servants from Ireland and England (cf. Zinn, pp. 23–25). These 20 African women and men were exchanged by hungry pirates for food stuffs. The colonial masters did not take the pirates into custody charging them for trafficking in human beings and returning the Africans to their ancestral lands. However, mainstream historians take a narrow view arguing that these trafficked Africans were not reduced to property and were therefore not slaves (for life) (Takaki, 2008, p. 52). But contracts and punishment regimes showcase one (de facto) reality for Africans and different one for servants (whites). Where they mingle, cohabitate, and run off to maroon communities, racist laws proscribe such fraternization beginning in the 1660s (Zinn, p. 31). The defeat of the multi-racial Bacon's rebellion, which had targeted both friendly Pamunkey Indians and austere English aristocrats in 1676, meant that differential punishment and incentives had to be instituted for Black enslaved persons and white servants to avoid such dangerous liaison in perpetuity. In the Carolinas, outlaw statutes prohibited Black persons' travel to Indian land—a policy to "create aversion" rather than fraternization and revolt against whites (Zinn, p. 54). Virginia instituted a systematic outlaw framework that proscribed interracial marriage and slave codes specified that children born to an enslaved woman would follow her "condition". A century later, the US federal government followed suit by giving maximum protection to slavers to thwart off slave insurrections (Zinn, pp. 89–90).

Of course, a case could be made that there existed protections for the subjugated and racialized Other. The transatlantic slave trade was abolished within a decade of the Declaration of Independence. Slavers could not torture, rape, or kill enslaved persons, including children. However, as most texts laconically state—such fancy legal protections were never enforced. Such de facto disregard for the law is never described as outlaw. There is one notable exception. When the fugitive slave law was passed, one rebel, J.W. Loguen, declares in 1850 that "it outlaws me, and I outlaw it!" (Zinn, 1980, p. 177). He provided for some 1,500 people safe housing in Syracuse, NY, en route to Canada. Loguen taunted his former slaver Sarah Logue, who wanted him to return or pay her $1,000 in compensation: "Have you got to learn that human rights are mutual and reciprocal, and if you take my liberty and life, you forfeit your own liberty and life?" (Zinn, ibid.). In fact, enslavers received ample compensation, especially during times of crisis, while freed people's legal petitions for reparations did not materialize (Hunter, 2019).

Possessive investment in whiteness—Black Lives Matter?

From 1619 to 1669 to the three-fifths compromise, to US Supreme Court decisions *Dred Scott*, *Plessy*, and *McCleskey*—the outlaw nation continues to disguise its exceptionalism. "The history of the United States has been a history of successive and cumulative racial projects" benefiting whites in every aspect of their lives and setting prohibitions regarding interracial fraternization or marriages (Lipsitz, 2011, p. 41). Specifically, Lipsitz faults the US Constitution for setting up "an elaborate federal system designed to protect the power of slaveholders" and for restricting rights of free Black people (*ibid.*). Slavery and indentured servitude remain codified in the Amendment that was supposed to set enslaved people free. Many critics of the "abolition" Amendment (i.e., 13th Amendment to the Constitution, 1865) have noted that slavery merely morphed from private to state-sponsored legal codification. However, the state has always been involved in the "peculiar institution", since slave codes and the US Constitution granted slavers policing power over their human chattel (Walters, 2013).[4] The Amendment along with the other two Reconstruction Amendments (14th and 15th) signified a bit of victors' justice, a hard-won demand by freed men who fought in the Union Army to outlaw slavery and bondage. In 1864, Senator Charles Sumner of Massachusetts proposed this abolitionist language: "All persons are equal before the law, so that no person can hold another as a slave" (Walters, 2013, p. 309). In the end, the compromise abolitionist language mimicked other emancipation laws such as Vermont's 1777 Constitution, which included this exception: "bound by law, for the payment of debts, damages, fines, costs, or the like" (Walters, p. 309). The Amendment's first section declares slavery and indentured servitude abolished, except "where duly convicted of a crime". Thus, the federal government preserves bondage under due process. Thus, the constitutional amendment magnifies the paradox of the outlaw state, which is the guarantor of the rule of law. The Reconstruction Amendments might rein in white supremacy, especially since they are the only amendments that each conclude with this imposition: "Congress shall have the power to enforce this article by appropriate legislation". However, Congress never made use of its power of enforcement mechanism—again, the hallmark of the outlaw state, which enforces laws only when it conveniently serves as severe punishment of the already dispossessed and soon-to-be disembodied. No Southern government was ever punished by Congress for systematically violating the Reconstruction Amendments.

How is it possible to enslave human beings at the same time to promise freedom from bondage? As Senator Sumner demanded, abolition of slavery must be categorical and absolute, binding. The United States is exceptional in this regard since the 1920s—when the League of Nations abolished slavery. The slave patrols and jails the plantation, the slave codes thus morph into police patrols who enforced the black codes and the convict-lease system, considered as "worse than slavery" (Oshinsky, 1996). Texas finally abolished the murderous convict-lease system in 1912, when its prisoner mortality rate got too high—3,500 prisoners died within a 40-year span. A mass grave of 95 prisoners was recently discovered (Groetzinger, 2019). Neoslavery through debt peonage and convict-leasing continues into the 1970s. By the 1980s, rural African Americans in Georgia still received a peculiar 'choice'. Sheriffs offered the following punishment to parolees or probationers: work on a farm or in logging or go to jail. White farmers also paid bonds and fees, and if the workers slipped, coming late to work, they were sent back to jail. Often, Black women and men worked for an indefinite period, since they somehow could never pay back the debt (Thompson & Copeland, 1987).

Federal complicity with the Jim Crow system was made explicit with the US Supreme Court decision *Plessy v Ferguson* (1896). Journalist anti-lynching crusader, Ida B. Wells-Barnett (1892, 1895) issued her damning judgment about the savage reality of white supremacist terror. White men in sheets justified torture and murder to control Black people's desire for uprisings, control their desire in political participation and lastly, to proscribe interracial relationships.

The Jim Crow outlaw decision, *Plessy v. Ferguson* (1896), made it clear that whites found it intolerable to share *public* spaces with Black free citizens. Equally important is the de facto proscription of sharing *intimate* spaces. Until 2000, interracial dating was prohibited in the state of Alabama—and 41% of voters fought to keep it that way—even though this law had already been overturned by the US Supreme Court in *Loving v. Virginia* (1967). Categorically and defiantly, the state law warned: "The legislature shall never pass any law to authorize or legalise any marriage between any white person and a Negro or descendant of a Negro" (cited in Stevenson, 2019, p. 29). Bryan Stevenson's courageous Equal Justice Initiative unearthed hundreds of lynching victims in the *Lynching in America* report (2017) and his organization initiated a first national memorial, the Museum for Peace and Justice, which opened in 2018. It memorializes victims of white supremacist terrorism. Lynch terror signaled to Black citizens that they would never receive the protection of the white supremacist legal system.

By suggesting that white women freely consorted with Black men, Wells-Barnett had to escape the South, as a bounty was put on her head. It led her to organize a world-wide anti-lynching campaign. To this day, the myth of the Black rapist has endured (Davis, 1983) and morphed into its own species: the trope of the "criminalblackman" (Russell-Brown, 2008). A powerful example of this moral panic is the recent attempt of eroding bail reform in New York State. A month before its enactment in 2020, police union and prosecutors warned about the premature release of violent people (without bail). In reality, bail serves to contain the poor, especially Black and Latinx people, presumed guilty *before* the court and plea system fix their sentence. New York's penal abolitionist groups worked hard to stop a proposal that sought to introduce a prediction of dangerousness as a new condition of confinement, which would have led to higher incarceration rates of Black men.

A call for abolition democracy

We need to write histories of the state's own outlaw behavior, exposing their legal reasoning in ideological terms. Their lawyers and judges use any rationale to "divide and conquer", make laws upon the subjugated Other, and they pass over in silence when it comes to their own terrorist behavior. Jailhouse lawyers such as Mumia Abu-Jamal breaks it down to another prisoner: "the System just make and break laws as it see fit!" (2009, p. 28). The elites' acts of transgression and acts committed by the imperial state are simply rendered invisible with impunity.

When penal abolitionists parse through the annals of history written from the perspective of the elites, they must note the Manichean logic which dictates that there are laws for 'decent' people who write and execute the laws, as much as they remain above the law. These laws are foisted upon 'indecent' people: the rabble, the racialized, the stateless denizens of the world. The club of the law comes down hard on the downtrodden, who are banished into carceral fortresses, warehoused in psychiatric hospitals, reform schools, boot camps, and other total institutions. The law is cavalier toward those who commit atrocities but exist within the pale—safeguarded by capital and social connections to those who write or administer the law.

A commitment to abolition democracy (Davis, 2005) entails a recognition and critique of the outlaw nature of a juridical state that *says* it enforces the rule of law and exacts punishment fairly but *acts* otherwise. The critical voices of Stand Watie, David Walker, and Ida B. Wells-Barnett still ring true today since the criminalizing system still has no ethical foundation in a rule of law that applies to all equally. Justice as fairness cannot be realized as long as the imperial, racist, and heteropatriarchal system continues to serve as bedrock for the outlaw nation-state's *raison-d'être*.

What is to be done? I join the choir of abolitionist voices who resist state and corporate violence; who use maroon strategies, unplugging and opting out of the surveillance machine; who establish sovereign and autonomous spaces and cooperatives and community structures with the call for dignity and abolitionist care practices (Kaba, 2017). Exploring visions for liberation, Julia Oparah (Sudbury, 2008) foregrounds the work of "maroon abolitionists", trans and gender-nonconforming activists of color, who contest the penal system (and gender-responsive prisons) and take their inspiration from the ancestors. Specifically, I support a call for *radical* maroonage, since, historically, some maroon communities collaborated with the hegemonic colonial state (cf. Lebrón Ortiz, 2020). These so-called treaty maroon towns had to chase freedom-seeking Black folks into the arms of the slavers (Saul, 2018). Radical maroonage is necessarily abolitionist because it rejects the Hobbesian, colonial legal ideology that criminalizes Indigenous and Black existence. Today, the Movement for Black Lives challenges us to work for transformative (social) justice:

> This agenda continues the legacy of our ancestors who pushed for reparations, Black self-determination and community control; and also propels new iterations of movements such as efforts for reproductive justice, holistic healing and reconciliation, and ending violence against Black cis, queer, and trans people.
>
> *(Platform, n.d.)*

Abolition democracy means nothing less than tearing down the entire criminalizing system and investing in transformative healing justice praxis.

Notes

1 Thanks to insightful comments and critiques from Alliyah Dookie, Michael J Coyle, Lucien Lombardo, and Bernhard Rohrbacher. Lucien also provided me with valuable legal resources.

2 I use Indian peoples or American Indian peoples to refer to *self-naming* nomenclature. "Native American" was popularized during the Clinton administration in the 1990s. Note, e.g., self-naming practices regarding AIM (American Indian Movement) and the National Museum of the American Indian.

3 Lipsitz (2011) expands on the racial logic in the following way: "Largely because of racialized space, whiteness in this society is not so much a color as a condition. It is a structured advantage that channels unfair gains and unjust enrichments to whites while imposing unearned and unjust obstacles in the way of Blacks. Of course, not all whites benefit equally from the possessive investment in whiteness, but even the poorest of the poor among whites do not face the degree of concentration in impoverished neighborhoods and schools or the levels of exposure to environmental hazards that routinely confront middle-income Blacks" (p. 3).

4 "The institution of slavery was created by positive law and could not exist without it. Slavery required that the general tort and criminal laws against kidnapping, false imprisonment, assault, and battery be exempted from applying to actions of the master toward the slave. The master-slave relationship was not necessarily about exploiting the labor of another; it was about the positive legal grant of the power, from the state to the master, to physically control and coerce the slave" (Walters, 2013, pp. 302–303).

References

Abu-Jamal, M. (2009) *Jailhouse lawyers: Prisoners defending prisoners v. the U.S.A.*, San Francisco, City Lights Books.

Bellamy, J. (1973) *Crime and public order in England in the later Middle Ages*, London, Routledge and Kegan Paul.

David Walker Memorial Project. (n.d.) David Walker: Unsung hero in the struggle against slavery. Retrieved 5/1/2020 from: http://www.davidwalkermemorial.org/david-walker

Davis, A. Y. (1983) *Women, race and class*, New York, Random House.

Davis, A. Y. (2005) *Abolition democracy*, New York, Seven Stories Press.

Desmond, M. (August 14, 2019) In order to understand the brutality of American capitalism, you have to start on the plantation, *New York Times Magazine*. Retrieved 1/1/2020 from: https://www.nytimes.com/interactive/2019/08/14/magazine/slavery-capitalism.html

Douglass, F. (1855) *My bondage and my freedom*, London, Partridge and Oakey.

Douglass, F. (1999) *Selected speeches and writings*, Foner, P. (ed.), Chicago, Lawrence Hill, 188–206.

Dunbar-Ortiz, R. (2014) *An indigenous peoples' history of the United States*, Boston, Beacon Press

Equal Justice Initiative (2017) *Lynching in America: Confronting the legacy of racial terror.* Retrieved 2/8/2020 from: https://lynchinginamerica.eji.org/report/

Gilmore, R. (2007) *Golden gulag: Prisons, surplus, crisis and opposition in globalizing California*, Berkeley, University of California Press.

Groetzinger, K. (March 26, 2019) Civil rights activists push lawmakers to confront Texas' dark history of convict leasing, *Texas Observer.* Retrieved 2/8/2020 from: https://www.texasobserver.org/civil-rights-activists-push-lawmakers-to-confront-texas-dark-history-of-convict-leasing/)

Hobbes, T, (1951/1982) *Leviathan*, New York, Penguin.

Hunter, T.W. (2019) When slaveowners got reparations, *New York Times*. Retrieved 5/1/20 from: https://www.nytimes.com/2019/04/16/opinion/when-slaveowners-got-reparations.html

Kaba, M. (May 8, 2017) Free us all: Participatory defense campaigns as abolitionist organizing. *New Inquiry*. Retrieved 2/9/2020 from: https://thenewinquiry.com/free-us-all/

Kennington, K. (2019) "To favor the side of freedom": Judicial opinions and the law of slavery, *Slavery & Abolition*, 40(2): 225–139.

Lebrón Ortiz, P. (2020) Resisting (meta) physical catastrophes through acts of marronage, *Radical Philosophy Review*, 23(1): 35–57.

Lipsitz, G. (2006 *The possessive investment in whiteness: How white people benefit from identity politics*, Philadelphia, Temple University Press.

Lipsitz, G. (2011) *How racism takes place*, Temple, Temple University Press.

Mauer, M. (2000), Plenary session, ICOPA conference, Toronto.

Miller, L. (1995) *From the heart: Voices of the American Indian*. New York, Knopf.

Mills, C. (1997) *The racial contract*, Ithaca, Cornell University Press.

Movement for Black Lives. (n.d.) Our platform. Retrieved 2/9/20 from: https://policy.m4bl.org/platform/

Nagel, M. (2014) Beyond the pale: Reflections on the vulnerability of black life in the U.S." *Diversity, social justice, and inclusive excellence: Transdisciplinary and global perspectives*, S. Asumah and M. Nagel (eds.), Albany, NY, SUNY Press, pp. 69–91.

Oshinsky, D. (1996) *Worse than slavery: Parchman farm and the ordeal of Jim Crow justice*, New York, Simon and Schuster.

Russell-Brown, K. (2008) *The color of crime: Racial hoaxes, white fear, black protectionism, police harassment and other macroaggressions*, 2nd edition, New York, New York University Press.

Saleh-Hanna, V. (2017) An abolitionist theory on crime: Ending the abusive relationship with Racist-Imperialist-Patriarchy [R.I.P.], *Contemporary Justice Review*, 20(4): 419–441.

Saul, Quincy (ed.) (2018) *Maroon comix: Origins and destinies*, Oakland, PM Press.

Stevenson, B. (2019) *Just mercy: A story of justice and redemption*, New York, Spiegel and Grau.

Sudbury, J. (2008) Maroon abolitionists: Black gender-oppressed activists in the anti-prison movement in the U.S. and Canada, *Meridians: Feminism, Race, Transnationalism*, 9(1): 1–29.

Takaki, R. (2008) *A different mirror: A history of multicultural America*, New York, Little, Brown and Company.

Thompson, T. & L. Copeland. (1987) Rural justice: Ex-convicts as cheap labor; an old habit that dies hard, *The Atlanta Journal*, A/1.

Walker, D. (1830) An appeal to the colored citizens of the world. David Walker Memorial Organization. Retrieved 2/2/2020 from: http://www.davidwalkermemorial.org/appeal

Walters, R.D. (2013) The thirteenth amendment "exception" to the state action doctrine: An originalist reappraisal, *George Mason University Civil Rights Law Journal*, 23(2): 283–331.

Wells-Barnett, I.B. (1892/2005) *Southern horrors: Lynch law in all its phases*. Project Gutenberg. Retrieved 2/3/2020 from: http://www.gutenberg.org/files/14975/14975-h/14975-h.htm

Wells-Barnett, I.B. (1895/2005) *A red record: Tabulated statistics and alleged causes of lynchings in the United States*, Project Gutenberg. Retrieved 2/3/2020 from: https://archive.org/stream/theredrecord14977gut/14977.txt

Zinn, 1980. *A people's history to the United States*, New York, HarperCollins.

6

NOT BEHIND BARS

The rippling of carceral habitus and corrective violence on the family and community life of prison guards

S.M. Rodriguez and Brittany Clark

Some of the most invisible actors of the criminal-legal system are its custodians: corrections officers, whose choice of work thrusts them into a violent environment, but who are expected to return, nonviolent, to their homes each day. Proposed reforms to or rejections of carcerality largely focus on the police and those labelled criminal or victim. However, the experience of corrections officers (henceforth COs) in many ways, mirrors that of those involuntarily held in jails, prisons, and detention centres. Like lower-level military, many COs enter the system through a bounded rationality, rather than idealism – choosing *violence work* because they have met socioeconomic constraints due to poverty, standard or low educational attainment, structural racism or geographically informed carceral expansion. It is our position that it remains important to understand how guards (similar to many of the incarcerated) embody both harm-doer and harmed in order to contest the logic of carcerality from a more comprehensive view.

Violence work describes the human representation of the inherent violence of state power. Coined by Micol Seigel (2018), violence work helps us understand the distribution of the state's monopoly on legitimate violence as a distinct unit of employment that coheres the efforts of the military and police. By integrating COs into the category of *violence worker,* we offer a clearer view on the tasks in their charge: embody and enact violence for the paradoxical aim of ending violence. Rather than follow the axiom that "violence begets violence" – at the core of the justification for violence work is the idea that it can somehow curb harm with superior harm. This is, ironically, also the logic of much of the interpersonal violence embedded within jails and prisons, or what has often been referred to as prison culture or the "convict code" (Trammell, 2012).

We maintain a queer feminist, anti-carceral focus on *corrections* as an inherently violent project. The state project to *correct* employs carceralist methods to neutralise and incapacitate people of colour, disabled, and neurodivergent people, queer people, and people who do not assimilate into a bourgeois understanding of order (Balfour and Comack, 2014; Ben-Moshe 2020; Whalley and Hackett, 2017). Corrections, in that sense, relies on pathologisation and the collapse of difference through punitive means. As an institution, it relies on vesting authority to the *corrections officer,* a title that describes those tasked as custodians and guards of jails, prisons, psychiatric institutions, detention centres, and other carceral fields.

To the detriment of a comprehensive anti-violence movement, criminological literature has a limited focus on the interpersonal violence between incarcerated people or between those incarcerated and those on guard. In response, we pen this chapter to challenge others to expand the idea of "prison culture" into the very understanding of our (carceral) state – what if, rather than a reflection of prison culture, the carceral habitus is just a stratum of the state's *corrective* violence? *What if – just as that code spreads to communities, neighbourhoods and households – corrective code returns home as well?*

Carceral habitus and the omnipresence of violence in CO workplace

The reasons that a CO may choose violence work vary. While the demands of the job cannot be briefly laid out on a one-page job description, applicants are typically aware that the job will surround them with violence. It is unlikely that many regard the jail, prison, or psychiatric facility as an abstractly chosen dream job. However, we know that there are some identifiable personality traits that lend themselves better to the field than others. Terrill Holland (1976) pulled groups of male applicants and placed them into pools of personality types, which were then used to compare COs to groups of the incarcerated and judge their potential in the field. What the study found was that the most successful COs had similar social experiences as incarcerated people; they experienced childhood trauma and abuse, they had feelings of being forgotten by the system, and they were often racialised as *other.* While this study could not account for the rapid growth in demand for corrections officers caused by mass incarceration, more recent studies have supported that COs in the United States disproportionately experienced family abuse in their childhoods (Valentine, Oehme and Martin, 2012). Reasonably, the social motivations for this state violence work were the "opportunities for advancement, job security, and early retirement with good pay" (Schlosser et al., 2010, p. 37). With the carceral expansion currently experienced in rural areas, guard work may exist as one of the only employment options, and therefore the position becomes a particularly constrained choice, made to provide for a family (Huling, 2002).

Consequently, for all those entrapped in the system, the next step becomes adjusting to the culture of violence of American correctional facilities. COs witness violence between the incarcerated; they can be harmed by interpersonal attacks from those incarcerated; and they enact interpersonal violence on the incarcerated as part of their work. And ultimately, COs enact the regularised violence of incarcerating people, which has its own well-researched psychological, emotional, and physical toll on those imprisoned (Scraton and McCulloch, 2008; Vervaet, 2010). Kimmett Edgar et al. (2003) focusses on how staff *should* address the violence among people in prison. While there are protocols meant to contain and de-escalate interpersonal violence, this protocol allows for ample discretion that privileges the use of physical force to contain daily interactions. Edgar states that "When problems between staff and prisoners are decided by the superior physical force of officers, the power values that many prisoners bring to prison are reinforced" (Edgar et al., 2003, p. 201). In this way, violence spirals, encircling the state, the violence worker on behalf of the state, to those in custody. While forceful responses are imagined as solutions, they, in reality, pollute the environment with omnipresent and obvious hostility.

Deirdre Caputo-Levine offers an analysis of the total institution that is the prison, which has limited forms of capital in circulation (2012). Violence becomes the preeminent currency, and although not everyone has equal capacity to utilise this capital, it remains the element that structures behaviour, hierarchies and success. This structuring, in turn, creates a subculture (Wheeler 1961, p. 711) and *habitus,* or the set of skills, habits, and dispositions that enable one to navigate the institution (Bourdieu, 1990). A *carceral habitus* relies on a recognition of the ubiquity of violence and a subconscious decision between reactive posturing and superior preemptory violence (Caputo-Levine, 2012). The carceral habitus is inculcated through sustained experience with prison, jail, and other institutions of imprisonment, where those within the institution internalise "the restrictions, authoritarian micromanagement, and routinized abuse of prison life" (Gowan 2002, p. 511). While carceral habitus has been used to describe the perceptions, habits, reactions, and disposition of those incarcerated, we put forward that the habitus is common between the incarcerated and the violence worker.

Workplace violence in violence work

As commonly accepted, workplace violence describes the violence or the threat of violence that the employed may experience, in the course of their work. The problem with addressing workplace violence in the violence work of corrections is that COs are tasked with de-escalating it, administering it, and may witness or experience it unexpectedly. It is pervasive interpersonally, but is also embedded systemically. Therefore, *not all of the violence that affects them is against them,* and they undoubtedly face the lasting effects that naturally come with sustained exposure to harm and death.

While, rightfully, most authors focus their research on violence in correctional facilities on those forcefully locked inside, we feel the need to assert that this work leads to wider-spread unwellness than a narrow focus can pronounce. The violence that is maintained is absorbed and embedded into the behaviour all those inside, including the workers. Whether managing, manipulating, de-escalating or escalating gang violence, sexual violence, or homicide, COs are steeped in a complicated nexus of violence with limited tools to remedy it (or themselves). Therefore, the mental, emotional, and physical health declines for all implicated.

Importantly, in this chapter, we imagine that implication to be as tentacular as carcerality itself. The effect of carceral violence extends beyond an instance's imagined dichotomy of "harmed" and "harm-doer". Because harm cannot be contained – it is carried to and from institution, by the violence worker – we have to understand that these harms follow the COs home. Disproportionately, loved ones experience (and at times, internalise) the carceral habitus through sustained correctional control in the form of family abuse and domestic violence.

We outline three levels of interpersonal violence embedded in the carceral institution, with particular focus on prisons and jails: that enacted against corrections officers, that enacted between imprisoned people, and that enacted by COs against the imprisoned.

Prisoner violence against COs

Due to the violent nature of correctional facilities, guards are explicitly promoted to act violently to secure their own bodies. Corrections officers can become the target of violence, particularly when they are working in large, racially diverse institutions (Lahm, 2009, p. 131). According to a multilevel study examining "inmate on staff" violence in prisons, crowding is one of the main contributors to violence targeting COs (p. 134). While at a micro level, it is easy to assume that violence occurs from a particular bias or motivation against a single staff member, the macro level is better able to explain structural variables. For example, Lahm (2009) found that when younger people were housed alongside older people, they were more likely than elderly prisoners to assault the staff. While police injuries or deaths are more likely to make headlines, COs and jailers actually experience more intentional injury from other people in the course of their occupation (BLS, 2015).

Nonetheless, mainstream news has attempted to make violence against COs visible. For example, ABC News offered a video called "Rikers Correction Officer: A Day in the Life" (Weinraub et al., 2016) featuring Officer Graham, who works at Rikers Island. Like a disproportionate number of people in United States' jails and prisons, Officer Graham is a young, Black male. In the three-minute video, we receive a brief look at Rikers from Graham's perspective, who begins by explaining that he prays for protection and "worries about his safety all the time" (Weinraub et al., 2016). He is equipped with a number of weapons, including a chemical agent used to burn other people and a gun to kill. Within a minute and a half, we watch Graham receive notice that two officers were assaulted the night before. The Rikers' facility is nothing less than degrading for all: people are locked in segregated housing, forced into madness by the lack of humanity. We cannot see their faces, but they can be heard screaming. Unironically, the CO says "it takes a special person to do this job" in reference to enduring "all kinds of smells" after a faceless, confined person attempts to splash workers with urine – his arm waving through a feeding slot.

It must be noted that the COs of New York City are disproportionately Black and/or Latino. The City informs us that 82% of corrections officers of the city are in these two demographics; 58% of which are Black.[1] The ABC video begins with Graham – a Black man – entering into a space where racialised people of low socioeconomic backgrounds are contained by the state and forced into productivity (through violence work or involuntary servitude) and/or madness (through violence work or captivity). It is with reason that the statement "I did my time" is often exclaimed by both the incarcerated and the CO (Lisitsina, 2015).

It is worthy to note that the threat level to COs may depend on the type of facility and its location, as labelling of "supermax" or "super-violent" may create self-fulfilling circumstances (King, Steiner and Breach, 2008). King, Steiner and Breach (2008) focus on Pelican Bay Prison, known for housing prisoners labelled most dangerous and uncooperative. They assert that "when inmates are locked up for being recalcitrant, they become recalcitrant" (p. 161), acknowledging the reciprocal nature of labelling, where labelling determines treatment, which determines behaviour, which determines further labelling. In segregated housing, maximum-security or "supermax" prisons, the exceptional confinement and use of force dehumanise those locked inside, which can lead to radically altered behaviours, sounds, and states of being.

While the motivations and methods of anti-CO interpersonal violence range, the environment likely causes more pervasive damage to COs than particular, interpersonal interactions (Bierie, 2012; Lopez, 2014; Violanti, 2017). A jail, prison, or detention centre creates mundanity of violence: the possibility of injury lightly foregrounds a routinisation of deprivation. The unpredictability of assaultive interactions further entrenches the carceral habitus – with markers of anxiety ranging from emotional dissonance (Thurston-Snoha and Mora, 2011; Lopez, 2014) to overreacting to routine situations (Wells, 2003). The posturing inhabited by prison guard parallels that of the prisoner.

Violence between incarcerated people

Within a site of incarceration, one of the primary responsibilities of the corrections officer is to maintain the social order. That order is, for all of the reasons previously offered, inherently violent. At times, COs are tasked with de-escalating interpersonal and group violence between prisoners (Bottoms, 1999), with threat, force, or manipulation. Hunt et al. (1993) for example, found that guards manipulated gang conflict in order to use the ensuing group violence to forge an environment where one group dominates others. The respondents of the study highlighted the devious nature of the relationship between California prison gangs and the corrections officers, citing three reasons that gangs are encouraged to survive. First, group violence between prisoners led to increased overtime (2003, p. 400). Second, corrections officers sometimes shared similar affiliations, and therefore supplied their associates with the forms of capital required to succeed in the prison environment (2003, p. 401). Lastly, COs "perpetuated the friction" between gangs in order to effectively quell a collectivism that can overturn the institution (2003, p. 401).

This was similarly witnessed by Shane Bauer, as he went undercover as a new CO recruit to investigate a Corrections Corporation of America (CCA)-owned private prison in Louisiana (Bauer, 2016). He reported that, during training, COs "boasted to [him] about inmate management tactics learned from seasoned officers", which included abstaining from intervening in violence and assaulting those who personally offend COs in even minor ways (Bauer, 2016). He was encouraged to follow simple advice during his CO training: "You just pit 'em against each other and that's the easiest way to get your job done" (2016, p. 17).

Incarcerated organisations and gangs operate in ways that encourage division. Gang violence can inadvertently control prisons through a myopic and racialised unity that encourages small-scale violence but ultimately discourages systemic, revolutionary violence. Following the ultimate logic of prisons (and of the state), that superior violence will quell slighter violence, the continued presence of gangs is a remark of allowance; gangs survive largely because they are a desired layer of a violent social order meant to support a greater peace.

Using actuarial science, Davis and Sorensen (2013) sought the significant predictive factors of potential violence, assaultive infractions, and injurious assaults among those incarcerated for capital murder. They found only two consistently significant, independent variables: age and prior prison incarceration. The older an incarcerated person, the more likely they are to avoid all three categories (potential violence, assaultive infractions, and injurious assaults). Prior prison incarceration was the strongest marker to encourage each of the three. Contrarily, while gang affiliation held the strongest effect on "potential violence", it actually did not as strongly relate to assaultive infractions and ultimately was not a statistically significant variable of the most serious category of injurious assaults (2013, p. 395). If understood through the lens offered here, it is perhaps carceral habitus at work: when carceral learning implants force as second nature. Although gang affiliation takes up a large space in the outside imagination of violent posturing, incarceration proves a worse phenomenon in our society.

In addition to the politics of collectivities and the presence of people marked as particularly violent, scholars have studied the more mundane variables that connect to increased interpersonal violence between the imprisoned. Bierie (2013) found that violence between incarcerated people increased in correlation to the increase in time it takes to reply to grievances that they have officially filed. Just as the 1971 Attica revolt taught us, there is a long history of ignored, delayed, or rejected grievances placed by those inside. Bierie reviewed seven years of federal prison data and found that 93.5% of grievances were denied or rejected on substantive or technical grounds between 2000 and 2007 (2013, p. 5). Rejections were typically issued within one day that the grievance was filed. Otherwise, 22.5% of official responses were late, leaving incarcerated people to wait for nearly three weeks for a reply to their concerns about issues such as wrongful discipline (17.78% of grievances), medical attention (16.64%), or even religious (1.94%) needs (p. 5). Intuitively, agitation increases with delays in attention or perceived neglect. Also, importantly, Bierie found no significant relationship between "distributive outcomes" (whether the grievance was granted or denied) and prisoner violence, just whether or not there was a high volume of late responses (p. 10).

Additionally, Bierie (2013) attended to other crucial effects, such as how the ratio of staff members to those incarcerated affected the number of violent incidents among those incarcerated. Bierie found that as the support staff (like counsellors or teachers) per prisoner increased, the lesser the amount of interpersonal violence between prisoners. On the other hand, as the custodial staff (CO) per prisoner increased, so too did interpersonal violence "within the same prison, compared to itself over time, and whether measured contemporaneously or lagged" (p. 13). This may have important implications worth looking at when considering the violence work of corrections officers in comparison to the support work of counsellors, teachers, and other staff working to reduce harm. It may actually be the overcrowding of COs that supports a more harmful environment.

Violence that COs enact against the incarcerated

One acknowledged form of violence in corrections facilities is that which COs enact on imprisoned people. Perhaps the most well-known study on guard psychology is the Stanford Prison Experiment, which showed that even in a role-playing experiment, those put into the authoritarian position of corrections officer adopted denigrating and brutal behaviours to coerce those labelled *prisoner* into degraded positions (Zimbardo et al., 1971). Within a week, the participants embraced a violent order to regulate the hierarchical environment, even in instances of slight (and arbitrary) infractions. Martin, a formerly incarcerated guest lecturer in a college course taught by Susan Phillips (2016) shared that as a result of his tardiness for count, a corrections officer handcuffed him and took him to an area where there were surveillance cameras, where he was beaten unconscious by a small group of COs (p. 44). He believes that he has sustained a traumatic brain injury as a result of the assault. In the official narrative to the hospital that treated Martin's injury, the CO reported succinctly that Martin fell. Other testimonies included "Duke", a white formerly incarcerated man from California, who was victimised in an incident when COs "stripped the inmates down to their underwear, hogtied them, and forced them to lie facedown (sic) on the asphalt in the middle of summer" (Phillips, 2016, p. 60). Rather than an individualised or exceptional encounter, Nancy Wolff and Jing Shi's (2009) data provide evidence that nearly one in four men and one in five women were assaulted by a staff member in the six-month period before their survey.

Violence is not limited to battering, however severe or unusual. Common harms perpetrated by COs also include sexual violence, deprivation, and other abuses of power that constitute torture (Phillips, 2016). In fact, over half (58%) of the sexual victimisation reported by incarcerated people is enacted by guards

(BJS, 2018). This violence also manifests psychologically, verbally, and emotionally, where the abuse of solitary confinement, sexual and nonsexual harassment, threats, and other verbal abuse cause significant damage (Phillips, 2016, p. 64). Phillips analyses this type of guard-on-prisoner violence and reconceptualises the acts of violence used in prisons as similar to wartime situations against terrorists (2016). This comparison, therefore, relates two forms of violence work and pushes her audience to question the acceptability of such grotesque carcerality.

Phillips asserts that "the many physical tortures found in US penitentiaries today belie Michel Foucault's assertion that the locus of punishment has moved from the body to the mind" (Phillips, 2016, p. 63). Therefore, while panoptic surveillance and psychological repression exist as elements of carceralism, detention sites still rely on physical force to a great degree. Through ever-present violence, COs attempt to maintain order and suppress behaviours that undermine state control.

However, it is both the insufficiency of formal training and the unique culture of prisons that explain the behaviour and coping mechanisms of officers. King, Steiner and Breach (2008) state that "formal training is not the only (or even most important) component in shaping correctional officers' behavior. New recruits must also understand and comply with the organizational culture that has developed" (p. 155). This subculture requires that most "exalt toughness and use and tolerate violence against inmates to maintain control" (p. 156). Rather than their formal training being the most important means of education prior to work, a gang mentality leads COs to submit to the officer subculture that exists (Bauer, 2016). In the court case *Madrid v. Gomez*, the court ruled "that there were inadequate written policies regarding the use of force, inadequate training in the use of force, inadequate supervision of the use of force, inadequate investigations of excessive force, and inadequate discipline for those excesses" (King, Steiner and Breach, 2008, p. 157). In Shane Bauer's (2016) undercover investigative work, he found that this encouragement of excessive force and embrace of community-making around prison violence was a feature of his training. Within the first few hours of training, a "veteran guard" taught new recruits to yell "stop fighting" or "stop resisting" in order to justify the enactment or continuation of assault on those imprisoned (Bauer, 2016, p. 8). Later, Bauer reveals that he was even coached to hurt any prisoner who spoke to him intelligently, as prisoners must speak at "inmate level" instead of "staff level" (Bauer, 2016, p. 38). Even a former Oklahoma Warden admits, "When we are not held accountable, the culture inside the prisons becomes a place that is so foreign to the culture of the real world that we develop our own way of doing things" (Gibbons and Katzenbach, 2011, p. 39).

The effects of prison conditions on COs

The aforementioned conditions all have an effect on the well-being of the staff throughout prisons. David Bierie (2012) conducted a study on the effects of various conditions, both physical and not, and the corresponding effects that those conditions have on COs. Bierie (2012) highlights that most of the "debate has generally centered on issues related to inmates alone, often ignoring the fact that staff live, to some degree, in these prisons as well" (p. 92). His study confirms that with "harsher conditions were associated with reduced well-being" (p. 89). The concept of *reduced well-being* is divided among the study between several dependent variable categories. The first of the categories, *sick leave use*, was used to describe the frequency of the use of sick days in COs with seemingly healthy young individuals. Bierie highlights that the amount in days that these individuals are taking is significantly higher than it would or should be in a healthy adult.

Bierie (2012) also discusses an increase in personal worries, and somatic and psychological symptoms that are associated with decreased mental stability. When asked of their substance use since becoming a CO, most guards answered that it "increased significantly" (p. 87). Somatic symptomatology – or the physical ailments that result from violence work – induces poor appetite, muscle aches and spasms, weak feelings, and recurring headaches and anxiousness. The measures of psychological symptomatology showed great increases in depression, anger, hopelessness, worry, and difficulty concentrating among COs (p. 87). Ultimately, roughly one in three COs suffer from PTSD (Spinaris et al., 2013; Barr and Thomas, 2019), which is "on par with veterans returning from armed conflict" (Lopez, 2014, p. 2).

Violence work is understood to transform a body physiologically, into a "constant state of fight or flight" (Lopez, 2014, p. 1). Daily interaction with conditions of deprivation, degradation, and torture are so damaging that they lead to an increased likelihood of suicide for COs. An abundance of research has tracked the frequency of suicides among law enforcement officers in general, but only recently has focussed on corrections officers as opposed to police officers. While the percentage of average adults in the United States who have reported having suicidal thoughts is only 3%, the trauma of the prison leads all within to experience elevated rates of suicidality (Barr and Thomas, 2019). Stack and Tsoudis (1997) found that the risk of suicide among prison guards is 39% higher than the general working population. More recently, in New Jersey, corrections officers were found to suffer a much higher rate of suicide than police officers (34.8 versus 15.1 per 100,000) (New Jersey, 2009). Likewise, in California state prisons, 10% of COs have considered taking their own lives, which, after retirement, increases to 31% (Barr and Thomas, 2019). These statistics demonstrate that the prison environment harms not just those who are involuntarily incarcerated, but those whose circumstances led them to work there.

However, the violence culture is not the only factor in a decreasing physical and mental state of COs. Exploitative employment conditions, such as mandatory overtime, force COs to work as much as a 16-hour shift before being able to return to their families. Caterina Spinaris (2019) describes that this mandatory job requirement is a leading cause of sleep deprivation in COs. Sleep deprivation, as she describes it, can result in cognitive impairments, mental disturbances, and physical symptoms/disease (Spinaris, 2019). Spinaris also notes that the effectiveness of the COs in their daily duties decreases as well, as many become "run down" and grow detached from the work. While many COs describe essentially living at their facilities because of mandatory overtime, this increases the presence of inappropriate relationships or abuse of those incarcerated (Spinaris, 2019). These factors aggravate and increase the likelihood of mental and physical harm. To Oscar Lopez (2014), the President of the NYC Corrections Officer's Benevolent Association remarks on his fear of the hidden repercussions of work stress, stating:

> If we don't do something about it, someone's going to pay the cost for it. And who's going to pay the cost? Your wife. Your husband. Your significant other. Your children. Your friends. The inmate. Because you're so stressed out, you lose it one day. And when you lose it, God only knows.
>
> *(p. 4)*

Bringing violence home

In "Confronting Confinement: A Report on the Commission of Safety and Abuse in America's Prisons" (Gibbons and Katzenbach, 2011), the Commission Co-Chairs begin:

> What happens inside jails and prisons does not stay inside jails and prisons. It comes home with prisoners after they are released and with corrections officers at the end of each day's shift. When people live and work in facilities that are unsafe, unhealthy, unproductive, or inhumane, they carry the effects home with them.

Despite the virtual silence about the effects of prison conditions on COs, there is passive acknowledgement that they, too, live a significant portion of their lives in a degraded environment. Unlike incarcerated people, COs have an ability to bring carceral habitus and trauma home *every day*. Therefore, it is reasonable for those beyond DOC employees and leadership to consider their unique capacity of the CO to affect households and communities at large.

While the effects of law enforcement on the community as a whole have been studied, as well as the reintegration of the formerly incarcerated into communities, the effects that come with being a CO on the community have rarely been considered. Additionally, research exists that explains the terrifying transfer of violence work-related skills to the home life for police officers (Lott, 1995; Ammons, 2005). Therefore, we know that police officers often become used to over-reliance on force, weapons, and authority – an often-dangerous combination when applied to home life. The skills that "spill over" into the home of law enforcement are often used to control, humiliate, and discipline lovers and family members (Graves, 2004; Johnson, Todd and Subramanian, 2005; Stinson and Liederbach, 2013).

While these are normative tactics within the criminalising system, they constitute abuse when in a household or community. According to a study that conducted the frequency of domestic violence incidents in homes where COs live, 26% of all surveyed COs had said they had engaged in violent episodes in their home (Valentine, Oehme and Martin, 2012). The survey also found that 32% of COs had been verbally abusive at one point in their household, and 11.3% had even been physically abusive at one point (Valentine, Oehme and Martin, 2012). In Florida, roughly 60 corrections officers are arrested each year for domestic violence (IFVS, 2009). This is, undoubtedly, a small sample of the number of COs who actually engage in violent practices at home, as the tremendous dark figure of domestic violence is acknowledged and the "code of silence" that allows for violence workers to acclimatise to not "snitching" on their peers, who are regularly witnessed beating, harassing, and coercing others (Klein and Klein, 2000; Ammons, 2005; Stinson and Liederbach, 2013). This applies even in cases when other COs are harming children, as the federal government investigation into New York City's Department of Corrections uncovered through interviews with teenagers who had been assaulted by law enforcement and corrections officers in schools, jails, and medical facilities (US DOJ, 2014). The state agents that witnessed the use of force that injured the kids neglected to file a report, or fabricated the details in order to protect their peers (US DOJ, 2014, p. 23).

Therefore, it is reasonable to believe that when COs bring violence management into what is supposed to be the comfort and intimacy of their own homes and communities, the transgressions generally go unnoted. This is worrying at various levels, including sexual abuse, which is a documented harm performed by guards. The omnipresence of sexual violence in prison is described by those incarcerated as extending from the constant surveillance when urinating or showering, to invasive cavity searches where people are forced to "lift their labia" or "spread cheeks" under threat of violence, to rape by guards (Jackson, 2013). When sexual assault, violations of privacy, and rape are systemic elements of one's job, it is improbable that a home would invite, or even comprehend, anti-violence.

Conclusion

While the carceral habitus of formerly incarcerated people and the risk factors of police officers applying violence work skills to their home and community life have been addressed with research, the unique situation of prison guards has been under-considered. Despite existing at the intersection of these issues – spending a significant time in prisons and jails *and* being trained in ways that may lead to life as a "batterer with a badge" (Ammons, 2005), corrections officers have gone unnoticed to perhaps all but those who hold the job and those who have cared for someone in the position. Beyond the importance of acknowledging the plight of those in the profession, this analysis provides a new basis from which to contest carceral logic. Put simply, *the inhumane reliance on retributive and incapacitating sanctioning is harmful to all.*

Corrective violence – the management of others' behaviours through punitive methods meant to neutralise, discipline, or assimilate – is a "skill" that must be mastered for guard work. The problematic nature of this violence, however, does not remain in the walls of any carceral site. Through the ritualisation of violence in prisons, jails, and other detention centres, corrections officers are imbued with authoritative harm-doing that translates into embodied trauma (the habitus) and carried home as corrective violence (the disciplinary inclination).

Therefore, anti-carceral logic should, in our opinion, extend to those whose bounded rationality led to the choice to engage in violence work. With a bifurcated geography of prison development in largely rural and urban settings, the connections made between corrections officers are that they are generally from working-class backgrounds, with lower educational attainment. In a neoliberal age of prison expansion and the collapse of organised labour and welfare, a segment of workers is caught between the growing demand for jail, prison, and detention work and the loss of workers' protections, benefits, and social services. This proves, for the aforementioned reasons, a perverse and deadly arrangement. While not all enter corrections with apprehension, gratefulness for any employment opportunity should not be conflated with idealism about the job or a particular pathology commonly shared for COs. We believe it is shortsighted and unconstructive to allow blame for violence workers' choice of employment to end our conversation of the pervasive harm of carcerality.

To conclude, we should move forward by soundly rejecting corrective violence. In order to do so, we need to consider the harm that affects all those corralled by state violence. This means acknowledging that the rippling of carceral harm extends far beyond those who opted into violence work.

Note

1 These data were presented through the City Council's fourth quarterly fiscal report in 2018.

References

Ammons, J. 2005. Batterers with badges: Officer-involved domestic violence. *Women Lawyers Journal*, vol. 90, no. 5, pp. 28–39.

Balfour, G. and Comack, E. 2014. *Criminalizing women: Gender and (in)justice in neoliberal times*, 2nd ed. Halifax: Fernwood Publishing.

Barr, L. and Thomas, P. 2019. Correctional officer suicides in 2019 tied for most in single year: Union president. *ABC News*. Accessed at https://abcnews.go.com/Politics/correctional-officer-suicides-2019-tied-single-year-union/story?id=65828169

Bauer, S. 2016. My four months as a private prison guard. *Mother Jones*. Accessed at https://www.motherjones.com/politics/2016/06/cca-private-prisons-corrections-corporation-inmates-investigation-bauer/

Ben-Moshe, L. 2020. *Decarcerating disability: Deinstitutionalization and prison abolition*. Minneapolis: Minnesota University Press.

Bierie, D.M. 2012. The impact of prison conditions on staff well-being. *International Journal of Offender Therapy and Comparative Criminology*, vol. 56, no. 1, pp. 81–95.

Bierie, D.M. 2013. Procedural justice and prison violence: Examining complaints among federal inmates (2000–2007). *Psychology, Public Policy, and Law*, vol. 19, no. 1, p. 15.

BJS – Bureau of Justice Statistics. 2018. Sexual victimization reported by adult correctional authorities, 2012–15, by Ramona Rantala. Accessed on: https://www.bjs.gov/content/pub/pdf/svraca1215.pdf

BLS – Bureau of Labor Statistics. 2015. Table 8. Incidence rates for nonfatal occupational injuries and illnesses involving days away from work per 10,000 full-time workers by selected worker occupation and events or exposures, all ownerships. Accessed on: https://www.bls.gov/news.release/osh2.t08.htm

Bottoms, A.E. 1999. Interpersonal violence and social order in prisons. *Crime and Justice*, vol. 26, pp. 205–281.

Bourdieu P. 1990. *The logic of practice*. Stanford, CA: Stanford University Press.

Caputo-Levine, D.D. 2012. The yard face: The contributions of inmate interpersonal violence to the carceral habitus. *Ethnography*, vol. 14, no. 2, pp. 165–185.

Davis, J. and Sorensen, J.R. 2013. Using base rates and correlational data to supplement clinical risk assessments. *Journal of the American Academy of Psychiatry and the Law Online*, vol. 41, no. 3, pp. 391–400.

Edgar, K., O'Donnell, I., Martin, C. and Martin, C. 2003. *Prison violence: The dynamics of conflict, fear and power*. Cullompton: Willan.

Gibbons, J.J. and Katzenbach, N.D.B. 2011. Confronting confinement: A report of the commission on safety and abuse in America's prisons: FSR FSR. *Federal Sentencing Reporter*, vol. 24, no. 1, pp. 36–41.

Gowan, T. 2002. The nexus: Homelessness and incarceration in two American cities. *Ethnography*, vol. 3, no. 4, pp. 500–534.

Graves, A. 2004. Law enforcement involved domestic abuse. *Law and Order*, vol. 52, no. 11, pp. 108–111.

Holland, T.R. et al. 1976. Personality patterns among correctional officer applicants." *Journal of Clinical Psychology*, vol. 32, no. 4, pp. 786.

Huling, T. 2002. Building a prison economy in rural America. In Mauer, M. and Chesney-Lind, M. (eds.) *Invisible punishment: The collateral consequences of mass imprisonment*. New York: The New Press, pp. 197–213.

Hunt, G., Riegel, S., Morales, T. and Waldorf, D. 1993. Changes in prison culture: Prison gangs and the case of the "Pepsi Generation". *Social Problems*, vol. 40, no. 3, pp. 398–409.

IFVS, Institute for Family Violence Studies. 2009. Module 1: The dynamics of officer-involved domestic violence. Accessed on: Law Enforcement Families Partnership website: http://training.familyvio.csw.fsu.edu/

Jackson, J.L. 2013. Sexual necropolitics and prison rape elimination. *Signs: Journal of Women in Culture and Society*, vol. 39, no. 1, pp. 197–220.

Johnson, L.B., Todd, M. and Subramanian, G. 2005. Violence in police families: Work-family spillover. *Journal of Family Violence*, vol. 20, no. 1, pp. 3–12.

King, K., Steiner, B. and Ritchie Breach, S. 2008. Violence in the supermax: A self-fulfilling prophecy. *The Prison Journal*, vol. 88, no. 1, pp. 144–168.

Klein, R. and Klein, C. 2000. The extent of domestic violence within law enforcement: An empirical study. In D.C. Sheehan (Ed.), *Domestic violence by police officers* (225–232). Washington, DC: U.S. Department of Justice.

Lahm, K.F. 2009. Inmate assaults on prison staff: A multilevel examination of an overlooked form of prison violence. *Prison Journal*, vol. 89, no. 2, pp. 131–150.

Lisitsina, D. 2015. Prison guards can never be weak: the hidden PTSD crisis in America's jails. *The Guardian*. Accessed on: https://www.theguardian.com/us-news/2015/may/20/corrections-officers-ptsd-american-prisons

Lopez, O. 2014. Prison officers need help, but they won't ask for it; in a constant state of fight or flight, corrections officers suffer high rates of mental health problems. *Newsweek Global*, vol. 162, no. 22, pp. 1–7.

Lott, L.D. 1995. Deadly secrets: Violence in the police family. *FBI Law Enforcement Bulletin*, vol. 64, pp. 12–16.

New Jersey Police Suicide Task Force Report. 2009. Submitted to governor Corzine. Accessed January 2020, on: https://www.nj.gov/oag/library/NJPoliceSuicideTaskForceReport-J anuary-30–2009-Final(r2.3.09).pdf

Phillips, S. 2016. Rewriting torture: Manufacturing a primer of abuse in US domestic prisons. *Social Justice*, vol. 43, no. 4, pp. 44–68.

Schlosser, L.Z. et al. 2010. "Reasons for Choosing a Correction Officer Career." *Psychological Services*, vol. 7, no. 1, pp. 34–43.

Scraton, P. and McCulloch, J., eds. 2008. *The violence of incarceration*. London: Routledge.

Seigel, M. 2018. Violence work: Policing and power. *Race & Class*, vol. 59, no. 4, pp. 15–33.

Spinaris, C., Denhof, M. and Morton, G., 2013. Impact of traumatic exposure on corrections professionals. White paper. Accessed at http://static.nicic.gov/UserShared/2015-02-03_nic12cs14gkm7_white_paper_122113_(1).pdf, 28, p. 16.

Spinaris, C. 2019. Mandatory overtime and partial chronic sleep deprivation – Part 1. *Corrections 1 by Lexipol*. Accessed at https://www.corrections1.com/officer-safety/articles/mandatory-overtime-and-partial-chronic-sleep-deprivationpart-1-apZHCJhDY3KHrWdQ/

Stack, S. and Tsoudis, O. 1997. Suicide risk among correctional officers: A logistic regression analysis. *Archives of Suicide Research*, vol. 3, pp. 183–186.

Stinson Sr, P.M. and Liederbach, J. 2013. Fox in the henhouse: A study of police officers arrested for crimes associated with domestic and/or family violence. *Criminal Justice Policy Review*, vol. 24, no. 5, pp. 601–625.

Thurston-Snoha, B.J. and Mora, N.S. 2011. Correctional workers and stress: Providing mental health support. *Corrections Today*, vol.73, no. 5, pp. 55–57.

Trammell, R. 2012. *Enforcing the convict code: Violence and prison culture*. Boulder, CO: Lynne Rienner Publishers.

U.S. Department of Justice (DOJ). 2014. *CRIPA Investigation of the New York City Department of Correction Jails on Rikers Island*. United States Attorney Southern District of New York. Accessed on: https://www.justice.gov/sites/default/files/usao-sdny/legacy/2015/03/25/SDNY%20Rikers%20Report.pdf

Valentine, C., Oehme, K. and Martin, A. 2012. Correctional officers and domestic violence: Experiences and attitudes. *Journal of Family Violence*, vol. 27, no. 6, pp. 531–545.

Vervaet, L. 2010. The violence of incarceration: A response from mainland Europe. *Race & Class*, vol. 51, no. 4, pp. 27–38.

Violanti, J.M. 2017. Suicide behind the wall: A national analysis of corrections officer suicide. *Sucidology Online*, p. 58.

Weinraub, C., Brown, J., Scott, T. and Valiente, A. 2016. Rikers Island officer describes what a day is like for him at the jail. *ABC News*. Accessed February 2020 on: ABCnews.go.com

Wells, D.T. 2003. Reducing stress for officers and their families. *Corrections Today*, vol. 65, no. 2, pp. 24–25.

Whalley, E. and Hackett, C. 2017. Carceral feminisms: The abolitionist project and undoing dominant feminisms. *Contemporary Justice Review*, vol. 20, no. 4, pp. 456–473.

Wheeler, S. 1961. Socialization in correctional communities. *American Sociological Review*, vol. 26, no. 5, pp. 697–712.

Wolff, N. and Shi, J. 2009. Contextualization of physical and sexual assault in male prisons: Incidents and their aftermath. *Journal of Correctional Health Care*, vol. 15, pp. 58–77.

Zimbardo, P.G., Haney, C., Banks, W.C. and Jaffe, D. 1971. The Stanford prison experiment: A simulation study of the psychology of imprisonment. Accessed on https://web.stanford.edu/dept/spec_coll/uarch/exhibits/spe/Narration.pdf

PART II

Creating anti-carceral knowledge

7

START

Emanuel "Eoz"

Where the aim is not to point at something because the theme is advancing.
Was I a child or am I still one? Who is worthy to define?
Why does that matter now, the feet move on the same place.
I should be innocent of evil, but there are plenty of excuses.
I am still in a wrap, covered with papers in ink landscapes.
I see a short way.
The faster I finish it, the whiter I will get to the end.
And the end, it is the end.
There's no hurry.
I take advantage of the landscape swimming in blue seas.
And with different colors I write stages.
Without wanting to use up all the ink, I try to get as much out as possible.
If in the end, only my wrap will remain.
My pieces of skin.
My papers.

8

THE ONLY ADVICE I GOT IS "STAY OUT OF TROUBLE"

David Head

I've been incarcerated for almost twenty years now, since the age of sixteen, in the state of Maryland. I would take full responsibility for my actions but it was a mistake and I did not do the actual act. I believe I should be held accountable but also given a chance.

In the state of Maryland there's no youth center to go to. I was first given a life sentence and I was told to stay out of trouble and find the right people to be around. These are the same people who are supposed to be the worst of the worst. I was sent to one of the worst prisons in Maryland. I made some mistakes and had to grow up. I then had my case overturned and now have a 40-year sentence. I wrote everyone from the governor to senators and the president asking for help. No one replied or if they did they said there's nothing they can do. I was evaluated for a drug program. They said I need the program and qualify for the program and had a bed space. The judge postponed it until further notice because of a ticket that was two years old, which was a drug ticket. Now I never had no help. No programs. The prison I was at for many years has no programs and for the programs they have, you had to be a few years from your release date. So that means if I need help I have to suffer until I get closer to my release date which is years away. If I get any drug tickets or dirty urine, they will hold it against me.

Let me give you a little background. I was molested inside of a church threatened and forced by a member. I was told by this person if I told anyone I would die and he would kill them. So I grew up with this fear. This person eventually got locked up for unrelated charges. I still live with that fear. Growing up my dad was an addict and my mom worked a lot. She also spent a lot of time in the church. My siblings were often doing their own thing and I turned to the streets and became an addict trying to escape the pain that was inside. I felt like I had no chance from start. I eventually ended up in prison for a precious life mistakenly lost. Throughout my years I've showed my remorse. I cry daily for the pain I caused on so many people and I vowed to change that.

To me paying your debt to society doesn't mean your time is over. It is making sure that the mistakes you made is not made again. It's about making sure you change your bad ways. Prisons can make you a harsher person. It's more drugs and violence in a little place. You can't go nowhere and hide. And you can't be a snitch. What's the purpose for prison other than punish you for your mistake? After that punishment then what?

If I pass away while I'm in here, I won't have no one to help me. They are not going to assign me a mentor to guide me. I have been beggin' for help. I go up for my first parole hearing in February. They say they will give me a hit because of the nature of the crime. They won't consider positive things I have done. Not only that, staff members are no longer allowed to write anything positive on your behalf, only negative. This is crazy. If they don't want you to be in prison why not talk about the positive things you are doing. I started a chess club here. I have professors and college students coming from out of state who want to come to court on my behalf and want me to join their chess club upon release. They were told by staff they cannot write anything positive. They were upset. How can parole determine the truth about a person if it's not all provided. This is crazy. Since being incarcerated I have made mistakes but I also received my GED.[1] Over 250 inmates sit for their GED. I have worked in MCE furniture plant and learned how to build and design furniture. I completed so many help groups. I am three credits away from an associate degree in business management. I've done so much positive, yet it's being ignored. When I first started working at MCE furniture plant, they asked me how much time do I have. I told them at the time "I have life". They said "that's good because we don't want no one with short time because with any someone that's going to be here for a long time we can continue to make money".

Note

1 Taking and passing the GED test and thus earning the General Equivalency Diploma gives those who did not complete high school, or who did not complete the requirements for a high school diploma, the opportunity to earn a high school equivalency credential.

9

DESIGNED TO BURY YOU IN A MENTAL GRAVE

Adrian Outten

I won't get into why I am here or the whole story of being raised from the streets, running with gangs getting into trouble and sent to prison at an early age (20). But the truth about having a lengthy prison sentence as long as mine is that even with good conduct credits, I won't be eligible for parole until I am in my 50s. Imagine being incarcerated since 2006. I was first jailed at the now-defunct Baltimore City Detention Center. At the age of 22 (2008), I was sentenced to an egregious life plus 55 years and was sent to a high-tech maximum-security prison called North Branch Correctional Institution.

When I first found out that I was being transferred to North Branch, I didn't know what to expect. North Branch is located in Cumberland, Maryland which is roughly a 150 miles away from Baltimore City where I and my family are from. Cumberland, Maryland has always been known for its mountains that sit at top of the Appalachian path that runs from parts of Pennsylvania all the way to Georgia. The bus ride to get to North Branch is just as treacherous. It takes roughly 2½ hours to get from Baltimore to Cumberland. That type of distance has diminished relationships and support from friends and family because it's unlikely people would want to travel back and forth just to visit someone inside of a prison. At times I feel as though I have been placed in a storage provided by the state at an undisclosed location to never be heard or seen again. The mountains that surround this place actually isolate it, for when it gets dark all you can see is darkness. The illusion makes it seem as though there's no world other than these prison walls.

I was a few months shy of turning 22 years old entering into what they called "the system". To make it worse, I walked right into the pit of hell when North Branch opened its doors. Surrounded by other men who were already years ahead of me in dealing with the ups and downs of being incarcerated. Honestly, could you stand the chance of interacting with someone who had been down 15 years or more on three consecutive life sentences or the person next to him whose doing life for murder and facing another life sentence for the murder he committed at another max-security facility. Surviving these conditions was real tough for me in the beginning. I have never seen racism in full force until I saw it the ways of these Caucasian Correctional Officers. Along with the emotions among us classified as "convicts", we knew the real match up was us against these hillbilly mountain white boys posing as COs. Having to battle with the fact that I could potentially get stabbed up by a lifer over something as small as a gambling debt to laying up in the hospital for weeks after being viciously assaulted by the hands and feet of them racist COs made me develop a set of thinking skills quick in order to stay alive.

Now as a 33-year-old, with 13 years of incarceration, I have been through some things that would have caused a mental breakdown but I'm one of the few who remains vigilant in not allowing this place to kill me. The reason why all prisons should be abolished is because it's designed to bury you in a mental grave until you die physically. With me experiencing the general population and the disciplinary segregation of both North Branch Correctional Institution and Western Correctional Institution (which is also located in Cumberland), I have seen how this environment led men especially those of color to an early death. The scene here is really gloomy these days. You would think that there's all sorts of help programs to help one rehabilitate into a law-abiding citizen but sadly in a region where roughly 3,000 inmates are held, there's not enough funded programs to provide one with the tools to transition into a better all-around person. Both prisons are maximum-security and they hold a majority of those who were sentenced to life sentences. Cumberland is what is known as "the last stop" among other inmates, as a way of saying that this is as worst as it get. It seriously plays a part of why a lot of inmate-on-inmate assaults happen because most of the general population don't have anything provided to them except for dietary and sanitation jobs. Everything else is limited and you have to meet certain criteria to even be recommended for the good, preferred jobs. Then race plays a huge factor on this location because with most of the Correctional Officers being white, they treat everyone differently. I don't need to explain because you should feel where I'm going with it.

But as one begins to do his time in here, you really can watch your years just wither away with no remorse. That's the most stress I feel that I go through because it seems as most everyone moves on in their lives without you. Even when I make collect calls home to family and friends, I feel like I'm such a huge burden to them. It's never easy being dependent on asking help from the outside world. I started out as just being a 20-year-old and now I'm in my 30s with more knowledge about how the world works. The only thing that holds me back is the fact that if none of my state (or federal) remedies grants any relief in my case then I'm looking to say goodbye to all my 30s and most of my 40s before I can say I'm eligible for parole. That's me having to deal with the constant changes prison makes as the years go by.

I understand that one should be punished if one breaks the law but the disparity among how one is treated while incarcerated has truly fallen to shit. Recidivism rates are so high not because one enjoys being locked up, but the turmoil and stress that prison took him through created the malice to build up in his soul. Once one steps back into society, you have to fight through so much that's against you and that creates more anger along with whatever you already brought home with you.

No one will truly know the psychological factor of being incarcerated until they have been incarcerated. You can do all the research in the world to get a grasp of what incarceration feels like but until you become just an ID number, you would never know the feeling. How can I better myself if those who dictate if I get my freedom again are against me? As soon as you walk through the prison doors gang intelligence will tag you as a member of one of the many security threat groups (STG) without any validations other than the tattoos on your body. Half of the time the tattoos are regular tattoos anyone gets. My problem is being faced with the possibility of being charged with additional charges after being found guilty for rule infraction. For example, I can get caught with a homemade knife in my possession which is a rule one infraction. A hearing officer found me guilty, gave me 180 days to do on lock up, and took away 120 days of good conduct credits pushing an already long release date back further. On top of that, I get re-booked for the same charges at the District Court in Cumberland and had to take a plea deal which added six more months to my sentence.

You might ask what I'm doing carrying around a weapon in the first place but after seeing on numerous occasions men dying from inmate-on-inmate knife fights, I usually need to keep access to some sort of weapon if a confrontation comes my way. These guards aren't equipped to come in and save you in record time, so through experience I learned that I have to defend myself. The dilemma between surviving a place like this and changing for the better is definitely far-fetched. I can be self-taught all day on acquiring the knowledge and skills to be productive once back in society but if the prison is not providing those adequate skills then what is one supposed to do?

No matter how much I say 'bout problems, involving being in prison, it seems as though it will fall on deaf ears. I can complain all day but the real question is "will we ever see a day when there's no more prisons?" Prison has become a huge commodity in the world of capitalism here in America. Anything that takes away from profiting and re-investing large sums of money is frowned upon. I'm only one of the 2.7 million that's incarcerated, so the $42,000 that I'm costing taxpayers every year might not mean much, but times that by the 2.7 million which frees up people not paying the government, and then we looking at a big problem.

Like right now, this institution is always testing the limits to what constitutional rights (an inmate holds) are basically being violated. What I mean is this place has in progress to move inmates out of one housing unit (until its empty) to make repairs to that building. But one of the fixtures they try to put in place is controlling how many times an inmate can flush his toilet. Meaning if I use the toilet and flush it twice then there's a timer in place to where I have to wait five minutes for the toilet to reset. If I flush a third time then I have to wait a full hour to be able to flush again. It creates a problem for when you have to defecate while locked in the cell with your cell mate and you can't use courtesy flushes to mask the smell because of the "3-flush rule". We already have one casualty with an inmate killing his cellmate in result of the new rule.

Then the kitchen and chow hall have been shut down until further notice due to repairs being made to sewage pipes. So, we will be fed brown bags breakfast, lunch, and dinner which contains nothing more than bread, fruit, and a snack. Rumors are swirling that repairs in the kitchen can take up to six months. The institution is trying to find a way for inmates to receive a hot meal but in all they could care less what we eat.

As all these problems relate to this institution, me being incarcerated forces me to just be immune to whatever happening and not make a fuss about it. As much as I want to change for the better, every day I wake up in here makes me feel as though I'm in a life-or-death situation. Changing for the better goes out the window when you have correctional officers overstepping their boundaries forcing one to become rebellious to everything. I look out my cell window and try to find hope but when barbed wires and steel fences are staring back at me, I just sit back down on the bunk look at the walls and wonder, "how did I end up like this?"

The penal system might never become abolished but what if people put plans in place for an ex-offender to truly have a second chance at life. I would love to have a second chance to show how much I never want to be in a position like this ever again.

10

THE COURTROOM

Phillip Johnson

I would like to describe a peculiar place, and how it feels to be in this place, with your freedom and life at stake. A lot of people have heard of and seen this place on TV, or have been in a position (seating) in this place; but not with life and freedom on the line.

In America, today and in the past, many people (especially African Americans) have lost their lives in this place, and the lives of family and friends. Here, your freedom, as you know it, your life, as you know it, hangs on how well you, and others, can act, talk, manipulate, persuade and quote the written word. It is a peculiar place. The courtroom.

As a child, many times, the courtroom for me was basically the bridge between the familiar, comforts and security of family (society), and the unknown, scary, dangerous and the abnormal (institutions and prisons).

The courtroom itself (its processes, procedures and participants) was a blur as it dictated my young life taking control, power and a child, from my parents. What a country we live in. I can remember standing in front of a judge, not understanding anything. Hoping that the nightmare would end and I could get back home, and in the streets.

I recall: judges ("white" and "black") sitting up high, in front of me, barely even looking at me, let alone asking me anything, as they determined my path. I was given lawyers I'd just met five or ten minutes ago, or in the courtroom, at that time. As I've gotten older, I've wondered: why aren't we taught about something that will be held over us; dictating how we live. Why aren't we taught the law, like we're taught math, science, reading and writing, in grade school? Like we're taught other subjects, meant to be tools, for our survival in life?

To be sure, I wasn't picked-up off the streets for no reason; at least not according to the law. I was "breaking" the law, but it's as if I signed an agreement to obey the law, which, really, I knew very little about.

The only time a judge spoke to me in court (with one exception) was if I was pleading guilty to something. The one time, as a juvenile, the judge asked me: "Do you do many or a lot of push ups?" I responded: "No." He said: "You must do a lot of something, to get arms like that." By the way, I'd plead guilty, earlier, but this was a deposition hearing, where he could send me home, or to a juvenile detention center. I'd memorized a speech to give, if he'd asked me if I had something to say. I gave the *spiel*, and he let me go home.

As an adult, the courts became a lot more serious, as far as my understanding of what type of consequence could be laid upon me, if I was convicted of a crime. It was as a young adult that I experienced the shenanigans and empty theatrics we call justice, or the pursuit of it.

I can recall: afternoons, sitting in a cold courtroom, feeling very much alone and the target of a slow, methodical attack. As the prosecutor, judge and marshals surrounded me. The courtroom would be empty, as far as curious citizens; the courtroom quiet, except for the voices of the prosecutor, my court appointed lawyer, and (occasionally) the judge interjecting, to make a ruling.

None of my family members were there, though I was in a fight for my life. I remember a feeling of melancholy, as I sat there beside my lawyer. I was very much grateful for her, and appreciated the fact that she was the only one fighting, for, and with me. I developed a superficial bond, that, I'm sure was one-sided as I reminisce, from the advantage of decades more experience.

But why should a young man experience this type of situation, in the United States of America? Many things and situation, met at an opportune time. One thing is undeniable: I was in part to blame, but not alone in responsibility. A courtroom is a microcosm of our society; what wasn't dealt with earlier, comes to the courtroom to be renamed, repacked (but with the same, earlier determined outcome and destination).

I recall: my first time being sentenced. I came into the courtroom, and stood beside my lawyer. Throughout the day, periodically, the judge would look at me, as my lawyer talked (as did the prosecutor). It just so happens: the judge had overseen another case I had, but had released me. When she pronounced the sentence, it was 15–45 years (ten mandatory). I walked out the courtroom, escorted by the marshals, and back to the "bullpen" (behind the courtroom). There, I saw a man I didn't know, but in traumatic times, camaraderie is a necessity.

Boldly, but in a sympathetic voice he asked, "How much time did they give you?" I told him and he said, "You won't have to do that much," referring to the ten-year mandatory minimum. For $100 of "crack" (or what people call crack) and a gun, I received that sentence, and have so far done 25 years of it. A courtroom is a peculiar place. I recall asking, myself, out loud, "How am I going to do 10 years?" (Right after I was sentenced, and talking to the man in the "bullpen.")

It seems: the courtroom of the late 20th and early 21st centuries shares similarities with places of the 17th-through-(early) 20th century (the auction block and minstrel shows.) The courtroom is the same tool used during the original Jim Crow era, being as though human beings are brought through the courtroom, as a "staging-ground." To be inspected, sized-up and softened up, distributed to whoever was able to secure the "bid," earlier, in backroom deals, attended by a select few. People, majority African Americans, are then shipped and transported to modern-day plantations and workhouses; privately owned or the Criminal Justice System's.

Every day, now that I've become aware of what I've become a part of, is a battle to unravel the tangled web, weaved by myself (as an unconscious youth) and the United States of America. Like the courtroom, the African American Experience in this country is peculiar, but, like a paper-trail, can be traced, through similarities in history, we can understand why we feel and act the way we do. Why we are, where we are, and what to do, and not do.

This all leads me back to me. So far, I've written about the negative things a courtroom can encompass, and lead to. Adversity breeds character (develops character). People who encounter adversity, who learn to overcome it, grow from it – fighters never know how good a fighter they are until they come up against another strong, good, fighter (adversity). It takes a worthy foe, to understand how good you are, for you to grow and become stronger.

The adversity I've faced in the courtroom and as a result of the courtroom and its advocates, has made me dig inside myself. And after searching myself, I've come to understand who I am, where I've come from, why I was there, and most importantly, where I want to go, and with whom. The adversity I've faced, as a result of my actions, has forced me to search, inside myself, for the reason why I made the decisions I made in the environment I was in (why I acted the way I did).

I feel better now, because I've come to understand myself, and people (my people) in similar situations. I want to get out of this "modern day plantation" and help rebuild my community. African Americans (fighters) have, and still do face adversity (a foe). We have overcome adversity and it has built our characters, enhancing America in the process.

11

GENERATING ABOLITIONIST AFFECT

Decarceral feminist methodologies and the closure of Holloway Prison

Carly Guest and Rachel Seoighe

Introduction: researching the closure of Holloway Prison

This chapter proposes that reflexive, feminist and affective methodologies can contribute to the intellectual and political project of abolitionism. We begin with a discussion of our work on the closure of HMP Holloway, London, and our decarceral feminist principles that have emerged from a critical analysis of the UK's prison system, particularly the incarceration of women. We then detail how we have developed decarceral feminist methodologies that centralise an ethics of care and practice of reflection and that seek to generate, utilise and take notice of affect. Describing two methods – archival engagement and a prison site visit – we illustrate how we generate what we term "abolitionist affect" – that is, an emotional engagement with and response to dominant carceral logic that is framed by and productive of abolitionist principles. Analysing the prison through our emotional and affective responses has enormous potential to unsettle the naturalisation of the prison and contribute to the abolitionist project by generating "abolitionist affect". The methodologies we detail here aim to disrupt the emotional and physical distance between the free and the unfree and trouble mainstream punitive discourses – make it more difficult to justify punitive sentiments and strategies and the way people are forced to live in carceral spaces.

Holloway was closed in the summer of 2016. Women imprisoned there were moved, in a matter of months and as a shock to both prisoners and staff, to prisons outside Central London. Working in collaboration with Islington Museum[1] and Reclaim Holloway,[2] we consider the meaning of the closure in terms of the policy and practice of imprisoning women in the UK. We adopt a necessarily and deliberately subjective standpoint in order to demonstrate how starting with an emotional engagement with the prison can generate readings that disrupt its legitimacy. This research project has presented an opportunity to develop methodologies that are responsive to the nuances of the lived experience of a contradictory institution, which is remembered as a unique, familiar and supportive environment by some, and as a punitive and devastating environment by others. In order to generate new insights that might prompt a meaningful societal response to women's imprisonment and the harms it exacerbates and produces, we argue for the use of reflexive, feminist methodologies that can generate abolitionist affect. We focus in this chapter on how we developed this approach through archival work and site visits. Methods driven by abolitionist affect demand we pay attention to our gut instincts and emotional responses as an avenue for challenging the seductiveness of carceral logic.

Decarceral feminism in the context of women's imprisonment in the UK

Decarceral feminism[3] is an intersectional movement that recognises the continuities of violence and injustice experienced by women both within and outside the prison. It calls not only for prison abolition but also the dismantling of structural injustices that shape practices of imprisonment and criminalisation (Carlton, 2016, p. 6; Sudbury, 2005). Institutions of criminal justice are a primary means of visiting structural violence upon women. Davis explains that our societal reliance on criminal justice institutions as the solution to crime, and to gender violence in particular – so-called "carceral feminism" – causes us to reproduce "the very violence that we assume we are contesting" (Davis, 2016, p. 139). Carceral feminism presents punishment and the prison as the only, natural solution to socially and structurally produced harm and violence. The prison is written through with vectors of oppression – sexism, racism, classism and heteropatriarchy (Carlton, 2016; Davis, 2016). Decarceral feminism acknowledges that the prison both mirrors and exacerbates oppressions experienced by women in wider society. It is "outside of and different from other spaces, but still inside the general social order" (Baer and Ravneberg, 2008, p. 214). Deeply unequal social structures sustain social marginalisation and disadvantage, inexorably drawing women (and, of course, not only women but men, trans and non-binary persons) into the prison system.

Punitive sentiments and strategies in society have intensified. Carvalho and Chamberlen (2018, p. 219) argue that we invest in punishment not because we believe in its utility but because of its affective dimension. We derive pleasure from punishment – "hostile solidarity" is generated through processes of scapegoating, othering, excluding and controlling others. This uncomfortable logic, however, is rationalised in various ways. Official discourses on women's punishment, for example, rely upon a rhetoric of care, rehabilitation and reform (Carlton, 2016; Malloch, 2016; Scraton, 2016), with discernible paternalistic inflections (Carlton, 2016; Corston, 2007). Imprisonment as the appropriate response to women's offending has been entrenched by the institutional co-option of rehabilitative discourses (Carlton, 2016; Shaylor, 2009). The women's prison system and wider institutions of criminal justice have been rebranded as "therapeutic" – places where women can access services for addictions, trauma or education, for example. This has occurred in the context of carceral expansion rather than reduction: reformist interventions have not disrupted social reliance on the prison (Carlton, 2016). Using the term "therapunitive", scholars have critiqued this element of the "exponential growth in the international women-prisoners reintegration industry" (Carlen and Tombs, 2006, p. 339; Malloch, 2016). As Chadwick and Clarke (2017, p. 53) note, state power is experienced by women as punitive and harmful in the "messy and complicated relationships between personal trauma and 'support' or unwanted interventions by state institutions and processes of criminalisation". Further, in the UK context, austerity measures have created enormous financial pressure on support organisations, leading to the retraction and reduction of essential services in the community. The racialised and classed impacts of these measures have been particularly evident in the declining economic security and quality of life of working-class women of colour, who are more likely to find themselves subject to criminalisation (Bassel and Emejulu, 2017; Cox and Sacks-Jones, 2017). Though prison is an inappropriate environment to access support services, Holloway's closure represented the dismantling of a support system that many women in London had come to rely on, in the context of austerity's assault on community-based support services.

Decarceral feminism calls for a response to women's offending that begins with the recognition of structural oppressions and vulnerabilities and advocates for support in the community rather than punishment and imprisonment. Real change, Malloch argues, "requires the reduction of poverty, inequality and social deprivation; addressing the process of criminalisation and reducing the social infliction of pain" (2016, p. 164). As decarceral feminists, we must be attentive to these structural realities if we are to bring about the imaginative, political and societal shift required for meaningful change. Davis (2003) has long argued that the prison's ideological function has been to absorb and disappear society's problems, in order to relieve us of the responsibility of tackling social problems that cause violence and harm. The prison diverts attention away from poverty, insecure and insufficient employment, structural racism and poor education, while simultaneously rationalising and giving expression to punitive sentiment. Disappearing women behind prison walls – no matter the services provided to them within – only disappears social problems (Davis, 2003).

Reflexive methods: generating abolitionist affect

Feminist methodological innovations are central to our decarceral feminist framework. We have developed a methodology explicitly seeking to generate abolitionist affect. We build on feminist scholarship that sought to instil alternative values within the academy through methodological innovations. This includes challenging the dominance of positivism and "its most acute methodological instrument – that of quantitative methods for its practice of detached and objective scientific research and the objectification of research subjects" (Doucet and Mauthner, 2006, p. 40). Feminist research is shaped by a claim for socially situated knowledges – centralising reflexivity and recognition of the role of the researcher in constructing knowledge, while actively developing diverse methodological innovations in order to unsettle positivist orthodoxies in collecting, analysing and presenting data (Doucet and Mauthner, 2005, p. 40). Feminist methodologies have much to offer prison scholarship, given the focus on reflexivity in terms of positionality and power, as well as its social justice imperative. Both demand consideration of how power influences knowledge production and construction processes – in both methods of data collection and interpretation of that data (Doucet and Mauthner, 2005, p. 41). In the context of prison research, this is important for researchers who have not experienced imprisonment, whose position as "distanced citizens" (Brown, 2009) shapes the production and interpretation of research data.[4] Feminist research asks us to consider the unseen influences on our interpretation of data and how our subject positionings ultimately affect knowledge construction (Doucet and Mauthner, 2005, p. 42).

We argue that feminist methodologies can contribute to the abolitionist project by altering ways of seeing and understanding the carceral system and its impacts. In deliberately evoking emotion and asking questions of what our responses can reveal, we aim to contest carceral logic, with its reliance on rational discourses of justice, punishment and desistance as a measurable, economic imperative. We draw on Ahmed (2017) and Lorde (1984) in constructing a methodology that centralises an ethics of care, practice of reflection and that generates, utilises and takes notice of affect. We do so in order to generate "abolitionist affect" – that is, an emotional engagement with and response to dominant carceral logic, framed by and productive of abolitionist principles.

We want to promote attention, as Ahmed (2017) recommends, to gut instinct as a kind of knowledge, and, further, as a kind of research method. Ahmed (2017, p. 28) asks us to "stay with the feelings that we might wish would go away", to embrace that feeling though it might seem too demanding and potentially world destroying. She suggests that wrongdoing is experienced as a sensation on the body (Ahmed, 2017, p. 22). Embodied sensations mark the phenomena out as unsettling, disturbing or simply wrong. It is this principle of staying with uncomfortable feelings, of noting them in and through the body, that we centralise in this work. We also actively seek to elicit discomfort with the carceral project through our reading of archival objects from Holloway and description of a prison site visit. We want to generate a sensation, in ourselves and others, that something is wrong, out of place and requires examination and disruption.

Our approach is indebted to autoethnographical work – a broad range of methodologies and studies that connect the personal to the cultural (Ellis and Bochner, 2000). While researchers disagree on precise definitions and conceptual boundaries, the blurring of distinctions between the personal and cultural are welcomed. Looking inward, these researchers expose "a vulnerable self that is moved by and may move through, refract and resist cultural interpretations"

(Ellis and Bochner, 2000, p. 739). The goal is to write "meaningfully and evocatively about topics that matter and might make a difference", inviting readers into the author's world, evoking feelings, sometimes by including sensory and emotional experiences, and writing from an ethic of care (Ellis and Bochner, 2000, p. 742). We are inspired by researchers concerned with using their whole "selves" – "all their senses, their bodies, movements, feeling" – to "learn about the other" (Ellis and Bochner, 2000, p. 741). Behar's claim that social science "that doesn't break your heart just isn't worth doing" (1996, cited in Ellis, 1999, p. 675) resonates with us. We hope, in our methodology, to follow those who have resisted the "trashing of emotion" in the social sciences, the war waged "against feeling, against women, against what is personal" (Tompkins, 1989, p. 138). Like Ellis and Bochner (2000, p. 747), we follow feminist and queer theorists who insist on the centrality of "emotion, intuition, personal experience, embodiment, and spirituality" to the research process.

Lorde (1984) emphasises the value and importance of attending to emotional instincts, intuitions and connections, dimensions of experience often dismissed and devalued as "women's work" and constructed as somehow outside of the political and academic realm. The "need and desire to nurture each other", Lorde (1984, p. 111) argues, "is not pathological but redemptive, and it is within that knowledge that our real power is discovered". Lorde's call for the recognition of that "women's work" – and its power – is a deeply feminist, political approach that can be applied to the extension of care to the imprisoned. In arguing for an explicitly affective engagement with the carceral state, requiring ourselves and requesting of others to stay with uncomfortable feelings, we aim to counter the impetus to rationalise our reliance on the prison.

Positionality

The act of production is integral to uncovering knowledge (Jungnickel and Hjorth, 2014) and this process brings our own positionality and auto-biography into focus. As women with no experience of imprisonment, we are what Brown (2009) describes as "distanced citizens". This distance is facilitated and encouraged by the state, as it is central to the acceptance and reproduction of carceral logic. Our positionality means there is little about the everyday experience of imprisonment we can fully understand. We are not claiming to voice women's experiences of Holloway,[5] rather, we use our position as distanced citizens as a point of critical intervention into and disruption of carceral logic. As distanced citizens, we are subject to the power and effect of carceral logic. The decarceral framework helps us to understand the ways in which the state naturalises and normalises incarceration and punishment, relying on emotional distance. We have sought to utilise and develop affective methodologies that insist we attend to the reach and impact of the carceral state, making uncomfortable the comfort this distance can generate.

Our emotion-led engagement demands we attend to that which, in our position, we could easily ignore. We offer readings that invite other "distanced citizens" to question the logic of the carceral (see also Guest and Seoighe, 2019). This understanding of the possibilities and limitations our positionality affords is at the forefront of how we understand our responses to and readings of Holloway. As described below, we handle objects and visit sites of incarceration from a place of relative security and comfort. From this place of viewing and engagement, the small, everyday pains and mundanities of punishment seem stark. We are not arguing that our responses to Holloway are more valuable, insightful or challenging to carceral logic than the voices and accounts of women who have experienced imprisonment, but that we can offer ways of thinking about how easily the prison can be made invisible, seem acceptable or be actively desired by "distanced citizens". In thinking, feeling, and writing from that position, we offer ways of bringing the devastating realities of the carceral into view.

Entering the archive

Shortly following the closure of Holloway in 2016 we ventured into the archives of Islington Museum. Curator Roz Currie collected various objects from the prison during her visit to Holloway after it closed, including signage and ephemera. Other objects, including vessels and cutlery, prayer books, a bed and a mirror were donated to the museum. Daniel Miller (1998) has demonstrated the importance of everyday objects to the stories we tell about ourselves and the world we live in. Things matter: they communicate emotion, identity, histories and biographies (Miller, 1998). The study of material cultures has shown us that the material and social are co-constructed realms (Bourdieu, 1977) and that everyday objects can offer insight into cultural processes (Miller, 1998). Everyday objects are "of significance precisely because being disregarded as trivial, they were often a key unchallenged mechanism for social reproduction and ideological dominance" (Miller, 1998, p. 3). Everyday prison objects hold significance for this reason; many of the objects that women handle and utilise in their everyday routines of washing, eating, dressing and sleeping are those provided by the state. They are instrumental in the reproduction and ideological dominance of the carceral state, communicated through the everyday. Some of the objects in the museum archive clearly communicated the power and operation of the carceral state, for example, signage dictating behaviour or the prison's safe for storing keys, while others were ostensibly designed for a different purpose – sanitary towels and toothpaste produced specifically for prison populations, for example – but revealed the everyday, mundane and apparently "innocuous" ways the carceral state exerts its control.

Moore et al. (2016, p. 29) argue that "all archives are produced under particular conditions that deserve scrutiny". Many of the items collected by Islington Museum relate to the everyday workings of Holloway. The museum's *Echoes of Holloway* project was concerned with giving an account of Holloway that did not just focus on its most famous women or histories. These items also reflect what was left behind and discarded after the closure of Holloway, free to be picked up by Roz on her walk around the prison. They are also, in part, reflective of what other museums did not want, what was perceived as having little monetary value for resale by the Ministry of Justice, and what was permissible for inclusion in the archive, with no security restrictions (keys or doors, for example, could not be included in the collection, for fear of replication). Tamboukou (in Moore et al., 2016, pp. 26–27) argues that the archive is necessarily fragmented, there is always something missing due to selection processes, restrictions and classifications, allowing "certain documents of life to be preserved and others to become obscure and marginalized". What is or is not included in the archive tells many stories about what is considered to be of value and worthy of preservation or documentation.

The objects were also being curated in particular ways through the way we three explored and engaged with them. Tamboukou (2014, p. 631) observes that while "working in the archive, the researcher is always creating an archive of her own, which gradually becomes part of wider fields and bodies of knowledge". The "researcher's cut", as Tamboukou terms it, "creates a unity, piecing together archival fragments, theoretical insights, spatio-temporal experiences and material conditions and limitations" (Tamboukou, 2014, p. 630). The items Roz selected, the ones we spent time with and discussed, or those we commented on and then left behind, what we were drawn to or less compelled by, were part of this "researcher's cut". Framed by an openness to abolitionist affect, this inevitably and intentionally propelled our engagement. We asked questions, shared responses to objects, returned to objects that affected us, and made links between them. This was a collective, subjective, affective exploration of the yet unsorted collection of these traces of Holloway.

Moore et al. (2016, p. 168) argue that, while the archive is necessarily fragmented, the researcher should not perpetuate this fragmentation, suggesting that we have an "epistemological and ethical responsibility" to offer meaning to the collection, and create possibilities for alternative understandings and interpretation. We have a responsibility, therefore, to make our own sense of the archive and to make explicit the "archival sensibility" (Moore et al., 2016) we approach the archive with, and develop while in it. Being explicit about our approach means acknowledging that we entered the archive open to the idea that we would be affected by it, and that the objects we spent most time with, and have subsequently written about (Guest and Seoighe, 2019), were those that evoked an emotional reaction in us. These included the well-worn plastic vessels and cutlery used by women in Holloway, marked by the usage of many women across time, and the austere metal bed frames that seemed to us too narrow to sleep in with any real comfort.

Our feelings of discomfort and unease with these items were shaped by our own position as "distanced citizens" and our reading of these items from a position of relative comfort and security. By focussing on our emotional engagement with these objects we do not claim to collapse the distinction between our experiences and those of women in prison, but to acknowledge that a feature of this distanced citizenship is to be discouraged from sustained critical attention to the everyday practices of punishment and incarceration. By staying with our feelings of discomfort and unease, and interpreting these objects through these feelings, and subsequently reflecting this emotional engagement and its meaning in writing, we generate an abolitionist affect. We ask what these affective responses communicate about the politics of and problems with imprisonment, and invite other researchers and readers to become attuned to affect underpinned by abolitionist sentiment. This is only one reading of the archive and one that is explicitly framed by feminist, decarceral principles. Our affective engagement with the archive allowed us to produce an account of it driven by and deliberately generative of abolitionist affect.

An emotion-mapping, collective site visit

We now reflect on a site visit to Bronzefield, a prison that many women were moved to following Holloway's closure. We consider how tracing the steps taken by many of the women's families on visits to their loved ones is a method generative of abolitionist affect. This prison is in Ashford, Surrey, approximately 18 miles from central London, but a distance that incurs significance costs in terms of both time and money. The extra distance created between the women and their families was central to concerns voiced by the women affected by Holloway's closure and women's support organisations (Cain, 2018). We wanted to experience the journey, to navigate the same route that loved ones would take if they were to travel by public transport and to emotionally engage with the prison site itself. We did this bearing in mind the substantial emotional weight that was missing from our experience in comparison to those visiting incarcerated loved ones.

Codd (2008), Comfort (2003, 2008), and Moran (2013) have drawn out the particular "pains" of entering the liminal space of the prison's visitors' area – for the visitors and the prisoner – where an emotionally loaded encounter between the "inside" and the "outside" occurs. Those emotional "pains" arise before and throughout the journey to the prison. Visiting the prison as a research collective – with others involved in the project and in Reclaim Holloway – made space for discussion and reflection. We talked through our observations and emotions at every stage of the visit, sharing our feelings and making sense of the affective experience of the visit together. From the considerable price of a return ticket (off-peak return tickets from London Waterloo to Ashford cost £10.60, "anytime return" tickets cost £14.50) to the busyness of the train and the long journey time – from home to Waterloo, a train ride up to 50 minutes and a 15-minute walk to the prison, we noted the various difficulties the journey might present to visitors (of differing ages and physical abilities) and their cumulative emotional toll. Beyond these important practicalities, the embodied experience of the visit sparked productive insights in terms of the prison's location and the local community's engagement with it.

The sensory implications of the prison's location were immediately obvious and intense. Proximity to Heathrow Airport means that planes pass overhead with startling regularity. In conjunction with the noise of passing trains on the tracks that run directly past the site, and the busy nearby roads, the sonic effect is overwhelming and oppressive. There is a constant hum of engines, a rushing of air disrupted by vehicles. We wondered how quickly, if at all, the women imprisoned in Bronzefield could get used to this noise and whether this noise could be considered punitive: a casual brutalisation of the senses, a collateral effect of purchasing a cheap but well-connected site to establish a prison. The planes flying overhead generate imaginative departures as well as noise: they signify freedom and might summon up dreams of travel to exotic places. For the women imprisoned in the flight path, the plans are likely reminders of their own stasis and lack of autonomy. Our site visit allowed us to speculate on another unfortunate effect of the prison's location, as a brutalisation by proximity to freedom, a brutalisation by imagination.

Our reflections on the building itself allowed for insights into how architecture is complicit in the emotional distancing between the prisoner and the "distanced citizen" (Brown, 2009). As Jewkes, Slee and Moran (2017, p. 293) suggest, the modern architecture of the prison, with its "bland external visual appearance" means that it has become less visible and less distinguishable. The speckled sandy outer wall of Bronzefield obscures the shape of the prison complex within. It is a tall, towering wall, with a metal rim at its top reminiscent of a container lid. Nondescript and located down a slip-road, tucked away from surrounding residential space, it looks like any other industrial building: a factory, perhaps, or a warehouse. Similar to Slee's description of another carceral site, Bronzefield's notable characteristics were its "sheer bulk" and "nothingy-ness" (Jewkes, Slee and Moran, 2017, p. 299). What was also striking for us, in considering the naturalisation of the prison in the local, lived environment, was the realisation that the perimeter of the prison is a popular walking route. We saw several people walking their dogs around the well-defined route; a path follows the walls, linking the parks accessible from both sides of the prison. It is, to the local residents, simply a building. It is "simply there, like everything else in the neighbourhood" (Jewkes, Slee and Moran, 2017, p. 303). In conversation, we reflected on how emotional distance can also be created by closeness, by normalisation. The women's presence, though hidden behind the walls, is a mundane, everyday reality for the local community. We talked about how local communities interact with prisons and the link between architecture and affect.

Centring an affective, emotion-led methodology such as this collective site visit allows for a reading and exploration of carceral spaces and their surroundings that challenge the tendency of these sites and buildings to render their function and inhabitants invisible.

The purpose of our visit was informed by an empathetic, abolitionist approach which subjected the site and the architecture to a critical gaze and allowed us to see the structural, ideological and deliberate decision to choose this peripheral site, this particularly bland architecture. Prison architecture was traditionally designed to generate affect, to prompt a very different engagement with the public to modern prison buildings. Jewkes, Slee and Moran (2017, p. 298) draw on Lefebvre (1991) to remind us that the "great power" of imposing prison façades, such as Holloway's original design, was to produce an affective response: "the great Victorian houses of correction were spatialized expressions of authority, invincibility and the uncompromising nature of the state's retribution". Now, as Fiddler (2007, p. 192) argues, the "[p]rison as the visual location of punishment is in retreat. Walls now mask the old gatehouses whose intent it was to deter". The visible, deterrent presence of the prison is no longer necessary in a society with a normalised "culture of punishment" and the everyday incarceration of more and more people, more and more women (Brown, 2009; Davis, 2003). Our site visit made clear that the purpose of today's prison is not to make visible the "criminal" and hold her up as a focus of deterrence or derision but to render her invisible, to subsume her into "non-places" (Jewkes, Slee and Moran, 2017), into an invisible system of punishment. The site visit helped us to understand that consigning practices of punishment to peripheral places, aided by the numbing and normalising architecture of the prison buildings themselves, aims to minimise affective responses to the prison.

Conclusion: generating "abolitionist affect"

In this chapter, we model an emotionally led methodology that foregrounds care, reflexivity and affect. We developed and mobilised these methods as a means of generating "abolitionist affect" – an emotional engagement with and response to dominant carceral logic. Drawing on the principles of decarceral feminism, and wider feminist methodological innovations, our explicit purpose has been to describe methods that reveal the violence of the carceral system through affective engagement with the material realities and lived experience of the prison. For those who have not experienced prison, ourselves included, this is an unavoidably limited endeavour. Yet we argue that these methods, in their explicit call for emotional engagement with the materiality and emotional experience of imprisonment, have the potential to forge connections that unsettle the naturalisation of the prison and our common-sense reliance on it as a response to social harm. The methods we describe push us to look beyond criminalisation, to acknowledge the structural production of violence and harm, and to recognise that imprisonment tends to compound suffering and exacerbate rather than address social harms. By opening up space for "real connection", as Lorde (1984) suggests we do, through care and affective engagement, these methods bring to bear/prompt a critical analysis of the carceral system and pave the way for an abolitionist politic.

Allowing ourselves as researchers to be guided by emotions – to use our emotions as method – sounds radical and somehow "non-academic" in the mainstream logic of Western academia and penal policy, with its very masculinist principles of rationality, cost-effectiveness and objectivity. But it is an imperative; it offers a way of puncturing carceral logic that offer only stale, continually broken promises of deterrence and a damaging reliance on retribution, warehousing and managing "risk". The punitive discourses that flourish in society are divisive, derisive and essentialising discourses that individualise crime and social harm, often in a racialised, gender and class-based manner. Carceral logic is dependent on emotional distancing, the othering of the criminal as reprehensible and deserving of punishment and the obscuring of structural reasons for offending such as poverty, addictions and a lack of employment and education. This logic is also dependent on our acquiescence as "distanced citizens" (Brown, 2009), our untroubled faith in the efficacy of the prison despite its failure to "rehabilitate" or prevent recidivism. Faith in the system can persist only because of our othering of the prisoner and our comfortable distance from the realities of prison life and its devastating emotional, physical and social impacts.

Abolitionist affect occurs where an encounter with the everyday, lived experience of punishment moves us to reconsider the appropriateness of punishment in society. It might generate discomfort or disgust in relation to the particularities of a particular practice, such as solitary confinement or the incarceration of mothers, or to the conditions in which prisoners are kept in an underfunded, understaffed and overcrowded carceral estate. Our methodology asks that we allow ourselves to be moved to act and bring about change. Lorde (1984, p. 141) tells us that: "Change is the immediate responsibility of each of us, wherever and however we are standing, in whatever arena we choose". We stand from the position of decarceral feminism and have developed methodologies that are shaped by this way of seeing. In deliberately generating abolitionist affect we consider how incarceration might be experienced and felt, and whether it is an adequate response to the "social problems" it claims to address, and invite others to enter this affective space alongside us.

Notes

1 The Islington Museum, London, *Echoes of Holloway* project and exhibition (2018–2019) was led by curator Roz Currie and funded by Heritage Lottery. See https://echoesofhollowayprison.com/.

2 A "coalition of local residents, campaigners, ex-prisoners and interested persons" collectively fighting for the site of the prison to remain in the hands of the local community of Islington (Mansfield and Wilson, 2017, p. 319). See http://reclaimholloway.mystrikingly.com/.

3 Decarceral (or anti-carceral) feminism does not deny that criminalisation and punishment are part of the male experience, nor seek to detract concern from male experiences, nor suggest that men are not subject to the same forces in society. It simply takes the particularities of women's experiences in the criminal justice system as its focus. Given that Holloway, a women's prison, is the focus of our study, a gender-specific analysis is particularly appropriate.

4 See McNaull (2017) for a compelling account of reflexive prison research.

5 Other dimensions of our work, using focus groups and narrative interviews, bring women's accounts closer into view.

References

Ahmed, S. (2017) *Living a Feminist Life*, Durham, Duke University Press.

Baer, L. D. and Ravneberg, B. (2008) 'The outside and inside in Norwegian and English prisons', *Geografisker Annaler B*, vol. 90, no. 2, pp. 205–216.

Bassel, L. and Emejulu, A. (2017) *Minority Women and Austerity: Survival and Resistance in France and Britain*, Bristol, Policy Press.

Bourdieu, P. (1977) *Outline of a Theory of Practice* (Vol. 16), Cambridge, Cambridge University Press.

Brown, M. (2009) *The Culture of Punishment: Prison, Society, and Spectacle*, New York, New York University Press.

Cain, C. (2018) 'After Holloway: Consultation with women affected by the criminal justice system', *Women in Prison*. Available at: http://www.womeninprison.org.uk/perch/resources/after-holloway.pdf (accessed 31 July 2019).

Carlen, P. and Tombs, J. (2006) 'Reconfigurations of penality: The ongoing case of the women's imprisonment and reintegration industries', *Theoretical Criminology*, vol. 10, no. 3, pp. 337–360.

Carlton. B. (2016) 'Penal reform, anti-carceral feminist campaigns and the politics of change in women's prisons', *Punishment & Society*, vol. 20, no. 3, pp. 283–307.

Carvalho, H. and Chamberlen, A. (2018) 'Why punishment pleases: Punitive feelings in a world of hostile solidarity', *Punishment and Society*, vol. 20, no. 2, pp. 217–234.

Chadwick, K. and Clarke, B. (2017) 'From 'troubled' women to failing institutions: The necessary narrative shift for the decarceration of women post-Corston', in Moore, L, Scraton, P and Wahidin, A. (eds) *Women's Imprisonment and the Case for Abolition: Critical Reflections on Corston Ten Years On*, Abingdon and New York, Routledge, pp. 61–80.

Codd, H. (2008) *In the Shadow of Prison. Families, Imprisonment and Criminal Justice*, Devon and Portland, Willan Publishing.

Comfort, M. (2003) 'In the tube at San Quentin: The "secondary prisonization" of women visiting inmates', *Journal of Contemporary Ethnography*, vol. 32, no. 1, pp. 77–107.

Comfort, M. (2008) *Doing Time Together: Love and Family in the Shadow of the Prison*, Chicago, University of Chicago Press.

Corston, J. (2007) *The Corston Report: A Report by Baroness Jean Corston of a Review of Women with Particular Vulnerabilities in the Criminal Justice System: The Need for a Distinct, Radically Different, Visibly-led, Strategic, Proportionate, Holistic, Woman-centred, Integrated Approach*, Home Office, UK.

Cox, J. and Sacks-Jones, K. (2017) *"Double Disadvantage": The Experiences of Black, Asian and Minority Ethnic Women in the Criminal Justice System*, London, Women in Prison and Agenda.

Davis, A. Y. (2003) *Are Prisons Obselete?* New York, Seven Stories Press.

Davis, A. Y. (2016) *Freedom is a Constant Struggle: Ferguson, Palestine and the Foundations of a Movement*, Chicago, Haymarket Books.

Doucet, A. and Mauthner, N. S. (2006) 'Feminist methodologies and epistemology', in Bryant, CD and Peck, DL (eds) *The Handbook of 21st Century Sociology*, Thousand Oaks, CA, Sage, pp. 36–43.

Ellis, C. (1999) 'Heartful Autoethnography', *Qualitative Health Research*, vol. 9, no. 5, pp. 669–683.

Ellis, C. and Bochner, A. (2000) 'Autoethnography, Personal Narrative, Reflexivity: Researcher as Subject' in Denzin, L. and Lincoln, Y. (eds.) *Handbook on Qualitative Research*, Thousand Oaks, CA, Sage, pp. 733–768.

Fiddler, M. (2007) 'Projecting the prison: The depiction of the uncanny in the Shawshank Redepmetion', *Crime, Media, Culture*, vol. 3, no. 2, pp. 192–206.

Guest, C. and Seoighe, R. (2019) 'Familiarity and Strangeness: Seeing everyday practices of punishment and resistance in Holloway Prison', *Punishment and Society*, vol. 22, no. 3, pp. 1–23

Jewkes, Y., Slee, E. and Moran, D. (2017) 'The visual retreat of the prison: Non-places for non-people', in Brown, M. and Carrabine, E. *Routledge International Handbook of Visual Criminology*, London, Routledge, pp. 293–304.

Jungnickel, K. and Hjorth, L. (2014) 'Methodological entanglements in the field: Methods, transitions and transmissions', *Visual Studies*, vol. 29, no. 2, pp. 138–147.

Lefebvre, H. (1991) *The Production of Space*, Oxford, Blackwell.

Lorde, A. (1984) *Sister Outsider: Essays and Speeches*, Trumansburg, Crossing Press.

Malloch, M. S. (2016) 'Justice for Women: A Penal Utopia', *Justice, Power and Resistance*, Foundation Volume, pp. 151–169.

Mansfield, M. and Wilson, A. (2017) 'Reclaim Holloway: Repeating the same mistakes, we can only expect the same results', *Justice, Power and Resistance*, vol. 1, no. 2, pp. 316–323.

McNaull, G. (2017) 'Critical feminist methodology: A reflexive account', in Fletcher, S. and White, H. (eds.) *Emerging Voices: Critical Social Research by European Group Postgraduate and Early Career Researchers*, London, EGPress, pp. 165–178.

Miller, D. (1998) 'Introduction: Why some things matter', in Miller, D. (ed.) *Material Cultures: Why Some Things Matter*, London, UCL Press, pp. 3–24.

Moore, N., Salter, A., Stanley, L. and Tamboukou, M. (2016) *The Archive Project: Archival Research in the Social Sciences*, London, Routledge.

Moran, D. (2013) 'Carceral geography and the spatialities of prison visiting: Visitation, recidivism, and hyperincarceration', *Environment and Planning D: Society and Space*, vol. 31, no.1, pp. 174–190.

Prison Reform Trust (2017) *Rates of Imprisonment for Women in Each Police Force Area in England and Wales, 2017*, London. Available at: http://www.prisonreformtrust.org.uk/PressPolicy/News/vw/1/ItemID/651.

Scraton, P. (2016) 'Bearing witness to the "pains of others": researching power, violence and resistance in a women's prison', *International Journal for Crime Justice and Social Democracy*, vol. 5, no. 1, pp. 5–20.

Shaylor, C. (2009) 'Neither kind nor gentle: The perils of gender responsive justice', in McCulloch, J. and Scraton, P. (eds) *The Violence of Incarceration*, New York, Routledge, pp. 145–163.

Sudbury, J. (2005) 'Introduction: Feminist critiques, transnational landscapes, abolitionist visions', in Sudbury, J. (ed.) *Global Lockdown: Race, Gender and the Prison-Industrial Complex*, New York, Routledge, pp. xi–xxvii.

Tamboukou, M. (2014) 'Archival research: Unravelling space/time/matter entanglements and fragments', *Qualitative Research*, vol. 14, no. 5, pp. 617–633.

Tompkins, J. (1989) 'Me and my shadow.' In Kauffman, L. (ed.) *Gender and Theory: Dialogues on Feminist Criticism*, Cambridge, Blackwell, pp. 121–139.

12

"THERE IS NO JUSTICE, THERE IS JUST US!" TOWARDS A POSTCOLONIAL FEMINIST CRITIQUE OF POLICING USING THE EXAMPLE OF RACIAL PROFILING IN EUROPE

Vanessa E. Thompson

> Jokes aside: I've got loads of issues. Although I drive my car slowly (and never fall for all the talk on European unification), or if I drive towards the border by bus or train, I ask myself why I'm the only one who has to provide identification! Is it so unusual when an Afro-German speaks his language, and isn't so pale in his face?

This is a quote from the track *Fremd im eigenen Land* (Stranger in Your Own Country) by the post migrant hip hop crew Advanced Chemistry. They published the song in 1992, following the racist pogroms in Rostock-Lichtenhagen, Germany. The group thematises the series of racist pogroms occurring at that time, also in relation to border regimes, as well as the structural racism that their members experience on a daily basis as black and other people of colour in Germany. Here, the experiences of police controls in which one has to "prove" one's identity are of fundamental importance.[1]

This article contextualises the deep rootedness of racism within the police apparatus by looking at the practice of racial profiling from a postcolonial feminist perspective and discusses it in respect of contemporary struggles against racial profiling in Germany, France and Switzerland.[2] Such a perspective allows a focus on entangled forms of policing, especially in their unspectacular everydayness. This also challenges the assumption that the function of the police changes from that of a guaranty of democracy to repression only in prominent incidents. I first present crucial gaps within dominant theories of policing. Second, I discuss lived experiences of racist policing along the lines of intersectional modalities of violence. Third, I focus on some of the practices of resistance. Lastly, I look at their abolitionist implications.

Dominant theories of policing and their white gaps

Strands of tradition within critical police studies, which in their heterogeneity analyse the forms, characteristics, mechanics as well as multiple histories of policing and understand them as intertwined with societal relations of power have been increasingly thematised in the German context (Künkel, 2014; Künkel and Briken, 2014; Loick, 2016; Pichl, 2014). With respect to Marxist and post-structuralist approaches, the police is analysed as a societal power relation, which reproduces discourses, arrangements and ideologies. Some of these approaches remain not only within the realm of a judiciary critique of the police but also radically question the legitimacy of the police on the basis of its inherent violence due to its contradictory relation with the law (Loick, 2016; Pichl, 2014). Here, police is also often conceptualised as functioning beyond the mere institution of police, as police interpellates subjects without being present.

Louis Althusser described the scene of modern subject formation through the interpellation by the police as such: through being hailed by police ("Hey, you there!") the person that turns around becomes a subject. And yet, the police interpellation does not require a constant police presence, as the policed law subject itself is prompted to act according to the law. Involved in the legal order, the modern policed subject not only recognises its subjectivity but further desires itself as a subject with rights that must be protected (Trautmann, 2013).

These theories undoubtedly belong to the most important approaches within a critical theory of policing. However, they also (re-)produce crucial gaps. I would like to outline at least two of these gaps and point to some of the shifts rendered possible through an analysis of the police in its relation to the history of European colonialism and racism (McCoy, 2009; Müller, 2014; Seigel, 2017).

Methodological Eurocentrism

It does not suffice to say that modern policing is constitutive of European nation-states, as European nation-states were also colonial empires (Bhambra, 2017). Merely discussing the genesis of the modern police within national framings obfuscates that police surveillance regimes are geographically as well as historically far more interlaced with each other (Browne, 2015; McCoy, 2009; Müller, 2014). Surveillance and punishment techniques which were developed in the "colonial laboratories" (Hönke and Müller, 2012; Loomba, 2005) of European colonial powers, spaces that were rather characterised through a juridification of "premature deaths" (Gilmore, 2007), often served as predecessors for the policed within the colonial metropoles. This was especially reflected in the presence of the police in many European colonies. As Frantz Fanon writes:

> The colonial world is a world cut in two. The dividing line, the frontiers are shown by barracks and police stations. In the colonies it is the

> policeman and the soldier who are the official, instituted go-betweens, the spokesmen of the settler and his rule of oppression. In capitalist societies the educational system, whether lay or clerical, the structure of moral reflexes handed down from father to son, the exemplary honesty of workers who are given a medal after 50 years of good and loyal service, and the affection which springs from harmonious relations and good behaviour – all these aesthetic expressions of respect for the established order serve to create around the exploited person an atmosphere of submission and of inhibition which lightens the task of policing considerably .... In the colonial countries, on the contrary, the policeman and the soldier, by their immediate presence and their frequent and direct action maintain contact with the native and advise him by means of rifle butts and napalm not to budge.
>
> *(1963, p. 38)*

Fanon points out the daily and violent presence of the police within the lives of colonised populations. Furthermore, he refers to the interplay between the police and military. A historicisation is also relevant for contemporary police studies. For example, the militarisation of police forces in the colonised suburbs of the global North cannot be detached from the continuations of the militarisation of police from a historical as well as transnational analysis along postcolonial North-South relations (Müller, 2014). The connection between the inclusion of colonised subjects into colonial police forces and neoliberal diversification strategies within police institutions serves as another example. Here, I am not aiming at a linear account of colonial continuities, but a contextualisation of postcolonial modes along their interwoven connections as well as discontinuities.

"Hey you there?" Who?

A postcolonial critique also raises questions on the level of subjectification. Doesn't the policed subject also turn around in Althusser's defining scene because they can be rather certain that they will *not* experience repressive violence from the police? Conversely, wouldn't it be more probable that individuals whose every day is directly or indirectly shaped by repressive encounters with police would try to avoid police encroachment? Here, I want to specifically refer to a quotation on a banner, made by racialised groups from the underprivileged suburbs of Paris during the protests for justice for Théo Luhaka and Adama Traoré. On the banner, which was tied to two columns of a building it reads: "Théo and Adama remind us why Zyed and Bouna ran away".[3]

Who, as a result of racist arrangements, is addressed even informally by the authorities (Kilomba, 2008)? How does racism changes the coordinates of interpellation conceptualised by Althusser? In *Black Skin, White Masks*, Fanon thoroughly illustrates racist articulations within institutions and in the everyday of colonised subjects. In his defining scene of the white gaze experienced by a black man who is sitting opposite of a white child and their white mother in a train, he writes:[4]

> "Look, a Negro!" It was an external stimulus that flicked over me as I passed by. I made a tight smile. "Look, a Negro!" It was true. It amused me. "Look, a Negro!" The circle was drawing a bit tighter. I made no secret of my amusement. "Mama, see the Negro! I'm frightened!" Frightened! Frightened! Now they were beginning to be afraid of me. I made up my mind to laugh myself to tears, but laughter had become impossible. I could no longer laugh, because I already knew that there were legends, stories, history and above all *historicity* ...
>
> *(Fanon, 1967, pp. 110–112, emphasis original).*

Admittedly, Fanon did not encounter the police in the train, but the white child's interpellations refer to the dimensions of everyday racism. A convergence of the two foils of interpellation raises the question whether the black man on the train would have really been interpellated in the way Althusser universally describes in his scene of police interpellation. Althusser's police interpellation does not only produce the modern subject as legal subject but as a white legal subject that can rest assured in the desire of being protected from the racialised and gendered other.

The banality of institutionalised racism

Racial profiling entails identity checks and searches/frisks without warrant, typically on the basis of skin colour and/or attributions such as (assumed) "national" heritage or language. Lived experiences of racial profiling amongst other things entail being criminalised, being publicly humiliated, and exposed, being addressed with racist language and experiencing psychological and/or physical violence as well as death (James and Thompson, 2016). In the past years, racial profiling has come to the fore of public and political debates, especially in countries in which institutional racism as a societal problem remains hegemonically denied and the effects of colonial continuities are not dealt with (El-Tayeb, 2015; Lentin, 2008; Salem and Thompson, 2016).

In Germany, France and Switzerland – three different but relational contexts – racial profiling is legally based on the framework of the nexus of the criminalisation of migration, the supposed war on crime and terrorism as well as the criminalisation of places in which racialised and/or disadvantaged groups work or live. Racial profiling does not receive any explicit legal attention in these countries; neither is there a judicial practice, nor do explicit prohibitions for their application exist.[5] At the same time, more and more black and people of colour initiatives, self-organised refugee networks as well as anti-racist groups and human rights organisations make racial profiling visible, scandalise the practice and offer support to those affected by it (see Cremer, 2013; Human Rights Watch, 2012; Open Society Justice Initiative, 2009, 2013).[6] The reports and documentations of these initiatives illustrate the multifarious and massive consequences of racial profiling. Stopped in their everyday lives, policed subjects are not just restricted in their freedom of movement and excluded from shared space. This is also a concurrent normalisation and legitimisation of police access to racialised bodies. In fact, we need to think of policing as a property relation, too (see Bhandar, 2018). Furthermore, the body itself becomes a border. Moreover, racial profiling contributes to the societal criminalisation of racialised subjects, because it leaves the hegemonic white public with the impression that the police has a reason to do so (James and Thompson, 2016). Thus, racist structures are re-produced (Basu, 2016). In addition, policed subjects have to de-criminalise themselves within their close environment and clarify that they were not "up to anything". In his article on urban policing in L.A., George Lipsitz writes that "policing takes time" (Lipsitz, 2016, p. 126). In Europe, racial profiling certainly does not *end* with being controlled. Rather, racial profiling *extends* the control in many ways.

Following Johan Galtung's concept of "structural violence" (1969) and adding Rob Nixon's concept of "slow violence" (2011), a violence that does not take place on the basis of spectacular incidents, but is spread over time and space, I define the consequences of racial profiling along modalities of structural violence, that do become visible and noticeable in their institutionalised form for those affected, but are characterised by their invisibility, slowness and silence.[7] Many of the initiatives against racial profiling, documentation centres and NGOs report psycho-social consequences such as anxiety regarding persecution or depression as a result of racial profiling (ADBs for NRW, 2017). Thus, people with mental vulnerabilities are not only exposed to police controls more often, but they also worsen because of them (Price, 2017; Shahar, 2019).

That police violations are difficult to report, and hence only seldomly done, also forms a part of this modality of structural violence. Thus, based on the lack of independent complaints bodies in Germany, France and Switzerland, the dehumanising practice cannot be documented or investigated, which continues the slow violence of policing.[8]

Moreover, factors such as residency and feared deportation play an important role and discourage victims of racist policing to speak out. In addition, racial profiling and the simultaneous production of racialised bodies as threatening often make it very difficult to find witnesses to provide testimonies. Solicitors and lawyers are also difficult to find and often reject mandates, especially because legal proceedings against the police are lost in most cases. Black people and people of colour also have to expect sanctions or counter charges for pressing charges against police, especially in the case of physical assaults. Therefore, the criminalisation of racialised subjects, who are hegemonically not recognised as victims of police violence, but considered as perpetrators, as a form of slow and structural violence continues.

This is illustrated in a recent case in Switzerland, in which the concerned person defended himself and is still doing so today with the support of anti-racist movements. After a meeting with friends in October 2009, Wilson A. was controlled whilst on a tram with a friend and, after asking why only him and his friend were being controlled, he was first physically forced to leave the tram and then brutally beaten. Although he informed the police that he had just had a heart operation, the officers continued to physically assault and verbally abuse him. With a weak heart, Wilson A. could barely breathe (Alliance against Racial Profiling, 2018, p. 2).[9]

Wilson A. pressed charges, whereupon the accused police officers also pressed charges on the basis of violence towards police officers. After an exhausting trial of eight years, which was attempted to be dismissed by court multiple times, the officers were acquitted. The sentencing is not yet final. The psychological, physical and financial pressures that come with such trials are also part of the slow violence through racial profiling.

Racial profiling takes place even when racialised subjects are the ones who called the police for support (like the case of Derege Wevelsiep from Frankfurt demonstrates), or are in need of support and care. The consequences often lead to death, also in continental Europe, where the structural problem of deadly racist police violence is considered a US-phenomenon. Ousman S. who died at a police station in Dortmund, Germany (July 2012) had previously called emergency services twice to request assistance (the medics diagnosed tachycardia but did not take him to the hospital, this demonstrates the racial profiling practised by medical staff as Ousman S. was not properly treated and not taken seriously, a manifestation of racial profiling in the medicine area), yet was arrested upon the arrival of the police and denied medical care after the neighbours called the police because of disturbance of rest. Amongst the many cases where racial profiling resulted in deathly consequences, the case of Oury Jalloh is probably one of the most well-known cases. Whilst in a police cell in Dessau, his body was found completely charred whilst fixated to a fire-resistant mattress (January 2005).[10]

The slow violence of racial profiling beyond the control is also illustrated in the institutional treatment of the victims' family members. Closed proceedings, stressful trials lasting over many years, everyday racism during court proceedings, investigations against family members (as in the case of the family members of the victims of the NSU murder series) or, for example, non-reimbursement of translation costs (as in the case of Oury Jalloh) contribute to family members and friends of the victims of police violence experiencing its continuation. The sudden death of Oury Jalloh's mother who, after her second "visit" in Germany during the proceedings in Magdeburg, departed deeply distressed and appalled, must also be seen as slow violence.[11]

But racial profiling does not only affect racialised masculinities. Rather, multiple marginalised people, women and LGBT*IQ/refugees/ poor black people and people of colour with disabilities are particularly vulnerable to racist police controls and their various consequences. The repeated shootings of black women by the police illustrate this (Mama, 1993). The cases of Christy Schwundeck, who was fatally shot in a job centre in Frankfurt am Main in May 2011 whilst enquiring about her unemployment benefits, and N'deye Mariame Sarr, who was shot by police in July 2000 in the house of her ex-husband, are crucial manifestations of how racism, gender, migrant status, social class and dis/ability intersect in policing (Bruce-Jones, 2015). In both cases, Schwundeck and Sarr were the only black women in these respective situations. Both were in a situation of crisis. Schwundeck was without money since 1 May as her unemployment benefits had not arrived. Sarr wanted to pick up her two-year-old child from her white husband, from whom she had separated, and who brought the child to his parents without letting her know in addition to having applied for sole child custody. Both shots were fired shortly after police arrived. Mariame Sarr was one of the first persons who was shot by the new PEP (*Polizei-Einsatz-Patrone*), a special bullet with a mushroom effect and created to gun down "very violent attackers".[12] In both cases, the public prosecutors closed the case on the grounds of self-defence.

These cases, as well as others, demonstrate that an intersectional perspective on racist policing is necessary to not only analyse the ways in which police violence draws on intersecting modes of murderous dehumanisation, but further to account for the specific forms of policing that multi-marginalised subjects and groups experience. Initial explorative studies as well as the accounts of support groups and initiatives active in continental Europe show that black women/women of colour, queer and non-binary folks are criminalised as sex workers and are exposed to identity checks and searches (El-Tayeb and Thompson, 2019, Plümecke and Wilopo, 2019). Black women/women of colour, queer and non-binary folks who work in the sex industry are particularly vulnerable to racist policing and its gendered implications, as they are controlled more often than their white colleagues and are under suspicion of working as illegal sex workers (Dankwa et al., 2019). A higher frequency of controls can have severe impacts on their lives, also in terms of, for instance, child custody regulations.

Black and racialised mothers in general are often constructed as "bad mothers" and over policed. This is also important with regard to the cases of Schwundeck and Sarr, as their children were implicitly or explicitly involved in both cases (in the case of Schwundeck, she was struggling to get her child out of foster care, which also exacerbated her depression). The recent case of Rita Awour Ojunge, a black female asylum seeker, who had been missing since April 2019, reveals this modality of intersectional policing. Though friends and her family continuously insisted that she was missing, she was never located until it was far too late. Ojunge repeatedly reported sexual harassment in the *lager* (carceral housing system for refugees and asylum seekers) Hohenleipisch in Brandenburg and her son repeatedly told his father that someone had violently beat her before she was brought from the camp on 7 April 2019. Ultimately, her body parts were found in the forests near the *lager* in June 2019. Her case demonstrates that active inaction by police is parcel to racist intersectional policing. Not only was Ojunge's son not believed, her reports on sexual harassment were further ignored, which points to the effects of s/exoticisation of black women and queer folks (dos Santos Pinto, 2018) as well as to the intersectional violence within the *lager* and camp system. She was further implicitly criminalised as a "bad mother" who would leave her children by themselves without letting anyone know. Observing or exhibiting benign neglect and not intervening when racialised bodies are insulted in a racist way, as well as physically assaulted, and sexually violated is also part of racial profiling. The "active inaction" (Tyner, 2016, p. 206) and the patterns of police non-prosecution (Melter, 2017) reproduce racialised subjects as a constant threat and subjects who do not deserve to be protected along the lines of colonial continuities (Samour, 2017).

Thus, a historicised and contextualised critique of the gendered policing of race and blackness, or gendered racial profiling (Ritchie, 2017, p. 145) must interrogate the interdependency of systems of policing and punishment (including carceral feminisms), regimes of welfare and social services, foster care, the lager and border control system, gendered and domestic violence, and their implicit orders.

Resistances

The resistances against racial profiling are multifaceted. Black people and people of colour have been reporting their experiences in various ways for decades, hence challenging the banalisation of racist police practices within the contexts of continental Europe. The documentation of these racist practices that are rendered socially invisible plays a major role. In Germany, the Campaign for Victims of Racist Police Violence (KOP) has been documenting racist police operations since 2000 and established a legal aid fund. Various cop watch groups like the group Copwatch Frankfurt based in Frankfurt have also been documenting cases of racial profiling since 2013 and have established a telephone support line to report incidents of racial profiling.

The Collective Against Stop and Search/Frisk Controls (*Le collectif contre le contrôle au faciès*), which was founded as an alliance of different anti-racist initiatives and civil society organisations in France in spring 2011, has established a phone line to report incidents of racial profiling and regularly hands out cards and further information on their documentation procedures in places that are heavily affected by racist policing (Keaton, 2013). In doing so, the collective stays in contact with those affected by racial profiling and encourages them to act against it. This documentation method that I call "counter-statistics" or "statistics from below" has its origin in the practice of policed subjects and their strategies. This is not just about statistical recording in the sense of having a legal onus of proof, as many of these collectives know about the institutional injustice of the justice system. Rather, documentation initiatives show people affected by racial profiling that they are not alone and hence contribute to the denormalisation of the problem.

Besides documentation, other forms of collective support are an integral part of the critical work against racist policing. For instance, creating spaces in which those affected by racist policing can share their experiences, identifying how they can combat this phenomenon, and making space to listen and be heard is foundational for the work against racial profiling. The abovementioned initiatives, as well as others such as the Alliance against Racial Profiling, have built support structures in which those affected by racial profiling are at the centre.[13] Raising awareness amongst the majority of society also plays an essential role here. Such initiatives contribute substantially to the scandalisation and denormalisation of racist policing, whether through their own research, reports and interviews or statements and campaigns. For instance, following the ruling at the Administrative Court in Koblenz KOP and the Initiative of Black People in Germany (ISD) started the nation-wide campaign *Stop Racial Profiling* that many anti-racist groups across Germany joined. In November 2011, the Collective Against Stop and Search Controls started a video campaign joined by some 30 black or public personalities of colour, sharing their first experiences of racial profiling and calling upon people to fight this institutionalised practice. Following this initiative, Copwatch Frankfurt has also initiated and recorded videos featuring people affected by racial profiling and their demands towards the majority society. This suggests that the interventions and practices of resistance are also articulated transnationally. Many of the groups also encourage critical observation of this practice. Thus, these initiatives contribute substantially to the democratisation of society that is threatened by the police.

The claims of the different organisations and collectives span from the abolition of preventive policing methods, to the inclusion of racial profiling in anti-discrimination law or trainings and labelling requirement for police officers (Adler et al., 2016; James and Thompson, 2016). Especially the establishment of independent reporting and investigations complaints commissions is part of the claims of anti-racist organisations. But there are also approaches that seek more foundational societal transformations beyond this and reject police "solutions" or "reforms" on the basis of a de-criminalising understanding of safety and the transformation of social relations towards structures that aren't based on violence.

Abolitionist visions

Strategies of looking out for each other, taking responsibility and being accountable that are "goal and also method against violence" (Brazzell, 2017) are necessary, especially when police practices not only render security impossible for subjects experiencing intersectional forms of violence and oppression – many would not call the police, regardless of their residence or citizenship status because of this (Loick, 2016) – but are constitutively based upon their exclusion from liberal understandings of safety. These abolitionist principles work alongside two directions. On the one hand, it is about looking out for each other, taking responsibility and caring for each other during police operations, as described above on the basis of practices of resistance.[14] Yet, looking out for each other, taking responsibility and caring for each other also refers to the abolitionist practices within our communities. In the past decades various groups, especially those affected by intersectional modalities of violence, have developed concepts and methods based upon historically marginalised knowledges that provide alternatives to the police and interwoven punishment regimes, for example, that of transformative justice and community accountability (Brazzell, 2017; Generation FIVE, 2007; LesMigras, 2011). These practices, though often associated with transformative and inspiring collectives in the US, have also been developed and created by multi-marginalised collectives in various parts of Europe, by undocumented sex workers, refugee and migrant women, and queer-feminists of colour (LesMigras, 2011). Further supporting and encouraging alliances between anti-police and anti-prison groups, self-organised refugee and migrant collectives and their supporters, anti-violence alliances and networks of sex workers that prioritise the realities, experiences and critique of especially poor black queer and trans* people of colour as well as establishing transformative, anti-capitalist and decolonial concepts of justice will also enable the creation of justice, as "we need justice, and, justice needs us!"

Notes

1 The cultural archives of Black artists and artists of colour especially illustrate a critique of policing, also within Europe. See inter alia tracks by BSMG, the track Black Lives Matter by LMNZ and 12 other MCs as well as tracks by Casey and Jorja Smith.
2 The empirical references and many of the theoretical reflections in this contribution arose within the course of my long-term activist work with groups and individuals fighting racial profiling in Germany and France, and more recently in Switzerland. I would like to take this opportunity to express special thanks to them here. An older version of this reactualised article was first published in German in Loick (2018). This article was translated by Joanna James.
3 Théo Luhaka was brutally abused by police in a Parisian suburb (2 February 2017). Adama Traoré died in police custody (19 July 2016). Zyed Benna and Bouna Traoré fled from a racist police control into a transformer house where they suffered deadly electric shocks on 27 October 2005.
4 I choose to leave the n-word in this quote instead of using the euphemism, because I'm of the opinion that Fanon was very considerate of also illustrating the violence of anti-black racism linguistically and the n-word refers to the violence of the white gaze here.
5 Whilst states such as the US or Britain following the three World Conferences against Racism in Durban adopted legal measures supposed to prevent this police practice, Germany, Switzerland and France (as well as many other European countries) did not establish a legal definition of racist profiling.
6 See the Campaign for Victims of Racist Police Violence (Kampagne für Opfer rassistischer Gewalt, KOP), the Initiative of Black People in Germany (ISD) and Copwatch Frankfurt in Germany, the Alliance against Racial Profiling (Allianz gegen Racial Profiling) in Switzerland and the Collectif against Stop and Search (Frisk) Controls (*Le collectif contre le contrôle au faciès*) in France.
7 Many thanks to Alexander Vorbrugg for making me aware of these concepts and for allowing me to learn about them from his own work and in conversations.
8 This also refers to cases of racial profiling in which black people and people of colour died in contact with the police. Institutional racism within the public prosecutor's office and the police thus hinders and complicates independent investigations.
9 I approach these experiences through a Fanonian framework and follow, amongst others, the crucial and material motif of un-breathing, a motif which sticks to the policing of race, especially of blackness, through time and space and refers to the physical as well as to the social breathing. This becomes clear in its continuity as expressed by

the last words of Eric Garner, who died in a police chokehold on 17 July 2014 in New York. Garner suffered from asthma and his last words were "I can't breathe". Fanon who intensely analysed the implications of social death in the colonial situation once wrote "When we revolt, then we don't do so because of a specific culture. We revolt simply because we can no longer breathe". (This is an edited version of a quote by Fanon that was mobilised by many social movements, see Fanon, 1965)

10 Laya-Alama Condé died by use of emetics through the police in Bremen (January 2005). Dominique Koumadio was shot by a police officer in Dortmund (February 2010). Slieman Hamade, whose parents called the police because of a conflict with the neighbours, died in the hallway of his parents' flat in Berlin Schöneberg. In Switzerland, Cemal G. died due to a positional suffocation and a police officer hitting him on his head in Bern (June 2001). Hervé M. died because a police officer fired multiple shots at him in Bex. Lamine F. is found dead in his police cell (October 2017) after being arrested. Mike B. P died during a police intervention in Lausanne (March 2018). These are only a few cases. It can be assumed that many others have not become known. Moreover, since 2005 over 100 people, most of them black or of colour, have died during contact with the police in France. See: http://www.urgence-notre-police-assaaine.fr/123663553

11 Within this context, one can also think of Erica Garner's death, Eric Garner's daughter, who died at the age of 27, and Venida Browder's death, Kalief Browder's mother (who hanged himself after three years of solitary confinement). The slow violence of racist policing expresses itself trans-generationally and trans-temporally, thus it goes beyond the individual subjects it addresses and affects communities.

12 It is important to think about how black subjects become laboratories and a testing ground for new forms and strategies of policing, like the PEP which was designed for "very violent attackers", and how Sarr was perceived in the anti-black gendered regimes of perception. Thanks to Zavier Wingham for bringing this to my mind.

13 The Alliance against Racial Profiling (*Allianz gegen Racial Profiling*) has especially received attention beyond the German speaking region for their support of Mohamed Wa Baile, who is also a member. Stopped by two city police officers (February 2015) for an identity control at a Zurich train station in Switzerland, he refused to give in to the racial profiling and in response received a fine which he unsuccessfully contested before the Appellate Court. Baile then took his case to the Federal Court. In March 2018, the Federal Court also upheld Baile's sentencing; together with his counsel, he now wants to take his case to the European Court of Justice for Human Rights.

14 Each and every one of us can document racial profiling and forward the information, observe or film the police during these controls (it depends on the situation, many groups offer workshops to feel better prepared for such situations) and signalise to the policed person as well as the police that they are not alone, but that there are people there who are watching the police.

Bibliography

ADBs für NRW/ Antidiskriminierungsbüro Köln (2017), *Menschen wie DU neigen zu Straftaten. (Rassistische) Diskriminierung bei der Polizei: Ursachen, Folgen und Möglichkeiten der Intervention.* Available at http://www.gleichbehandlungsbuero.de/docs/Rassistische%20Disktiminierung%20bei%20der%20Polizei*Brochure%20vom%20ADB*Köln.pdf (Accessed 16 April 2020).

Adler, J., Digoh, L., and Haruna-Oelker, H. (2016) 'Racial Profiling – Eine Menschenrecht swidrige Praxis', in Bergold-Caldwell, D. et al. (eds), *Spiegelblicke*, Berlin, Orlanda, pp. 251–254.

Allianz gegen Racial Profiling (2018) *Rassistischer Polizeigewalt schutzlos ausgeliefert. Der Fall Wilson A. zeigt: Das Polizei- und Justizsystem ist institutionell rassistisch*. Available at https://www.facebook.com/allianzgegenracialprofiling/posts/1489429861166214 (Accessed 15 April 2020).

Althusser, L. (1977) 'Ideologie und ideologische Staatsapparate (Anmerkungen für eine Untersuchung)', in Althusser, L. (ed), *Ideologie und ideologische Staatsapparate: Aufsätze zur marxistischen Theorie*, Hamburg/Berlin, VSA, pp. 108–153.

Basu, B. (2016) 'Die Lüge von der Neutralität. Überlegungen zu Rassismus in Polizei, Justiz und Politik', in Kampagne für Opfer rassistischer Polizeigewalt (ed), *Alltäglicher Ausnahmezustand. Institutioneller Rassismus in deutschen Strafverfolgungsbehörden*, Münster, Unrast, pp. 85–101.

Benjamin W. (1965) *Zur Kritik der Gewalt und andere Aufsätze*, Frankfurt/M, Suhrkamp.

Bhambra, G. (2017) The Current Crisis of Europe: Refugees, Colonialism, and the Limits of Cosmopolitanism', *European Law Journal*, 23(5): 395–405.

Bhandar, B. (2018) *Colonial Lives of Property: Law, Land, and Racial Regimes of Ownership*, Durham, Duke University Press.

Brazzell, M. (2017) 'Sicherheit von Links. Der Transformative Justice-Ansatz', *Luxemburg. Gesellschaftsanalyse und linke Praxis*. Available at https://www.zeitschrift-luxemburg.de/sicherheit-von-links-der-transformative-justice-ansatz/ (Accessed 16 April 2020).

Browne, S. (2015) *Dark Matters: On the Surveillance of Blackness*, Durham, Duke University Press.

Bruce-Jones, E. (2015) 'German Policing at the Intersection: Race, Gender Migrant Status and Mental Health', *Race and Class*, 56(3): 36–49.

Bruce-Jones, E. (2016) *Race in the Shadow of Law. State Violence in Contemporary Europe*. New York, Routledge.

Cremer, H. (2013) 'Racial Profiling – Menschenrechtswidrige Personenkontrollen nach § 22 Abs. 1 a Bundespolizeigesetz. Empfehlungen an den Gesetzgeber, Gerichte und Polizei', in Deutsches Institut für Menschenrechte (eds). Available at https://www.institut-fuer-menschenrechte.de/uploads/tx*commerce/Studie*Racial*Profiling*Menschenrechtswidrige*Personenkontrollen*nach*Bundespolizeigesetz.pdf (Accessed 16 April 2020).

Dankwa, S. et al. (2019) 'Profiling und Rassismus im Kontext von Sexarbeit', in Wa Baile, M. et al. (eds), *Racial Profiling. Struktureller Rassismus und antirassistischer Widerstand*, Bielefeld: Transcript, pp. 155–171.

dos Santos Pinto, J. (2018) 'Besitzen, s/exotisieren, vergessen – Sklaverei, Einbürgerung und Rassisierung um 1798', paper presented at *Von der Kolonisierung zur Globalisierung. Warum wir Schweizer Geschichte neu denken sollten*, Bern, University of Bern.

El-Tayeb, F. (2015) *Anders Europäisch. Rassismus, Identität und Widerstand im vereinten Europa*, Münster, Trancsript.

El-Tayeb, F. and V.E. Thompson (2019) 'Racial Profiling als Verbindung zwischen alltäglichem Rassismus, staatlicher Gewalt und kolonialrassistischen Traditionen. Ein Gespräch über Racial Profiling und intersektionale Befreiungsprojekte in Europa', in Wa Baile, M. et al. (eds.), *Racial Profiling. Struktureller Rassismus und Antirassistischer Widerstand*, Bielefeld, Transcript, pp. 311–29.

Fanon, F. (1963) *The Wretched of the Earth*, New York, Grove Press.

Fanon, F. (1965) *A Dying Colonialism*, New York, Grove Press.

Fanon, F. (1967) *Black Skin, White Masks*, New York, Grove Press.

Galtung, J. (1969) 'Violence, Peace, and Peace Research', *Journal of Peace Research*, 6(3): 167–191.

generation FIVE (2007) *Toward Transformative Justice*. Available at http://www.generationfive.org/wp-content/uploads/2013/07/G5*Toward*Transformative*Justice-Document.pdf (Accessed 5 April 2020).

Gilmore, R. W. (2007) *Golden Gulag: Prisons, Surplus, Crisis, and Opposition in Globalizing California*, Berkeley, University of California Press.

Goldberg, D. T. (2006) Racial Europeanization, *Ethnic and Racial Studies*, 29(2): 331–364.

Human Rights Watch (2012) *The Root of Humiliation. Abusive Identity Checks in France*. Available at https://www.hrw.org/report/2012/01/26/root-humiliation/abusive-identity-checks-france (Accessed 5 April 2020).

Human Rights Watch (2018) *Themendossier Rassistisches Profiling (Racial Profiling)*. Available at http://www.humanrights.ch/de/menschenrechte-schweiz/inneres/strafen/polizei/polizei-beschwerdestellen-unabhaenige-untersuchung (Accessed 5 April 2020).

Hönke, J., and Müller, M-M. (2012) 'Governing (in)security in a postcolonial world: Transnational entanglements and the worldliness of 'local' practice' *Security Dialogue*, 43(5): 383–401.

James, J. and Thompson, V. E. (2016) 'Racial Profiling, Institutioneller Rassismus und Widerstände', in Drücker et al. (eds.), *Geflüchtete, Flucht und Asyl*, Düsseldorf, Informations- und Dokumentationszentrums für Antirassismusarbeit e.V. (IDA), pp. 55–59.

Jobard, F. (2013) 'Zur politischen Theorie der Polizei', *WestEnd. Neue Zeitschrift für Sozialforschung*, 13(1): 65–77.

Kampagne für Opfer rassistischer Polizeigewalt (eds) (2016) *Alltäglicher Ausnahmezustand. Institutioneller Rassismus in deutschen Strafverfolgungsbehörden*, Münster, Unrast.

Keaton, T. D. (2013) 'Racial Profiling and the "French Exception"', *French Cultural Studies*, 24(2): 231–242.

Kilomba, G. (2008) *Plantation Memories. Episodes of Everyday Racism*, Münster, Unrast.

Kollaborative Forschungsgruppe Racial Profiling (2019) *Racial Profiling. Erfahrung, Wirkung, Widerstand, Studie*, Rosa Luxemburg Stiftung (eds), Berlin. Available at. https://www.rosalux.de/publikation/id/40493/racial-profiling/ (Accessed 5 April 2020).

Künkel, J. (2014) 'Intersektionalität, Machtanalyse, Theorienpluralität. Eine Replik zur Debatte um kritische Polizeiforschung', *sub\urban. zeitschrift für kritische stadtforschung*, 2(2): 77–90.

Künkel, J. and Briken, K. (eds) (2014) 'Restrukturierung der Polizeien', *Kriminologisches Journal*, 4: 210–212.

Lentin, A. (2008) 'Europe and the Silence about Race', *European Journal of Social Theory*, 11(4): 487–503.

LesMigras (2011) 'Handlungsmöglichkeiten im Umgang mit Gewalt und Diskriminierung. Unterstützung geben', Antigewalt- und Antidiskriminierungsbereich der Lesbenberatung Berlin e.V. (eds). Available at http://lesmigras.de/tl*files/lesmigras/Tapesh/LM*Broschuere*Tapesh*UnterstuetzungGeben.pdf (Accessed 5 April 2020).

Lipsitz, G. (2016) 'Policing Place and Taxing Time on Skid Row', in Camp, J. T. and Heatherton, C. (eds), *Policing the Planet. Why the Policing Crisis Led to Black Lives Matter*. New York, Verso, pp. 123–140.

Loick, D. (2016) 'We Look Out for Each Other. Für eine Welt ohne Polizei', *Prager Frühling*, 2.2016. Available at https://www.prager-fruehling-magazin.de/de/article/1270.we-look-out-for-each-other.html#*ftn6 (Accessed 5 April 2020).

Loick, D. (ed) (2018) *Kritik der Polizei*, Frankfurt am Main, Campus.

Loomba, A. (2005) *Colonialism/Postcolonialism*, London and New York, Routledge.

Mama, A. (1993) 'Black Women and the Police. A Place Where the Law Is Not Upheld, in Inside Babylon', in James, W. and Harris, C. (eds), *The Caribbean Diaspora in Britain*, London, Verso pp. 135–153.

McCoy, A. W. (2009) *Policing America's Empire. The United States, the Philippines and the Rise of the Surveillance State.* Madison, University of Wisconsin Press.

Melter, C. (2017) 'Koloniale, nationalsozialistische und aktuelle rassistische Kontinuitäten in Gesetzgebung und der Polizei am Beispiel von Schwarzen Deutschen, Roma und Sinti', in Fereidooni K. and El, M. (eds), *Rassismuskritik und Widerstandsformen*, Wiesbaden, VS Verlag, pp. 589–612.

Müller, M.-M. (2014) 'Polizieren als (post-)koloniale Praxis. Ein Beitrag zur Debatte um kritische Polizeiforschung', *sub\urban. zeitschrift für kritische stadtforschung*, 2(2): 71–76.

Müller, M.-M. and Ostermeier, L. (2014) 'Decolonizing German Police Building: The (Post-) Colonial Afterlife of the Deutsch-Afghanische Freundschaft', paper presented at *Empires: Social Control, Political Transition, (Post-)Colonial Legacies*, Brüssel.

Nixon, R. (2011) *Slow Violence and the Environmentalism of the Poor*, Cambridge, MA, Harvard University Press.

Open Society Justice Initiative (2009) *Profiling Minorites: A Study of Stop-and-Search Practices in Paris.* Available at http://www.cnrs.fr/inshs/recherche/docs- actualites/rapport-facies.pdf (Accessed 10 April 2020).

Open Society Justice Initiative (2013) *Equality under Pressure. The Impact of Ethnic Profiling.* Available at https://www.opensocietyfoundations.org/sites/default/files/equality-under-pressure-the-impact-of-ethnic-profiling-netherlands-20131128*1.pdf (Accessed 10 April 2020).

Pichl, M. (2014) 'Zur Entgrenzung der Polizei – eine juridische und materialistische Kritik polizeilicher Gewalt', *Kritische Vierteljahresschrift für Gesetzgebung und Rechtswissenschaft*, 97(3): 249–266.

Plümecke, T. and Wilopo, C. (2019) 'Die Kontrolle der »Anderen«: Intersektionalität rassistischer Polizeipraktiken', in Wa Baile, M. et al. (eds), *Racial Profiling: Struktureller Rassismus und antirassistischer Widerstand*, Bielefeld: Transcript, pp. 139–154.

Price, J. M. (2017) 'Psychic Investment in Cruelty: Three Parables on Race and Imprisoning the Mentally Ill', *Contemporary Justice Review*, 20(4): 491–504.

Ritchie, A. J. (2017) *Invisible No More. Police Violence against Black Women and Women of Color*, Boston, Beacon Press.

Salem, S. and Thompson, V. E. (2016) 'Old Racisms, New Masks: On the Continuing Discontinuities of Racism and the Erasure of Race in European Contexts', *Nineteen Sixty Nine: An Ethnic Studies Journal*, 3(1): 1–23.

Samour, N. (2017) 'Zwei Beispiele für Rassismus und Repression im deutschen Jugendstrafrecht', in Brazzell, M. (eds), *Was macht uns wirklich sicher? Toolkit für Aktivist*innen*, Münster, Edition Assemblage, pp. 41–44.

Shahar, Z. (2019) 'Black Liberation Requires Making Room for Uncomfortable Manifestations of Mental Illness', Black Youth Project. Available at http://blackyouthproject.com/black-liberation-requires-making-room-for-uncomfortable-manifestations-of-mental-illness/ (Accessed 10 April 2020).

Seigel, M. (2017) 'The Dilemma of "racial profiling": An Abolitionist Police History', *Contemporary Justice Review*, 20(4): 474–490.

Stam, R. and Shohat, E. (2012) *Race in Translation: Culture Wars around the Postcolonial Atlantic.* New York and London, NYU Press.

Trautmann, F. (2013) 'Polizey, Begleitheft zur Ausstellung', in Frankfurter Kunstverein (eds), *Ohnmacht als Situation. Democracia, Revolutie, Polizey*, Frankfurt, Frankfurter Kunstverein.

Tyner, J. A. (2016) *Violence in Capitalism: Devaluing Life in an Age of Responsibility*, Lincoln and London, University of Nebraska Press.

Wekker, G. (2017) *White Innocence: Paradoxes of Colonialism and Race*, Durham, Duke University Press.

Wa Baile, M. et al. (eds) (2019) *Racial Profiling. Struktureller Rassismus und antirassistischer Widerstand*, Bielefeld, Transcript.

13

AGAINST PENAL HUMANISM

A Foucaudian critique

Clécio Lemos

Introduction

We usually associate Michel Foucault's work on criminology with the early 1970s: in 1971, he founded the Prisons Information Group with Jean-Marie Domenach, Pierre Vidal-Naquet and Daniel Defert, and penal matters were at the center of his lectures at the Collège de France until 1975, when he published *Discipline and Punish*. However, this half decade represents only a small part of his intellectual output, and if we use his thought as a "toolkit" (Foucault, 2006, p. 251), we will find resources to think through criminology in all three phases of his intellectual trajectory: the archeology of knowledge (1961–1969), the genealogy of power (1970–1979) and ethics (1980–1984). These three phases weren't contradictory, as Foucault himself pointed out the circularity between knowledge, power, and the subject (Foucault, 2010d, p. 5), and we will use all three to elucidate our hypothesis.

By the 1970s, Foucault had already taught us that "it is not possible to separate the truth from the processes of their production, and that these processes are both of knowing and of power" (Ewald, 1993, p. 21). He formulated the expression "knowledge-power" to emphasize that truth regimes produce power, and power relations produce truths; the two are independent and advance together. From 1980 onwards, he began focusing on the third essential element in his analysis of modernity: subjectivation (Foucault, 2014a, p. 13).[1] These three elements or facets of his analysis (knowledge, power, and ethics) were used to overcome the four forces of humanism, economism, state-centrism, and repressivism.

This article investigates how Foucault's departure from humanism in particular can make a relevant contribution to contemporary criminology. Foucault's discourse analysis and the work of Luigi Ferrajoli and James Q. Wilson will be used to understand how humanist philosophy is present in some of the main theories of penal punishment legitimation, and can be understood as "punitive humanism."

Having established the presence of humanism in criminological discourse, the hypothesis of this article is that Foucault's theory of subjectivation can lead us away from punitive humanism. If the subject is a historical creation that is constantly changing, then public policies not only react to the subject, but also influence the change of subject types. Criminal justice does not punish simply because the population wants punishment; the appetite for punishment has to be created, as there is no immutable and innate desire for it. Punishment is only one possible form of political action to promote social security, and not necessarily the most efficient one.

Humanism versus subjectivation

The human sciences of the 18th century were largely based on a static and universalist view of the subject, which presupposed a discoverable human essence that served as the foundation for all forms of positivism.[2] Foucault questions this "transcendental-empirical being," arguing instead that the subject is a recent and historically situated invention: "does man really exist?" (Foucault, 2007, pp. 443–444).

Using the genealogical work of Nietzsche as a starting point, Foucault never stops confronting humanist theories with the imperative to historicize not only knowledge and practices, but also the subject itself. Foucault believes that the transcendental individual is an untenable fiction that mainly serves as a political tool: if this is human nature, then this is the politics we need.[3]

This "pure cognoscent subject" presupposes the possibility of finding a "free subject in relation to power," a pre-power subject who must be rescued (Senellart, 2014, p. 316). To Foucault, this dialectical reading of human nature that seeks a final synthesis free from contradictions is sterile: there is no space for a metaphysical[4] belief in the ultimate truth about man (Foucault, 2010b, pp. 49–50).

The Foucauldian conception of the subject has advanced since 1980: by insisting on the "active role" of the subject, Foucault makes clear that subjectivity is not merely the passive product of relations of governmentality (Senellart, 2014, p. 314). Contrary to certain critical schools that submerge the individual in the power structures and material conditions that shape it, Foucauldian ethics preserve a necessary condition of freedom in the constitution of the self. The subjectivation process explored in Foucault's final phase refutes the possibility that ideas spring automatically from the combination of power structures, which would amount to a form of positivism. The ideas cannot be explained solely by the facts (Butler, 2016).

Paying attention to the ways in which power and truth mutually create each other is not a way to enclose the subject, but rather a tool that the subject can use to unravel the learned subjectivation. Foucault increasingly replaces "subject" with "subjectivation" to insist upon the fact that the creation of the subject is an open and ongoing process. This does not ignore the normative power of truths and governments over the self, but recognizes the simultaneous production of the self by the self (Foucault, 2016, pp. 25–26).

Within Western civilization, it is important acknowledge that there are "techniques of the self," by which individuals make changes to their bodies and souls—a freedom that is never lost in any state of domination (Pelbart, 2016, p. 277). Starting from the premise that humans are without origin and without end, there are "indefinite possibilities of transformation of the subject," which are not exempt from the context of truth and power, but are never fully constrained by these factors either (Foucault, 2010c, p. 475).

Truth and government can only act upon free subjects, and modernity can only be understood by acknowledging that it is simultaneously produced by a totalizing and individualizing process. Modern power updates the technology of pastoral power (Foucault, 1995, p. 236): the "government of the self" is just as important as the "government of the others" (Gros, 2010, pp. 474–475).[5]

To invoke an active subject is not to accept the universal rationality of the subject; it is rather to recognize that historicity operates on subjectivation without ever burying its active capacity. One cannot be attached to a past or future image of the subject: the self is a producer and a product, produced in the relation (Dreyfus and Rabinow, 1995, p. 286). Self-constitution includes not only an investigation into forms of power and knowledge, but also an understanding of how "the individual finds himself tied, and accepts to be tied, to the power exerted over him" (Foucault, 2014b, p. 19).

This matrix of subjectivation allows Foucault to *deanthropologize* history, combining the "discontinuity" of the facts with a dynamic vision of the subject. It is a political philosophy that invigorates the subject, and in doing so, opens a fundamental field for the comprehension of the present (Castro, 2004, p. 517). Refusing an "*a priori* theory of the subject" is the only way for Foucault to reconcile his political theory with the constant changes in the practices of power. There are "different forms of subject," and the care of the self is always susceptible to new ethics (Foucault, 2004, p. 275).

According to Foucault, humanism[6] is an attempt to "color and justify the conceptions of man," but this fixed conception is "too inconsistent to serve as an axis for reflection" and can be put to the service of authoritarian regimes like Nazism and Stalinism (Foucault, 2005, p. 346). The subject, far from being determined once and for all, is a product of bilateral action—of power formations upon the self, and of the self upon the self. This theory of subjectivation completed Foucault's diagnosis of the West. To incorporate this truth-government-subjectivation method of the late Foucault is to repudiate humanism, since the subject is precarious. The subject of modernity is neither determined by its material conditions nor unmoored from its historical conditions: it is an unending process that passes through the government of the self.

Two discourses of punitive humanism

Is humanism present in criminology and in the creation of criminal policies? Is it still relevant in the current theories of punishment? To what extent is our confidence in the benefits of punishment attached to a particular understanding of human nature?

The heart of every criminal justice justification can be found in its answer to the simple question, "Why punish?" (Cohen, 1988, p. 29). How can the state justify punishment for certain acts, given that it has many other possible avenues of action (reparations, mediation, etc.)? If criminology has made great advances in problematizing the concept of crime, especially since the advent of the Labeling Approach, the very act of punishing remains relatively undisturbed. The feasibility of replacing punishments altogether has not yet received the serious consideration it deserves, which has left restorative justice and penal abolitionism in the background of leading criminological debates.

To understand the largely unquestioned centrality of punishment, we have to analyze the underlying conception of the human mind and subject, what may be called as "punitive humanism." Humanism has influenced all Western thinkers since the 18th century, and all the great "critical" matrices are like "fish in water: that is, ... [they are] unable to breath anywhere else" (Foucault, 2007, p. 360). Thus, we can suppose that humanism is also present in the traditional and critical strains of Criminology. An attentive reading shows a common humanist outlook in both "conservative" and "minimalist" thinkers, and this humanist underpinning is exemplified in the work of Luigi Ferrajoli (Roman law tradition) and James Q. Wilson (common law tradition). Despite significant divergences in their proposed policies, both justify punishments using the assumption of a fixed subject.

In his important work, *Law and Reason*, the Italian scholar Luigi Ferrajoli states that there are two main grounds for penal punishments: crime deterrence and the avoidance of blood revenge. However, he writes that punishment is not a very effective deterrent, given the complex social, psychological, and cultural motivations behind any crime. The second justification is more plausible, and he believes it is sufficient to use "modest punishments little more than symbolic" (Ferrajoli, 2006, p. 310).

In other words, criminal punishments are necessary because humans naturally seek revenge, and punishments mediated by public, impartial, and "rational" rules allow civilizational advancement in the social organization. Public revenge in the form of punishment saves the guilty person from the vicious caprices of the avenger, and thus the criminal himself has an interest in its maintenance (Ferrajoli, 2006, p. 312).

According to Ferrajoli, it is a "naturalistic fallacy" to believe that society can be controlled without punitive practices; penal abolition would lead to an unacceptable civilizational "regression" (Ferrajoli, 2006, p. 320). But how can he assume that man is doomed to be punitive and vengeful? Is he not just "naturalizing" a specific human reaction?

Ferrajoli relies on a universalist understanding of human nature: that humans are fated to deal with their conflicts in a violent and vindictive way, and that without regulation, society will devolve into vengeful anarchy. But this restricted understanding of the subject, which anchors his defense of penal practices, is not exclusive to Ferrajoli, who was chosen because he is one of the most famous proponents of the view that punishment is necessary to prevent violence.

Our second example, James Q. Wilson, is a co-author of the "Broken windows" theory (along with George L. Kelling) that gave rise to the notorious "zero tolerance" policy in New York City. Wilson is author and coauthor of several celebrated works, of which *Thinking about Crime* is perhaps his seminal contribution, published almost 50 years ago and now in its third edition.

His premise is that it's futile to attempt to alter human nature (whether through general progress or individual rehabilitation), and thus his book focuses on protecting society by "altering the choices facing would-be offenders" (Wilson, 2013, p. XXVII). Wilson divides his topic into two major strategies: changing the costs of crime through criminal sanctions, and elevating the benefits of legal compliance through better job opportunities and higher income. He recognizes that both options depend on the same assumption and present "only modest" scientific and philosophical implications: both the "tough minded" and the "tender minded" agree that human nature is to make rational choices in one's self interest (Wilson, 2013, p. 234).

These two policies are the only viable options in a free society, where behavioral control cannot rely on surveillance and direct coercion. Wilson believes that "family structure, moral development, [and] the level of personal freedom" most strongly influence criminal behavior (Wilson, 2013, p. 235), but that liberal values preclude the state from intervening in these spheres. Thus, the freer a society intends to be, the more it has to depend on punishments, and America with its static culture, is no exception to this rule.

Wilson not only works out an abstract theory of rational choice; he also limits the scope of public policies to labor adjustments and the penal sector, concluding that punishments are necessary to deter criminal conduct. Crime is a market choice, and the American constitution and American society are Hobbesian (Wilson, 2013, p. 237), centered on individualism and three human passions: desire for wealth, desire for glory, and fear of violent death. Since this is human nature, the state of war is permanent unless a superior force (the Leviathan State) is built to protect people from one another.

Wilson points out that Hobbes is the basis of classical penal thinking, starting with Beccaria and Bentham; for Bentham in particular, state punishment is the decisive element that leads the rational, pain-minimizing individual to avoid crime. Since humans are calculating creatures, we must offer a risk of suffering that is greater than the risk of the benefit of the crime, and only a punishment will weigh heavily enough to tip the scales (Wilson, 2013, p. 230). Wilson's humanism is exposed when he links the need for a threat of punishment to the selfish and violent character of his "culture," thereby naturalizing punishments. His theory outlines punitive humanism: punishment as a mandatory consequence of the type of citizen that the writer takes for granted.

Wilson is not just another Anglo-Saxon liberal, but remains a major influence on the criminological thoughts of the Anglo-Saxon world, having promoted the rise of "administrative criminology" in the late 20th century. The juxtaposition of Wilson and Ferrajoli suggests that punitive humanism is indeed a major presence in contemporary criminology. Now, it is time to think how the Foucauldian perspective can offer a qualified response to this traditional way of legitimizing punishments.

Disengaging from punitive humanism

Using Foucault, and in particular his work on subjectivation, we can respond to punitive humanism with two arguments: (1) the desire for punishment is not innate, and (2) public policies are both products and producers of subjectivities.

If Foucault's "anti-humanist position" (Foucault, 2014a, p. 74) is fully taken into account, it becomes obvious that the desire for punishment in Western society is typical of humanist philosophy, but not of human nature in general, as many societies throughout history have used other forms of social governance (agreement, reparatory, forgiveness). The brutal response of contemporary Western states is not natural or inevitable, and there is abundant documentation proving that the pre-modern West was not as barbaric as we assume (see Clastres,[7] Rouland,[8] Larrauri[9]).

Punishment as the answer to conflict is not an anthropological fact; it is the result of a particular regime of veridiction. As punishment is incorporated into the process of subjectivation, it begins to appear as the only possible lens through which to interpret social reality. It is not surprising that proposals for the reduction or abolition of criminal justice are seen as dystopias by many people, instead of as "real utopias" (Scott, 2013; Scott and Bell, 2016).

Foucault made clear that the answer to a policy based on a pessimistic understanding of human nature is not a policy based on a "noble savage" perspective, which would remain a form of determinism (Cohen, 1988, p. 128). He did not ask for a return to the "pure soul" of the original man, a supposed human being without the vices of the civilization. The real rebuttal is a perspective that does not promise a new "theory of the subject," a new way to point out the "true human nature", but that recognizes the subject—and every culture—as an incessant construction. Contemporary attitudes toward punishment are records of modernity, not of human nature (Foucault, 2010a, p. 149). Or in other words, Punishment is a *historical* truth that has infiltrated the Western subject and made the punitive response look like the *natural* consequence of unwanted acts. Or as Nietzsche puts it, our education is guided by the "fantasies of jailers and executioners" (Nietzsche, 2004, p. 21).

The relationship between harm (cause) and punishment (consequence) is not causal in the way we assume: this connection is the result of a process of co-emergence promoted by a historically situated discourse. Punishment as a way of doing "justice" is an invented normativity, and many others remain possible.

Since the demand for penalties is a modern "event," we can wonder whether the most appropriate act might be, instead of creating policies in accordance with this rationality, to encourage ways of altering this subjectivation: to invent and foment new politics, truths and "practices of the self" to destabilize the present culture.

We have the possibility to invent a "philosophical clinical practice of the subject that enables subjects to loosen themselves from the identities by which they are governed." Instead of giving vent to punitive supplications, which unquestionably have drastic social effects, we could dispute the "speech acts by which individuals constitute themselves as subjects and tie themselves to identities given as their truth" (Harcourt and Brion, 2014, p. 310).

In other words, we can resist the "truth of punishment." To doubt the necessity of a certain form of government is also to doubt the necessity of a certain way of thinking, and it seems commendable to foster the creation of a society that will be "uneasy with the permanence of its code and its laws, criminal institutions and its punitive practices." What the humanist perspective seems to ignore is that there is the possibility of producing new ways of subjectivation, and that new forms of "truth" can gain great social expression (Foucault, 2010e, pp. 325–360).

With all its suffering and dramatic social consequences, punishment can become an intolerable truth. The punitive pretension can be recognized as a trait of an authoritarian sociability that is neither natural nor inevitable. Even if we desire punishment today, nothing binds us to this desire. History has not ended, nor have truths, political forms, or human subjectivities. Putting the subject in the position of self-construction gives her the autonomy that many believed had been taken away by a philosophy that sees individuals as puppets of power (Harcourt, 2018, p. 305).

We must keep in mind that ways of governing are not mere effects of ways of thinking. Forms of power, knowledge, and subjectivities are in a complex and uninterrupted relationship of reciprocal construction. Criminal justice is not merely a consequence of human nature or of a particular culture; it also shapes society and thus its field of application.

Punitive humanism ignores the dynamic character of penal institutions—including their role in creating truths and subjectivities—instead acting as if justice were a mere consequence of society, rather than a powerful part of it. The punitive social pleas of modernity are encouraged by the example offered by the criminal justice system,[10] and the criminal model of modernity has trapped us into questions that always lead back to the same answers (Moore and Roberts, 2016, p. 130). To create alternatives to the punitive format is also to encourage new forms of social interactions, new ways of thinking about our relationships, and new values.

Repressive law enforcement techniques shape our perceptions about who is engaged in unwanted behavior; they project a specific view of "disorderly persons" and what to do about them. We must urgently think about "how those proposed policies are going to shape us as contemporary subjects of society" (Harcourt, 2004, p. 242) and how they encourage punitive ways of thinking.

We must recognize "subjectivity as the effect of multiple and varied processes of government," not as an "a-historical subjectivity" (Voruz, 2010, pp. 7–8). This is one of the reasons punitive responses now appear "natural" or inevitable to us. Penal logic is a form of government rationality, and the forms of knowledge historically associated with crime and punishment (criminal law, popular crime narrative, and criminology) have become "available outside their limited original subject domains as powerful tools with which to interpret and frame" other forms of social action (Simon, 2007, p. 17).

Punitive logic modulates "the society's view of certain disturbances of the public road," especially those of populations who end up enmeshed in the penal apparatus. This criminal style of dealing with conflicts becomes a lens through which to see social problems, a "bureaucratic-mediatic theater" that actively shapes the culture, providing forms of explanation and hypothetically solving the disorders for the purpose of social pacification (Wacquant, 2007, pp. 11–29).

Thus, it does not make sense to argue that the punitive model is justifiable because we must respond to the current punitive culture; the relationship between the two is symbiotic: change one, and you will eventually change the other. It is not possible to view public policies as pure effects of culture, because they also create and reinforce cultures. Truth is mobile and unstable because the subject itself is a malleable creation. This second point confirms the absurdity of defending punishment based on a static understanding of the subject or society, both of which are in constant flux. Moreover, even if the culture is punitive, this does not mean that institutions should reproduce the worst elements of the culture.

The point is not to establish the primacy of the subject over power or vice-versa, but rather to recognize that they are mutually constitutive (Foucault, 2006, p. 172). One is not the origin and other the result, as punitive humanist theories might have us believe. There is a possibility to escape the vicious punitive cycle, through both institutions and culture.

Power has no "intrinsic legitimacy," and this does not mean a suspension of all certainties, but the "the non-necessity of all power of whatever kind" (Foucault, 2014a, p. 13). Criminal justice is not a necessity arising from what is human; it is a dated construction (about three centuries old) that is no more immutable than the subject. If penal punishment is justifiable, the justification cannot be humanist: neither "human nature" nor the presence of a "culture in the present" is sufficient to legitimize a form of justice that can be summarized as "suffering in the name of peace."

Notes

1 He believed that these three concepts (knowledge, power, subjectivation) provide the key to understanding modernity (Foucault, 2011b, p. 10). He stresses the existence of a "rule of immanence" to show that there is no exteriority to these elements, since they are mutually constitutive (Foucault, 2011a, pp. 108–109). Thus, there is no metaphysical truth, power, or subject, and thus, Foucault refused to make a "theory of the truth," "theory of power," or a "theory of the subject." Truth is always a precarious

knowledge that interacts with a conjuncture of power and processes of subjectivation. Government should be understood as an act of influencing and directing the conduct of others (action over action). Subjectivation is the process by which the self is formed and that induces and reflects regimes of truth and governmentalities. It is this three-fold articulation that the author called the "focal points of experience" (Foucault, 2010d, p. 4).

2 Foucault's critique of humanism did not begin in the 1980s, but it was rounded out during this period. By 1966, he had already dedicated himself to this theme in *The Order of Things*, which provides a different interpretation of the great forms of knowledge (biology, economy, language) of the beginning of modernity (Foucault, 2007).

3 In the lectures in Rio de Janeiro of 1973, entitled "Truth and juridical forms," he immediately points out that the purpose of the lectures is to show that political conditions are "not a veil or an obstacle for the subject of knowledge, but that through which the subjects of knowledge are formed." Power is not the effect of a ready and finished subject, nor what disrupts an original human nature; the subject is constituted in the interaction with its political conditions (Foucault, 2002, p. 27).

4 As Daniel Defert wrote, to break away from "original man" is to break away from the ultimate space of metaphysics in the human sciences. This has always been one of the main postulates of Foucault's philosophy, and can be recognized as the fundamental landmark of all his analyses on the discourses and practices of power (Defert, 2014, p. 254). The subject must be found in the "interior of a historical plot." Hence his whole critique of the idea of ideology as "false consciousness," the belief that there is a right awareness beyond power, a truth that can be revealed and that will liberate man. On the contrary, what Foucault demonstrates is that subjects of knowledge are always formed in relation to their historical circumstances (Harcourt and Brion, 2014, p. 285), and thus his goal was not to find a truth outside power, independent of power, but to show how all truths also stem from processes of power, since all relations are relations of power.

5 Recognizing the ceaselessly productive aspect of the human mind over its own individual configuration, Foucault teaches that subjectivation processes deserve the same attention as government processes if the goal is to understand what is happening in the Western world (Foucault, 1995, p. 244).

6 There is no room left for a primordial ethics from which to depart; all humanisms are interpretive barriers, insofar as they promise an "unalienated essence." The last two books published by Foucault, volumes 2 (*The use of pleasure*) and 3 (*The care of the self*) of his history of sexuality reaffirm that the relation of self to self is fundamental key to understanding contemporary life, since the "desiring man" also has a history (Foucault, 1984, p. 11).

7 The Hobbesian presumption of widespread warfare in savage societies was based on accounts of primitive American societies (Hobbes, 2014, p. 109). However, such records have already been seriously questioned by Pierre Clastres, whose scientific evidence points to the fact that the original people of America were not actually "stateless" but actually "against the state." The existence of leaders without power to punish did not lead to chaos; on the contrary, there was social cohesion (Clastres, 2004, p. 47)(contrário, havia coesão social.uth-tellingessantes).

8 One notices the absence of punitive logic in many Indigenous societies, such as the Eskimos of Greenland, the people of Corsica, the Zunhis of North America, the Mbutis (hunter-gatherers) of the Congo, the Bedouin of Jordan, the Gamos of Ethiopia, and the Mountags of Chad. The common factor is that the vast majority of disputes are resolved with the non-violent interaction of the parties (Rouland, 2008, pp. 108–110).

9 Before the modern state, many institutions were called upon to help resolve disputes: even for very serious offenses the solution often relied on agreements, indemnities, or even forgiveness (Larrauri, 2005, pp. 18–20).

10 Larrauri recalls a survey pointing out that the US states with the death penalty are also those that have the highest records of urban lynchings against suspected criminals (Larrauri, 2005, p. 22).

References

Butler J. (2016) 'Meramente cultural', *Ideias* 7(2), pp. 227–248.

Castro E. (2004) *El vocabulario de Foucault,* Buenos Aires, Universidad Nacional de Quilmes.

Clastres P. (2004) *Arqueologia da violência: pesquisas de antropologia política,* São Paulo, Cosac & Naify.

Cohen S. (1988) *Against criminology,* New Jersey, Transaction Books.

Defert D. (2014) 'Situação do curso', in Foucault M. *Aulas sobre a vontade de saber:* curso no Collège de France (1970–1971) (trans. Rosemary Costhek Abílio), São Paulo, Editora WMF Martins Fontes, pp. 239–264.

Dreyfus H. and Rabinow P. (1995) *Michel Foucault, uma trajetória filosófica*: para além do estruturalismo e da hermenêutica (trans. Vera Porto Carrero), Rio de Janeiro, Universitária.

Ewald F. (1993) *Foucault, a norma e o direito* (trans. Antonio Fernando Cascais), Lisboa, Veja.

Ferrajoli L. (2006) *Direito e razão*: teoria do garantismo penal, 2. ed, São Paulo, Revistas dos Tribunais.

Foucault M. (1984) *História da sexualidade 2*: o uso dos prazeres (trans. Maria Thereza da Costa Albuquerque), 8. ed, Rio de Janeiro, Edições Graal.

Foucault M. (1995) 'O Sujeito e o Poder', in Dreyfus H. and Rabinow P. (eds.) *Michel Foucault, uma trajetória filosófica*: para além do estruturalismo e da hermenêutica, Rio de Janeiro, Universitária, pp. 231–249.

Foucault M. (2002) *A verdade e as formas jurídicas,* 3. ed, Rio de Janeiro, NAU editora.

Foucault M. (2004) *Ética, sexualidade, política* (Ditos e Escritos V) (trans. Elisa Monteiro e Inês Autran Dourado Barbosa), Rio de Janeiro, Forense Universitária.

Foucault M. (2005) *Arqueologia das Ciências e História dos Sistemas de Pensamento* (Ditos e Escritos II), Rio de Janeiro, Forense Universitária.

Foucault M. (2006) *Estratégia, saber-poder* (Ditos e escritos IV) (trans. Vera Lucia Avdlar Ribeiro), 2. ed, Rio de. Janeiro, Forense Universitária.

Foucault M. (2007) *As palavras e as coisas:* uma arqueologia das ciências humanas (trans. Salma Tannus Muchail), 9. ed, São Paulo, Martins Fontes.

Foucault M. (2010a) *Vigiar e punir,* 28. ed, Petrópolis, Editora Vozes.

Foucault M. (2010b) *Em Defesa da Sociedade:* curso no Collège de France (1975–1976), 2. ed, São Paulo, editora WMF Martins Fontes.

Foucault M. (2010c) *A hermenêutica do sujeito:* curso no Collège de France (1981–1982) (trans. Márcio Alves da Fonseca and Salma Annus Muchail), 3. ed, São Paulo, Editora WMF Martins Fontes.

Foucault M. (2010d) *O governo de si e dos outros:* curso no Collège de France (1982–1983) (trans. Eduardo Brandão), São Paulo, Editora WMF Martins Fontes.

Foucault M. (2010e) *Repensar a política* (Ditos e escritos VI) (trans. Ana Lúcia Paranhos Pessoa), Rio de Janeiro, Forense Universitária.

Foucault M. (2011a) *História da sexualidade 1: a vontade de saber,* 21. ed, Rio de Janeiro, Graal.

Foucault M. (2011b) *A coragem da verdade:* curso no Collège de France (1983–1984) (trans. E. Brandão), São Paulo, Editora WMF Martins Fontes.

Foucault M. (2014a) *Do governo dos vivos:* curso no Collège de France (1979–1980) (trans. E. Brandão), São Paulo, Editora WMF Martins Fontes.
Foucault M. (2014b) *Wrong-doing, truth-telling*: The function of avowal in justice (trans. S. W. Sawyer), Chicago, The University of Chicago Press.
Foucault M. (2016) *Subjetividade e verdade:* curso no Collège de France (1980–1981) (trans. Rosemary Costhek Abílio), São Paulo, Editora WMF Martins Fontes.
Gros F. (2010) 'Situação do curso', in Foucault M. (ed) *A hermenêutica do sujeito:* curso no Collège de France (1981–1982) (trans. Márcio Alves da Fonseca and Salma Annus Muchail), 3. ed, São Paulo, Editora WMF Martins Fontes, pp. 455–494.
Harcourt B. (2004) *Illusion of order*: The false promise of broken windows policing, Cambridge, Harvard University Press.
Harcourt B. (2018) *The counterrevolution: How our government went to war against its own citizens,* New York, Basic Books.
Harcourt B. and Brion F. (2014) 'The louvain lectures in context', in Foucault M. *Wrong-doing, truth-telling*: the function of avowal in justice (trans. Stephen W. Sawyer), Chicago, The University of Chicago Press, pp. 271–322.
Hobbes T. (2014) *Leviatã* (trans. Rosina D'Angina), São Paulo, Martin Claret.
Larrauri E. (2005) 'Criminologia crítica: abolicionismo y garantismo', *Revista de Estudos Criminais* 20(5), pp. 11–38.
Moore J. and Roberts R. (2016) 'What lies beyond criminal justice? Developing transformative solutions', *Justice, Power and Resistance,* Foundation Volume, pp. 115–136.
Nietzsche F. (2004) *Aurora,* São Paulo, Companhia das letras.
Pelbart P. (2016) 'Da dessubjetivação nomádica à subjetivação herética: Foucault, Agamben, Deleuze', in *Reinvenções de Foucault,* Rio de Janeiro, Lamparina, pp. 270–281.
Rouland N. (2008) *Nos confins do direito*: antropologia jurídica da modernidade (trans. Maria Ermantina de Almeida Prado Galvão) São Paulo, Martins Fontes.
Scott D. (2013) 'Visualising an abolitionist real Utopia: principles, Policy and praxis', in Malloch et al. (eds.), *Crime, critique and Utopia,* London, Palgrave Macmillan, pp. 90–113.
Scott D. and Bell E. (2016) 'Reawakening our radical imaginations: Thinking realistically about utopias, dystopias and the non-penal', *Justice, Power and Resistance Foundation,* Vol. sept, pp. 11–32.
Senellart M. (2014) Situação do curso. in Foucault M. (ed.), *Do governo dos vivos:* curso no Collège de France (1979–1980) (trans. Eduardo Brandão), São Paulo, Editora WMF Martins Fontes, pp. 295–326.
Simon J. (2007) *Governing through crime: How the war on crime transformed American democracy and created a culture of fear,* New York, Oxford University Press.
Voruz V. (2010) 'Politics in Foucault's later work: A philosophy of truth; or reformism in question', *Theoretical Criminology* 15(1), pp. 1–19.
Wacquant L. (2007) *Punir os pobres: A nova gestão da miséria nos Estados Unidos [A onda punitiva]*, 3. ed, Rio de Janeiro, Revan.
Wilson J. Q. (2013) *Thinking about crime*, revised ed, New York, Basic Books.

PART III

Case studies pointing to radical alternatives

14

FEET ON THE GROUND

Emanuel "Eoz"

Do not imagine a different present
Do not bring up illusions about a better future
Release that past of beautiful moments
I no longer love the person, I love the memories

Unexpected encounters made me improvise
The fact that is not what I thought help me land
By walking heavy I got tired
I did not let go my experiences, I was not going to return

I began to believe that, by living, I would never die
I began to notice that my air was down
I fulfill a plan that even I wouldn't understand
And from this place, the days responded.

15

THE SYSTEM IS DESIGNED FOR ME TO FAIL

Douglas Knakmuhs

I'm 38 years old and I've been locked up since I was 16, but even before that I was in and out of group homes and juvenile hall since the age of 11. I've spent more of my life inside a cage then on the streets as a free man.

I was released for the first time in December 2010 at the age of 30. I only lasted two weeks before I went on the run and was arrested a month and a half later.

Nine months later while back in prison, I slit my wrists due to a deep depression that had descended upon me. The officers found me unconscious in my cell from blood loss and had to life-flight me from the prison. When I came too, I was in a "suicide watch" cell at the prison. I was diagnosed with bi-polar manic depression. The medications they gave me seemed to help.

I was released two years later and I immediately relapsed with my drug of choice, which is meth, and I stopped taking my meds. Within six months, I found myself at a motel room having a complete psychological meltdown from the extreme use of drugs, coupled with my lack of the use of my medications and what I now believe to be PTSD in the extreme. I held my ex-girlfriend hostage with a knife. After an hour or so, I stabbed her in the neck, took 80 Ambien pills and woke up three months later in the ICU at a local hospital. I didn't know my own name, why I was laying in that bed, or where I was even at. It took me months of rehabilitation to get back to "normal." I was sent back to prison until the remainder of my first, sentence; then I was released to the county jail to face the charges of stabbing my girlfriend. My family was able to bond me out and true to form I quit taking my meds again, began to use meth and within six months I was caught with a large amount of meth and a gun, but this time I was immediately released because the "war on drugs" in America is a broken system with no end in sight. I knew the Feds were probably watching me, so I tried to lay low.

Because I was out of jail on bond for the assault on my ex-girlfriend, and with the additional charges of the drugs hanging over my head, a month after I got caught with the meth, I swallowed 50 Elavil pills in my third attempt to kill myself. Once again, I was in a coma for two months with no recollection as to how I got there.

I've been locked up ever since then. I'm now scheduled to be released in 2021 and I fear my pending release. Mainly because prisons in Missouri don't offer any help for us while we're here. They warehouse us without much thought of rehabilitation.

I've recently attempted to enroll in college class, but while I'm incarcerated federal law prohibits inmates in prison from receiving any student aid. So, if I can't pay out of pocket, then I can't better myself. To me, that proves that the system is designed for me to fail. I'd love to further my education to give me the confidence I need to become successful in life, but society passes laws that tell me I can't get any help.

With no rights whatsoever once I'm released, I have no voice in this world. A wise man once said, "The only difference between a free man and a slave is his right to vote." We all know from history that blacks were not allowed to vote as a way to take their rights away from them. Laws were passed to hold them back, and until the last 50 or so years, they were not treated as American citizens.

What does it mean to be an American citizen? The word "citizen" is defined as: "A person owing loyalty to and entitled by birth of naturalization to the protection of a state or nation." The word "right" is defined as: "Something due to a person or governmental body by law, tradition or nature."

So, don't I have a right as an American citizen to better myself? Don't I have a right as an American citizen to help decide what that "something due to a person" by our government is? How many convicted citizens in America can't vote? Estimated ten million! That's enough to decide entire elections. That's enough to change racist, biased laws in our land. But because the system decides that I can't vote, I have no voice.

What do you think it does to a man when he knows he's a "second class" citizen? Just ask any black American, and they'll tell you. I'm white, but I totally understand their plight.

At the age of 12, I became institutionalized. I came from a broken home and never had a chance. Prison at such a young age caused me to develop mental health issues. It's not something I'm proud of, but it is what it is.

Right now, as I write this, I'm in the "hole" where I've been for the past eight months due to an assault. Since I've been in the "hole" the mental health department at the prison is short of staff, so I haven't seen a therapist in a while. Sometimes I wonder if anyone even cares.

I've sat and I've thought about this extensively and I've come to realize that America will always have prisons because let's face it, prisons are big money. In my opinion, it's the new form of slavery. Companies like Securus, GTL

(Telmate), ICSolutions and many others are making millions of dollars off of the poorest Americans in this country. Families are forced to pay exuberant prices to companies like J-Pay to send the little bit of money they have to incarcerated family members. The costs of phone calls home are unregulated it seems. The system created "work-release" programs as a way to legalize slavery. Prison industry jobs pay 25 cents to 50 cents an hour with no real work place protections. The goods made at these industry jobs are sold at a premium price.

The medical services here in Missouri are non-existent it seems. CMS is the company contracted through Missouri DOC to provide medical services to inmates, but since it's a "for profit" company, they don't make money if they pay for inmates to get medical help. So, we are denied medical treatment for pretty much everything.

I've had Hepatitis-C for 16 years and even though medical professionals in the free world can cure the disease, CMS refuses to treat 99% of inmates with Hep-C. The ACLU of St. Louis currently has a lawsuit against them right now because of CMS unconstitutional treatment against Hep-C inmates. This is just the tip of the iceberg really. I could go on for days.

So, what do we do? That's the big question.

I believe we must attack the problem on many fronts. Starting with at-risk kids. Most children living in poverty turn to crime. Not all, but being poor makes us more susceptible to crime. School programs help, but we got to start early. If you can deter the man from prison before he ever gets here, then being in prison never becomes a problem for him.

For those of us that's in here, I believe certain laws need to be changed so inmates can apply for student aid. Education is the biggest key to success. Schools should be giving incentives for educating prisoners. Long-distance learning classes should be expanded to where the prisons have college class inside the prison walls, with real college professors teaching us. In each state, an entire prison could be designed for "college" where inmates would have to sign up to get transferred there thru good behavior. Certain criteria would apply. Only non-violent offenders or something like that. It could be minimally staffed and the professors would receive some type of bonus for doing it. Think about it, it could all be done TV remote viewing or like Skype.

I also believe the mental health system in prisons needs to be overhauled. Far too many inmates in here are in need of serious professional help and they ain't receiving any at all.

I also believe that more programs need to be set up to help inmates once they are released from prison. It's not enough to simply "hope" that people will do right once they are free, you have to take steps to ensure they stay out by offering them the "protection of a state or nation" because that is their right; "something due to a person … by law, tradition or nature."

So, if society fails to protect the poorest Americans in our country, then how can we ever have a piece of the American dream?

Let's think about that for a minute; the "American Dream." What does that mean to you? To me it's every person's right to be given a chance to succeed in this country. No matter who you are, where you've been, or what your problems were. What matters is what direction are you going in? What are your intentions in life? Where do you want to be at in 5; 10; 20 years? How do you want to be remembered when you are gone?

I believe this is the greatest country on this planet. I also believe that the Declaration of Independence said it all when it stated, "We hold these truths to be self-evident, that all men are created equal, that they are endowed by their creator with certain unalienable rights, that among these are life, liberty, and the pursuit of happiness."

I am a firm believer of our Constitution. I believe it to be the greatest set of civil rights to ever be enacted in human civilization. I believe that piece of paper is what makes our country so great. But I also believe that because of certain caselaw our country has allowed the civil rights of certain citizens to become eroded over time. I am now, and will forever be a second-class citizen. Being convicted of a crime doesn't make me any less human, or any less of an American.

I understand that I've committed crimes that landed me in prison, and in most cases rightly so. When the court sentenced me, the punishment was in reality a life sentence, because I will be forever punished. Whether it's in prison or outside of prison. My punishment will follow me to my grave.

I also believe that America suffers from a "class" system. We have upper, middle and lower classes. As a democracy, we are supposed to all be equal, but in reality that ain't true. The great equalizer in this country is the almighty dollar. With enough money, anything is possible; but at the same time if you don't have any money then all the doors are closed to you. It's the way of the world and always has been.

At the end of the day I truly believe that education can solve a lot of the problems that inmates face once they are released. Until our politicians pass laws that allow better schooling, better drug rehabilitation, better mental health and more pre-release programs to inmates, then the prison industrial complex is going to continue to become the modern-day slavery that it is. Slavery is defined: "A condition of hard work and subjection. In a state of bondage." Bondage meaning servitude, or to serve.

So while I serve a prison sentence, I am ordered in "a condition of hard work and subjection," and while "in a state of bondage," my government has stripped me of all my rights "endowed by my creator," so that I am forever unequal in society once I'm released.

Our Forefathers in all their wisdom and knowledge wrote the Bill of Rights as a way to guarantee that no American citizens would ever be subjected to tyranny by their government. Never in a million years did they ever expect that when the 13th Amendment was enacted, that the "Punishment Clause" of Section 1 of said Amendment to mean that slavery was OK as a punishment. The 13th Amendment abolished slavery. It stated, "Neither slavery nor involuntary servitude, except as punishment for a crime where of the party shall be duly convicted."

So why is the prison system allowed to hold us as slaves when the 8th Amendment (The Original Bill of Rights) states, "nor cruel and unusual punishment inflicted." Clearly the 8th and the 13th Amendments are in conflict as it refers to punishments, because isn't slavery the very definition of "cruel and unusual punishment"? So then why is the greatest nation on this planet still allowing a form of slavery to exist within its borders?

Amendment 15, Section 1 states, "The right of citizens of the United States to vote shall not be denied or abridged by the United States or by any state on account of race, color, or previous condition of servitude."

Servitude means: "Forced labor imposed as a punishment."

Now you may say I'm not a slave, but I've been sent to the "hole" for refusing to work inside prison walls. I've been punished for not wanting to work in here, so that makes me a slave. The judge sentenced me to a term of prison, not hard labor.

So, let's recap what we've learned today, kids: we learned the definitions citizen, rights, slavery, bondage, servitude and a few others. We learned that people in our country are making millions off of prison by holding the poorest citizens in "slavery." We learned a few of the conditions of the state-sponsored slavery are a lack of education, mental health institutionalization and a total lack of medical care. We learned that American citizens have every right to be free from slavery, be free to vote and live their lives in a "class system." But more importantly we learned that I don't have the same rights as you do. We learned that I am in fact a slave. For all intents and purposes, I'm no longer an American, even though I've lived my whole life in this country. America, the land of my birth.

I proposed a few useful solutions, namely, focus on poverty and at-risk kids as a deterrent; change laws to allow me to obtain an education and more job training; provide more pre-release and after care programs designed to help me succeed.

My life is what's at stake. In a way, America is what's at stake. Until we face the facts lined out in this message, our country will be guilty of crimes against humanity. But as a "civilized" nation, we can't look in the mirror and see that I am you, and you are me …

16

INCARCERATION AS THE WORST POSSIBLE TREATMENT FOR MENTAL ILLNESS

Richard Sean Gross

My crime was a selfish act conceived in isolation. An arrogant response to abuse both real and imagined, most of which occurred decades earlier. It was not a rational act and I made no effort to get away with it or deny responsibility. I wrongly believed that I would receive top notch psychiatric care, while the truth of my maltreatment came to light. I confessed before I ever spoke to a lawyer.

Ineligible for an insanity defense under the M'Naghten rule, I was found competent to stand trial. Formulated by an English court in 1843, M'Naghten determines that if you knew what you did was wrong you are guilty. When asked if I knew I would get in trouble for it, I replied "yes," proving I knew it was wrong. The prosecution sought the death penalty, but the judge sentenced me to death by incarceration (life without parole).

Though never recognized by the court, my treatment for mental illness began immediately. On suicide watch I was stripped naked, given a flimsy and short paper gown, then placed in a cold cell without sheets or blanket. I spent my first night ever in jail naked and afraid. I don't know why they thought I was suicidal, and I still consider suicide watch to be the worst punishment they got.

Soon I was prescribed a heavy dose of Thorazine by a visiting psychiatrist who spoke to me for 90 seconds and then shouted "NEXT!" Conveyor belt psychiatry is common in prison due to the massive numbers of patients. In all the years I took psych meds I never saw a doctor more than ten minutes once every few months. Most appointments lasted only a minute as the Doctor found that I had no intentions of hurting myself or others, while other patients were moments away from causing harm.

Arriving at State prison after my conviction, the doctors were in disbelief at how much Thorazine I was taking. Developed in the 1950s as a "chemical lobotomy," the drug is seldom used in this century except maybe to help the accused sleep-walk through their convictions. The term "Thorazine shuffle" is still used to describe the gait of an over-medicated inmate. Over time, I was taken off Thorazine and, eventually, all psychiatric medications. These meds don't cure mental illness while prolonged use can be dangerous to organs and cause tremors. Slowing down activity in the frontal lobe, psychiatric medications can prevent patients from "acting out" and are great for warehousing inmates. Prisons are usually generous with medications while being stingy with mental health staffing and programing.

I ended up at a prison known as "the fort" on I block – a "special needs" unit housing a mixture of the mentally ill and intellectually/developmentally disabled. People who would be ridiculed or exploited in general population. Everyone took psych meds and was generally asleep by 9 pm. Many slept 10–16 hours a day; doing little in their waking hours aside from eating and smoking. Most had no family in contact with them, didn't get visitors, and received very little mail. They didn't leave the block to work or participate in programs. Having no money, they just sat in cells so void of belongings that they echoed. They would just lay there and decompensate until someone reached out to them.

Some staff would try to engage them in art therapy or other activities on the block. Bingo was especially popular if the staff would come up with prizes. Not allowed to bring anything into the prison they had to find snacks, etc., on the inside. A budget for art supplies was difficult enough to get; money to give prizes to "criminals" was much harder. But there was always money for medication, cameras, and barbed wire.

In the case of *Madrid v. Gomez*, California's treatment of mentally ill prisoners was found lacking. A Federal Judge stated his opinion: "sedating all inmates with a powerful medication that leaves them in a constant stupor would arguably reduce security risks; however, such a condition of confinement would clearly fail constitutional muster."

In my view this is the condition of numerous prisoners – I have seen it. If the corrections officers feel they're having a problem with a mentally ill resident, they call the psych department. All they can really do is increase the patient's dose until he or she no longer causes problems for the staff. Whether the person has the energy to get up and go to the yard, or meals, is not the officer's concern. Psychiatric medications play an important role in the warehousing of prisoners made necessary by mass incarceration and the overcrowding that results.

After a decade or so, I entered general population still finding many with obvious mental illness. I have met thousands of convicts from all walks of life finding that they are not who the media portray them to be. I've met no mobsters, safe-crackers, wheel men or cat burglars. Instead: addicts, the mentally ill and the intellectually/developmentally disabled. I meet people who couldn't hang on to a job or a romantic partner. People who couldn't control their addictions or manage their finances. People who made stupid decisions and irrational choices which they didn't even seriously expect to get away with. Not cold and calculating as prosecutors describe; much more confused and chaotic. People who couldn't keep it together and fell apart in a desperate, unknowing cry for help.

The State responds to this cry for help with punishment to deter others from committing crime. Deterrence works only if people are expecting to get caught and convicted, are aware of the punishment, and are making rational choices to begin with. Only a small percentage of crimes, even serious violent ones, result in a conviction and prison sentence. Many are not reported, not solved, or dropped for lack of evidence. Few people walking the streets are familiar with the State legislature's most recent "tough on crime" sentencing act. Deterrence has no impact when the crime was not a rational act decided upon after a sober evaluation of pros and cons. If the people who commit crime were making rational choices, the mere existence of prisons would be enough to scare them without the long prison sentences that make district attorneys and other politicians so popular. If there are "career criminals" weighing the odds and making clever choices, then they are probably getting away with their crimes which would explain why I've never met any of them in prison.

The focus on deterrence is misguided and the recidivism rate proves it. We need to shift the focus to crime prevention and treatment for people who have problems that lead them to "criminal" behaviors. We ignore these problems at our peril. To spend billions on incarceration and still not address the core problem that is driving the behavior is folly. In most cases I believe the core problem is some degree of mental illness.

Wellness programs have gone a long way to reduce cost for health insurance companies. By investing in the health and fitness of people, they ultimately profit because of the reduced claims which come from healthy people.

I see mental illness much like physical fitness: it is a matter of degrees. Certainly, an aerobics instructor is fit while the person so obese they can't get out of their house is not (and likely mentally ill as well). Most of us fall somewhere between these extremes. Mental health is the same way. Certainly, a deranged serial killer who eats his victims is insane while a successful person, loved by family and friends, living in a comfortable home they can afford, appears sane. Most of us fall somewhere between these extremes.

Truth is, all of us could be in better shape physically and mentally. We need to de-stigmatize mental illness and promote mental health among all people to prevent crime from happening. We need to create stability and sanity in the lives of those most likely to commit crime. The young, the poor, the homeless, and most of all the mentally ill.

People voice sympathy for the mentally ill but don't really want them around and have always wanted a place to ship them off to. Bizarre behaviors in any neighborhood will trigger a call to the police. Police in the USA shoot about 1,000 people per year. It is estimated that one quarter to one half are mentally ill. Some of those are intending to get killed, committing what is often called "suicide by cop."

In most principalities, the police have little choice but to arrest and jail the mentally ill. Most mental health hospitals have been closed, and where they exist they might also warehouse patients without much treatment. Conditions were often inhuman and, when made public, led to the closure of such institutions. Today, America's largest jails are also its largest provider of mental health care, yet the warehousing and inhuman conditions in jails and prisons are not so easily brought to the public's attention nor do they care about the "criminals."

When you consider that sex offenders are frequently mentally ill persons who could benefit from mental health services, the public's attitude toward them is one of open hostility combined with an erroneous belief that they cannot be cured. As much as people want them to be punished, no one is giving them life sentences; so we need to treat them before they walk the streets again. Like all mental illness it can be treated and managed if addressed with compassion by trained professionals.

Even within prisons, there is hostility toward sex offenders and other mentally ill residents. Far from a get-out-of-jail-card, mental illness exposes an inmate to ridicule from staff and residents, reduced employment opportunities, and diminished probability of parole. Those designated as mentally ill are simply not trusted or understood by anyone and are isolated as a matter of practice even when it is not policy.

Prisons don't know what to do with the mentally ill. There are Special Needs Units – SNU, Mental Illness Units – MHU, Secure Residential Treatment Units – SRTU, Forensic Treatment Centers – FTC, Security Housing Units – SHU, and Special Management Units – SMU, among others. An alphabet soup of housing units which the mentally ill are shuffled between. The staff are constantly torn between promoting socialization that will help such people in prison, and the isolation that will protect others from them. Due to training and temperament, corrections officers are better at the latter. The design of the prisons is, of course, better suited to isolation than socialization.

The effect of isolation on prisoners, especially the mentally ill, is well known and has been since prisons were new. Eastern State Penitentiary in Philadelphia was an early effort to use isolation, and penitence, to correct "criminal" behavior. Prisoners could not speak and spent much of their time alone in their cells with only a Bible. Charles Dickens visited Easter State in the early 1840s and had this comment on the effects of isolation. "I hold this slow and daily tampering with the mysteries of the brain, to be immeasurably worse than any torture of the body." I fail to see how exacerbating one's mental illness in anyway makes society a safer place.

Today's special management units and "supermax" prisons are places where this lesson is once again ignored. A Federal Judge, ruling in *Madrid v. Gomez* described the placement of the mentally ill in California's Security Housing Unit at Pelican Bay Prison as: "The mental equivalent of putting an asthmatic in a place with little or no air to breathe." I fail to see how exacerbating one's mental illness in any way makes society a safer place.

The simple truth is that prison is not the place to treat mental illness or drug addiction: the two main reasons people end up in prison. We may think of prison as a sure-fire cold turkey quit, but drugs do get in. Taxpayers don't want to subsidize drug treatment programs for "criminals" especially when they don't always work, yet they pay billions to incarcerate them and it doesn't always work.

Certainly, there are times when people need to be separate from society. Nobody wants a serial rapist running loose. However, to place that person in a facility for x number of years, a facility where he may be raped himself, and then release him with the same mental problem as before is lunacy, madness!

Imagine a hospital which treats a person's disease for two weeks. If the patient recovers in two days, they must still remain for two weeks. If they do not recover in two weeks they still have to go; their treatment after that point would be optional and at their own expense. Now imagine that said disease is contagious and actually harms others more than the carrier. For God's sake let's treat this person until they are better and then welcome them back among the healthy. The idea that helping an offender with their problems is "letting them off easy" is foolish.

A crime is a rip in the fabric of society and requires an examination of the harm done and the needs of all stakeholders: the victim, the perpetrator, and the community. It is the obligation of the offender to address the harm and the community's needs. People who advocate for victim's rights always assume that the victim wants revenge and punishment delivered by the state when most would rather see remorse and reparations. Politicians assume that only deterrence can prevent crime and so seek more extensive and expensive punishments. They promise to "lock 'em up and throw away the key," and then spend public money on endless prison construction projects.

Many assume that a small number of evil people are committing all the crime and we just need to build enough prison space to incapacitate them all. Soviet writer and dissident Aleksandr Solzhenitsyn described the problem this way:

> If only there were evil people somewhere insidiously committing evil deeds, and it were necessary only to separate them from the rest of us and destroy them! But the line dividing good and evil cuts through the heart of every human being. And who is willing to destroy a piece of his own heart?

We have a system predicated on false assumptions supported by voters and politicians who have never seen the inside of a prison and hope they never do. We are so focused on punishing the "criminal" and not caring what effect that has on them that we lose sight of the fact that society may not be gaining anything from the costly practice of incarceration. If the taxpayers are not well served by the current system, it should be changed.

Harsh punishments do not bring the remorse that the victim wants and often makes the offender a victim of the state. In a case filled with examples of people who die from medical neglect, Federal Judge Henderson concluded that:

> there is a common lack of respect for medical staff, and custody staff far too often actively interfere with the provisions of medical care, often for reasons that appear to have little or nothing to do with legitimate custody concerns.

My experience has been that custody staff have no respect for the other departments (medical, psychiatry, education, drug treatment, etc.) and frequently thwart the efforts of those trying to have a positive impact on the incarcerated people. There are staff dedicated to taking good care of their charges and solving the problems that bring people to jail. There are many volunteers who are forced to jump through hoops to be allowed to enter institutions where they can help. The wall keeps people out as well as keep people in.

It is compassion that brings remorse and a determination to change on the part of the resident. Organizations like Inside/Out and the Alternatives to Violence Project (AVP) venture into maximum security institutions to help and humanize people. Other volunteers come in to make possible workshops on Restorative Justice, creative writing, art, poetry, and Bible study. These activities are the real life of the jail and the place where hearts are softened, and people change.

I have benefited greatly from workshops and the course offered by Villanova University free of charge. I have become someone better and more educated than I would have if I had never come to prison. Many people need a time-out to take an exacting personal inventory, to heal themselves, and to grow into a better human being. It often happens in prison but is more in spite of the place than because of it. Prison is solely concentrated on restraining dangerous people. It is designed to isolate people from each other as well as the outside world.

Prison can and should be used when an individual is a danger to others. It should only be used for as long as the person is a danger and the focus should be on identifying the illness and applying treatment. When it is obvious to the court that addiction or mental illness is driving the anti-social behavior, treatment should begin at once under the circumstances conductive to healing. The ideal setting is probably not a prison or not prison as we know it.

Prison burdens the entire family, leaves everyone broke, often renders the felon permanently unemployable, and promotes mental illness. It is as harsh a punishment as electro-shock is a harsh therapy and should never be the first choice to deal with any problem. Yet prison has become our go-to solution, a default setting for dealing with difficult people. Incarceration is the most expensive and ineffective way to address social problems.

Crime prevention would be better for victims than after-the-fact state retribution. Ultimately, it could be cheaper too, just as a wellness program can prevent costly illness. Healthy, stable, well-adjusted people don't make victims out of their spouses, children, neighbors, or strangers.

Punishing those who make bad personal choices such as violence, theft, or drug use comes natural to society. Behaviors like alcoholism and obesity are also caused by bad personal choices yet there is sympathy for these problems despite their cost to society. Our first instinct is to help these people, not to punish them. We should feel the same way toward drug addicts, sex offenders, and those acting out of mental illness.

The overall effect of incarceration is to take those who have problems (poverty, addiction, mental illness, learning disability, etc.), and place them in a setting which is *known* to not help, or exacerbate those types of problems. The dubious satisfaction of seeing "bad people" punished should not lead us to support a system which is not helping people or preventing future victims.

There should not be a department of caging people but a Department of Redemption which supervises the treatment and recovery of those people who have caused harm. Virtually everyone who enters prison is not at their peak mental health. Incarceration is isolation and isolation causes insanity.

17

THE RHETORIC OF DEHUMANIZATION

Japanese American concentration camps and the US criminalizing system

Michael J. Coyle and Stephen T. Young

Introduction: the rhetoric about Japanese Americans and Criminalized Americans

This chapter is a study in the *engineering of consent*, as Edward Bernays disturbingly coined it in his loving embrace of *Propaganda* (1928). We compare two productions of consent by the US government: one is now broadly accepted by historians as one of the most shameful acts in US history, whereas the other goes broadly unrecognized in almost all sectors of society to this day. The first is the engineering of consent around the mass incarceration of Japanese Americans from the Pacific coast in concentration camps during World War II (WWII).[1] The second is the engineering of consent performed daily by the US criminalizing system (law, police, courts and prisons). By exposing the striking similarities in these two productions of consent, we demonstrate that any narrative promoting the criminalization system as preoccupied with justice, public safety and accountability is unmasked as false and the need for penal abolition is made apparent.

Our purpose is to highlight – through two examples of government action – how government engineers mass consent. Our thesis is that the dehumanizing rhetoric used against Japanese Americans by the US government during WWII has deep parallels with the dehumanizing rhetoric against Criminalized Americans produced by the US government's *criminal justice logic* (Coyle, 2018a; Hulsman, 1997). Our hope is that these similitudes inspire recognition, repugnance and demand for restitution, in that this second group of targets are entitled to the same redress as the first: acknowledgement that propaganda and consent production deliberately dehumanized, cessation of targeting, and ultimately apology and reparations.

Language, rhetoric and dehumanization

This chapter is a study of rhetoric, a study of language. As our examination of both *Japanese Americans* and *Criminalized Americans* will show the action is centered on the use of language to dehumanize a population. This language is highly political and faces a difficult task: to neutralize and make innocuous speech and action that in any other circumstance would be called out as completely unacceptable. Dehumanization includes three different rhetorical maneuvers to make violent and cruel action tolerable: 1) language that depicts humans as less-than-human, 2) language that erases the human entity as the object of violent action, and 3) language that erases the human as agent of violent action.

As George Orwell (1946) noted, in order to make the unpalatable digestible, political language must incorporate as many rhetorical devices as possible to distance the horror: euphemism, clever phrasing and generic or global terms are but a few common strategies:

> Defenseless villages are bombarded from the air, the inhabitants driven out into the countryside, the cattle machine-gunned, the huts set on fire with incendiary bullets: this is called *pacification*. Millions of peasants are robbed of their farms and sent trudging along the roads with no more that they can carry: this is called *transfer of population* or *rectification of frontiers*. People are imprisoned for years without trial, or shot in the back of the neck or sent to die of scurvy in Arctic lumber camps: this is called *elimination of unreliable elements*.
>
> *(p. 261)*

Language work that enables the dehumanizing treatment of human beings for political ends is difficult to accomplish, but when done well, as Orwell demonstrates, it can make people comfortable with the most violent actions by hiding them in plain sight or placing them in a narrative that hides the dehumanizing acts. Fortunately, no amount of euphemism, clever phraseology or rhetorical devices can withstand the unmasking that close examination achieves.

The dehumanizing rhetoric about Japanese Americans

Government work to shape and manipulate public opinion has a long history in the US (Brewer, 2009). While the passage of time makes it easier to distinguish individual cases of the government's work to build conformity of thought, in the moment, the manufacture of consent and propaganda can be difficult for most to spot – even in a highly rhetorical or dehumanizing case. At the time, the 1940s mass incarceration of Japanese Americans in concentration camps was described as sound national policy and thoughtful protection of Japanese Americans; today it is commonly referenced, at best, as an example of misguided military policy and anti-Japanese racist sentiment before and during WWII (Navarro, 2010). This contrast in opinion provides an instructive case study for how oppression, dehumanization and violence are made palatable to publics via rhetorical language.

The history of how the US incarcerated people solely because of their Japanese ancestry – citizens and immigrants alike – has been studied in great detail (e.g., see Nishiura Weglyn, 1996; Reeves, 2015). It began when US President Roosevelt signed Executive Order 9066 authorizing the military to exclude civilians from any US region without trial or hearing. By the end of WWII, more than 120,000 US citizens and immigrants of Japanese descent had been incarcerated and their property and wealth largely – in most cases entirely – appropriated. Within a year, all persons of Japanese ancestry living in the Western portion of the Pacific states had been taken hostage. Executive Order 9102 followed, and it created the War Relocation Authority – a body whose use of the word 'Relocation' is only matched by the title given to its first act of forced removal: 'voluntary evacuation'. Legal exoneration from such detainment did not come until after the war (1945), and it would be more than another 40 years before US President Ronald Reagan offered a formal apology and HR 442 – a law recognizing the incarceration of Japanese Americans as worth a reparation payment of $20,000 per individual person imprisoned. As the final government investigative body summarized its findings:

> … the Commission on the Wartime Relocation and Internment of Civilians (CWRIC) report takes the absence of 'true' military necessity as the relevant fact: the internment occurred "despite the fact that not a single documented act of espionage, sabotage or fifth column activity was committed by an American citizen of Japanese ancestry or by a resident Japanese alien on the West Coast" (as cited in Lee, 2007, p. 3)

In time, scholars have come to view the Japanese American concentration camps with very different eyes than those who designed and established them. Often the titles of scholarly works convey horror, shock and revulsion: *Years of Infamy: The Untold Story of America's Concentration Camps*; *The Shocking Story of the Japanese American Internment in World War II*; *The History of an American Concentration Camp, Pomona, California*. No scholarship has uncovered evidence to support the original claim of military necessity driving the concentration camps and the incarceration of Japanese Americans (Lee, 2007), whereas historians have substantiated the influence of anxieties around power and war (Daniels, 1981), as well as strategies of dominance (Feeley, 1995). While early scholarship centered on the impact of white farmers of the Pacific Coast applying economic lobbying and wartime hysteria (Renteln, 1995), later scholarship has drawn connections to the preceding century of racist and xenophobic law concerning Japanese immigrants and the rights of Japanese Americans (Reeves, 2015). Frequently, these works raise concerns about how European Americans saw themselves as racially superior to Japanese Americans (Dower, 1986), and scholarship points to the influence of racial considerations in the treatment of Japanese Americans while incarcerated (Rock, 2014). Commonly, these scholars point to the absurdity of the language: 'evacuation' to describe the acts of intentional exclusion and forced removal; 'relocation' to describe incarceration; 'non-aliens' to describe US citizens of Japanese ancestry; 'may be excluded' to describe being evicted from one's home; 'assembly centers' to describe detention spaces; and 'relocation centers' to describe concentration camps (National, 2013).

The dehumanizing rhetoric about Criminalized Americans

The US criminalizing system performs a unique role in the dehumanization and *othering* of specific groups. The basis of this is the differing of certain behaviors and individuals as 'crime' or 'criminal'. Criminalizing discourse insinuates that a specific population takes part in a limited behavior deserving of 'management' by and through the criminalizing system (Coyle, 2018a). This ideology clings to the ideals of white supremacy and focuses much of the consent production on the 'criminality' disproportionately associated with people in communities of color (Alexander, 2012). This narrative is flawed. 'Crime', and thus 'criminals', can exist due to the perception of a violation of a desired societal norm. However, these terms are counterintuitive to supporting our understanding of the language behind the criminalizing system as the majority of 'criminal' behavior is commonplace in our society (Coyle, 2018a; Kappeler, Potter, and Blumberg, 2005; Mathiesen, 2015).

Why then does the criminalizing system continue to warrant the use of such terms as a means of dehumanization? The answer specifically concerns power, the use of oppression and discriminatory behaviors through the *othering* of individuals/groups (Epps and Furman, 2016). The process of using terminology to dehumanize particular groups supports the social method of identifying individuals different from the white hetero-normative capitalist culture for the purposes of creating a dominant and subordinate group. This use of language to separate groups follows the pattern discussed by Carpentier (2017), in which language is used to destroy the 'enemy', homogenize the 'self' or the dominant group opposed to the 'enemy', and present the radical difference of the enemy as inferior to the dominant. This radical difference making allows for the 'destruction' of the 'enemy' as they represent dangerous, threatening or 'criminal' behavior (Baysha, 2020).

Much of this process is reaffirmed through the everyday language used by actors within the criminalizing system. The discourse surrounding the system is rooted in the "implicit values and hidden assumptions in words and/or phrases" (Arrigo, 2001, p. 164) used to express the attitudes and judgments of the individual or institution. The language used through this discourse provides unconscious hidden value through particular descriptors, providing definitions or dehumanizing labels to describe others. This means someone spoken of as 'criminal' or a 'threat' also represents an active 'evil' that must be feared, controlled and thusly punished. All of this is a part of the broader use of *The Language of Justice*, which allows for the use of symbols and language to understand the process in which this discourse becomes legitimized. Specifically, as mentioned earlier, studying the language of the criminalizing system pushes us to understand "the power and process of those defining behavior, people and discourse" (Coyle, 2018a, p. 328). Examining language allows scholars to identify everyday justice discourse rarely acknowledged but often accepted as self-evident (Coyle, 2018b). Specifically, studying *The Language of Justice* centers our understanding on how the language of moral entrepreneurs within the criminalizing system has always worked as a powerful tool. As will be demonstrated, language becomes a tool to subjugate those of lower economic status, particular gender identities, and people of color (Coyle, 2013), and is a subjugations that is presented to these populations as for their own 'protection' when in fact it represents a system built on racial oppression/violence and imperialism.

The rhetorical techniques of dehumanization

Edward Bernays noted that, "The conscious and intelligent manipulation of the organized habits and opinions of the masses is an important element in democratic society" (1928, p. 10). The constant nature of rhetorical work in public life – the inventing, the framing, the arranging and the stylizing toward particular ends – is often hard for us to swallow given our idealism around 'democracy'. This is especially the case when we look to history and examine some of the rhetoric of the past (e.g., on slavery, women, or GLBTQ+ issues). Time and distance often make obvious what is very difficult to see in the moment. For example, though Senator Joseph McCarthy's rhetoric literally emboldened and captured the imagination and behavior of a 'red scare' age, a handful of decades later his name is synonymous with making accusations without evidence and abusing the values of loyalty and pride in one's community. Today, McCarthy's dehumanizing rhetoric seems so obviously ideological and manipulative that its contours frequently occur as comical (we even have an -ism for it: McCarthyism).

The rhetorical work of government, as seen in the example of Senator McCarthy, is frightening for at least two reasons. First, the power differential any person (or any group they belong to) faces when stacked against the government is daunting, and frankly overwhelming. Second, and even more terrifying, if dehumanizing rhetoric can be broadly unrecognized even at its height, *unseen* if you will, what dehumanizing rhetoric is fully at work today that – as we would expect – we do not currently *see* (Coyle, Forthcoming)?

Consistently *seen* and routinely *unseen* rhetoric, then, is an important distinction. Our purpose in this chapter is to take advantage of some likenesses to bring together some *seen rhetoric* to point to some *unseen rhetoric*. We seek to show *the now recognized* rhetorical work of government in the production of consent for the mass incarceration of Japanese Americans in concentration camps, to point to *the now unrecognized* rhetorical work of government in the production of consent for the mass incarceration of Criminalized Americans.

The rhetorical techniques of dehumanizing Japanese Americans

To complete its mission of eliminating Japanese Americans from the free society of the mainland Pacific coast, the US government had a difficult task. It required a rhetoric that would permit and make palatable three things: (1) the kidnapping of US citizens and immigrants (of distant or near Japanese ancestry), (2) their forced ejection from free society into concentration camps and (3) the confiscation of their businesses, personal property and material connections. In short, it needed to re-frame Americans as 'Japanese' and re-categorize abduction and concentration-camp-internment as 'relocation'.

There is no better reflection of the rhetorical labor done to accomplish this dehumanization work than the jaw dropping, ten-minute, 1942 film, produced by the US government for this occasion.[2] This one exemplar of US propaganda can be used to distinguish an array of rhetorical strategies that were used throughout the 'internment' period. The name given to the film, *Japanese Relocation*, immediately identifies the two rhetorical devices it will employ to hide objectionable acts and neutralize potential outrage: the story is about the 'Japanese' (not about fellow US citizens and immigrant residents) and it is about 'relocating' (not about forcing people into concentration camps and using armed threat against them). All the rhetorical work of the film is arranged in *an underlying logic that depends on the frames of war, protection (from simulated danger, threat, and fear), and aid.*

The *war* frame dominates the film. For example, the language is frequently militarized: the events are described as an 'operation' completed by the 'War Relocation Authority'; the film narrator is Milton Eisenhower, brother to the famous general; and the first spoken words are, "When the Japanese attacked Pearl Harbor our west coast became a potential combat zone." Further, the justifications for the acts are also militarized: "houses and hotels occupied almost exclusively by Japanese were within a stone's throw of a naval air base, ship yards, oil wells."[3]

The *protection* frame is also evident in the above quotes. Suddenly US citizens are simply called 'Japanese', a turn of phrase that is hardly unimportant in the context of WWII. Implied is that the public should be afraid and feel threatened by these US citizens, and recognize that protection is required. As the film continues, "Japanese fishermen had every opportunity to watch the movement of our ships; Japanese farmers were living close to vital aircraft plants."[4] The *protection* frame is constant, and even applied to those terrorized by the government, as the film describes how the government "encouraged the Japanese to leave voluntarily." As the narrator notes: "The trouble for the voluntary evacuees" was they "soon felt threatened at their new locations. So the program was quickly put on a planned and protected basis." The blatant suggestion here is that people are being protected. They were in "trouble," and "felt threatened" at their "new locations." Therefore, a "plan" for "protecting" them was built. In one swift repositioning, forcefully removed and concentration-camp-interned persons are renamed as "volunteer evacuees" who "made plans."

In this fashion, the building logic promotes a frame of *aid*. The wider US public are aided by being protected from the – no longer Japanese Americans – Japanese. The abduction and concentration-camp-internment of US citizens is called a "mass migration," a "relocation" or a "transfer" of "evacuees." However, such characterizations are ludicrous. When people are forced, by armed guard, to a concentration camp, they have not migrated, transferred or relocated. Language such as "forced removal," "incarceration" or "concentration camp" is never used. Instead, people are described as being "evacuated" to "evacuation areas" – phrasings suggesting aid from an impending natural disaster, such as a hurricane.

In describing the events, the narrator exclaims, "Now the actual migration got under way … The evacuees cooperated whole heartedly … The many loyal among them felt that this was a sacrifice they could make on behalf of America's war effort." But neither words asking a viewer to imagine "whole hearted cooperation" from someone being herded off to a concentration camp, nor the exciting, adventuresome, happy music, nor the camera ready image of a smiling child waving off a bus departing for a concentration camp are enough to dislodge the eerie similarity of these scenes to the 'migration' of Jews in Europe: armed soldiers around the bus, train depots with piles of suitcases and parcels, and the down-town, boarded-up businesses of the "evacuees."[5]

For those taken, the narrator says, "Behind them they left shops and homes they had occupied for many years. Their fishing fleets were impounded and left under guard." But even the passing film shots show the blatant lie. In shop windows the signs read of a knowledge of what was to be lost forever: "Selling out Entire Stock," "Must be Sold at Once" and "Closed for Good." The complete loss is obvious. The "relocation" is not described as one to temporary prisons and then to actual concentration camps, but instead to what the narrator tells us are "relocation centers" and "assembly centers," that is, "until new pioneer communities could be completed on federally owned lands in the interior." Here the language of concentration camps as "pioneer communities" defies description.

The film's rhetorical presentation of what was done to Japanese Americans entirely erases a process of dehumanization. The viewer is constantly assured that what is being done is on the one hand "protecting us all from the enemy Japanese," and on the other hand "helping American citizen Japanese and Japanese aliens." Accordingly, it is done for their "consideration," and done "democratically." What has been done is that we have "evacuated" people in danger; we "encouraged" them to move, we "transferred" them on a "volunteer" basis, and then as they were in "trouble" and "felt threatened" a "plan" was put in place to "protect" them. Though the kidnapping and concentration camp placement can only be imagined as a horrific experience to undergo, the narrator describes an almost festive event that was actually "aid (that) was financed by the government":

> Notices were posted. All persons of Japanese descent were required to register. They gathered in their own churches and schools, and the Japanese themselves cheerfully handled the enormous paperwork involved in the

> migration. Civilian physicians made preliminary medical examinations. Government agencies helped in a hundred ways; they helped the evacuees find tenants for their farms, they helped businessmen lease, sell or store their property.

Unbelievably, in the film the kidnapping and incarceration of these Americans is described as experienced "cheerfully." The powerful frame of a government providing aid is returned to repeatedly: with "physicians" and "government agencies" they are "helped in a hundred ways." Continuous "aid" is afoot: "they helped the evacuees find tenants for their farms, they helped business men lease, sell or store their property," and they do not even have to pay for this, as uncle Sam foots the bill: "financed by the government." The horrendous theft Japanese Americans suffer in business, property, and personal belongings is never recognized, and any mention of it makes it seem like a *voluntary loss* by transforming it into a self-willed *sacrifice*: "quick disposal of property often involved financial sacrifice for the evacuees." Not a theft, but a voluntary "sacrifice," something from someone who is being "helped" since they are an "evacuee." The accompanying film imagery is equally striking: a smiling doctor putting a stethoscope on a child held by a seemingly grateful parent; white men advising Japanese Americans at tables under signs that read "Farm Security Administration: Farmers, Nurserymen" and "Federal Reserve Bank – Evacuee Property Department." And just in case there was any doubt, the narrator supplies the final nail to secure the coffin lid:

> Neither the Army nor the War Relocation Authority relished the idea of taking men, women, and children from their homes, their shops and their farms, so the military and civilian agencies alike determined to do the job as a democracy should: with real consideration for the people involved.

Thus, all the rhetorical work of the film is organized around *an underlying logic that depends on the frames of war, protection (from simulated danger, threat, and fear), and aid.*

The rhetorical techniques of dehumanizing Criminalized Americans

There is little difference between the now *seen* rhetoric used to kidnap and imprison Japanese Americans during WWII and the *unseen* rhetoric currently used to justify the caging/surveillance of millions of Criminalized Americans. This latter rhetoric exists in the societal consciousness as appropriate and has yet to be unveiled for being as violent, racist and dehumanizing as the former rhetoric. The same linguistic tools used during WWII by the government (through the military), are used today by the government (through the criminalizing institutions of law, police, courts and prisons). Today, a category of Criminalized Americans has been created to distinguish them from other Americans and to justify their separate treatment. This contemporary language carries a similar societal *weight* to that demonstrated in the 1942 film as it works to enemify particular groups.

In broad conceptualizations, the language used to dehumanize Criminalized Americans works in two distinct ways. The first way is to broadly criminalize people in communities of color and/or people in poor communities and thereby justify their disproportionate incarceration. The use of the word 'criminal' works similarly to 'Japanese' in this sense as it creates an enemy deserving of containment and punishment. More specifically, it supports the separation of the intended audience from those whose presence and participation in American life represent a threat (Carpentier, 2017) to a common understanding of safety in a country shaped by white supremacy and racial capitalism. While the state often softens this language, criminalizing institutions use their positions as moral entrepreneurs to construct a discourse around those identified as 'criminal' in a way that advances the continuance of harm of communities, groups and individuals (Coyle, 2013). Second, the rhetorical language and practices surrounding the current dehumanization of Criminalized Americans utilize the same logic as that identified in the case of Japanese Americans: one that equally depends on the frames of war, protection (from simulated danger, threat and fear) and aid.

The production of Criminalized Americans is facilitated by a similar militaristic rhetoric to that used against Japanese Americans in WWII. The *war on crime* frame, the militarization of police and correctional cohorts, the expansion of punitive 'criminal' legal system policies and the political accelerations of surveillance post 9/11 have led to a repurposing of such enemifying language. Specifically, those criminalized are now framed as a 'threat' to a society now depicted as requiring protection. Instead of *seeing* that criminalizing institutions selectively pursue a small percentage of committed 'crime' (e.g., although 1 of every 5 women are sexually assaulted in their lifetime, 1 in every 13 households annually experiencing property victimization, and 1 in 3 persons uses unlawful drugs – only a fraction of these 'crimes' or 'criminals' are given any attention whatsoever from the criminalizing system), they are presented as broadly successful institutions protecting and aiding the public. At the same time, those held accountable for committing 'crime' are not acknowledged as a small segment of those who break laws but are instead presented as the proof that 'crime' is being addressed by 'public safety programs'. Furthermore, their incarceration and extreme surveillance are justified as benefits for receiving 'correctional' programs. Their targeted bodies and lives warrant danger assessments and control in order to maintain a governing through 'crime' logic (Simon, 2007). This threat assessment uses the same calculus demonstrated in the film to transform Japanese Americans into 'Japanese' who warranted containment as protection against potential threats. However, varying from the acceptance of such cruelty committed during WWII, much of the current dehumanizing rhetoric remains unrecognized, thus allowing continued violence by the state against already oppressed populations.

To uncover this hidden language, this section uses similar techniques utilized above. Specifically, drawing out the unseen language of criminalization and dehumanization requires a focus on the discourse present on the Federal Bureau of Prisons (BOP), Federal Bureau of Investigation (FBI) and the Immigration and Customs Enforcement (ICE) websites. Each of these agencies plays an important role in the construction of consent and societal understandings about Criminalized Americans. This alone makes the analysis of their language a useful tool in unmasking the dehumanization rhetoric present in the criminalizing system. To accomplish this unmasking, our analysis includes, but is not limited to, press releases, transcripts of speeches/presentations and all other information provided on various pages of each agency's website.[6]

Two central themes develop from the rhetoric of these websites relating to the creation of Criminalized Americans. Each is individually important in supporting our demonstration of how these criminalizing institutions use the language of 'criminals' to convey the same logic as that explored above in the case of Japanese Americans: one that depends on the frames of war, protection (from simulated danger, threat, and fear) and aid. As discussed by Carpentier (2017), the dehumanizing of a group involves the process of homogenizing the self or the dominant group. A key piece of this process is defining not only an 'enemy' but also a 'protector'. All of the analyzed websites make very specific symbolic statements to identify officers, personnel or agents working for these institutions as the 'protectors' of society. Labeling state actors in such a way draws on historical tools discussed above. It first declares an 'enemy' that is dangerous to society. Instead of 'Japanese', our current 'enemy' is the 'criminal' symbolized as a destructive force bent on harming those needing protection.

The separation of the threats and the protectors also feeds the state rhetoric of militarized glorification of law enforcement as necessary tools used to hold society together. The use of such language as ingredients for varying justice recipes shapes these individuals as 'protectors' (see Coyle, 2018b) and firmly supports their role of moral entrepreneurs concerning the labeling of those worthy of 'justice'. The Federal Bureau of Investigation (FBI), arguably more than other agencies, uses this rhetoric to ensure the separation of the 'threat' and 'protector'. The mission statement of the agency clearly demonstrates their 'protector' status by stating their purpose is "To protect the American people and uphold the Constitution of the United States." They later go on to discuss their agency priorities. Each point of the list solidifies their narrative as 'protectors' in our cultural space. Examples of this include; "Protect the United States from terrorist attack" and "Protect civil rights."[7]

The Federal Bureau of Prisons (BOP) also demonstrates this type of rhetoric in discussing the purpose of their agency. Their website clearly states that "we protect public safety ..." and under their mission statement the agency states they exist "to protect society by confining offenders in controlled environments."[8] Additionally, their website states "The BOP will provide for public safety and national security by focusing on the prevention, disruption, and response to terrorist activities via secure institutions and proactive management practices which mitigate terrorist threats."[9] Like the FBI, they subtly discuss their direct role in acting against those who might 'harm' the society/public and state that they 'protect'.

The Immigration and Customs Enforcement (ICE) uses a very similar rhetoric. Specifically, ICE states "US Immigration and Customs Enforcement employees protect America from the cross-border crime and illegal immigration that threaten national security and public safety."[10] Their website continues with "combating cross-border criminal activity is the largest single area of responsibility of Homeland Security Investigations (HSI), and is a critical component of the overall safety, security, and well-being of our nation."[11] This level of 'protector' rhetoric is also noticeable in various press releases on the ICE website. One such release provides a statement by an agent: "When we raised our hands we swore to protect our nation from all enemies, foreign and domestic, overseas we fought foreign enemies, now our mission is our domestic enemies."[12]

These statements situate agencies at the forefront of creating the homogenous self that is present within the predominantly white hetero-normative capitalist culture. Specifically, they support the creation of frames such as an 'enemy' deserving of 'combat' in a *war*, a populace in need of *protection*, and government as providing *aid*. The result is the creation of Criminalized Americans. These agencies' speech acts, like the government film discussed above, are able to use language as a tool to dehumanize those which they must "protect society against." In many cases, without clearly referring to the threat, these agencies construct a societal consent that their actions are virtuous and that those they 'fight', Criminalized Americans, deserve the harm they experience. Additionally, while not explicitly stated, this language makes clear who represents the threat. By using words such as "border" and "terrorist," the language of these agencies works subtly to ensure that the public understands that the enemy is not a white middle-class citizen. The subtle use of this language pairs with decades worth of coded discourse to ensure that the image created represents a vilification of communities of color, immigrants, and the poor. The construction of these groups as 'enemies' that society is at *war* with, requires *protection* from, and owes itself and them *aid* for, is a tool used to ensure the seemingly self-evident truth perpetuated by social power dynamics that allow the criminalizing system to perpetuate harm against already oppressed populations.

Conclusion: ending dehumanizing rhetoric about Criminalized Americans

This chapter has been a study in the engineering of consent. We have examined two examples of government-induced rhetoric that attempt to produce conformity of thought about Japanese Americans and Criminalized Americans. While initially successful, the work of the US government to produce mass consent for the dehumanizing of Japanese Americans in WWII was ultimately unmasked. Further, this dehumanization work was recognized as such by the government, apologized for, and some reparations were made for it. To this day, the work of the US government to produce mass consent around the category 'criminal' and the millions of dehumanized Criminalized Americans is profoundly successful. The rhetorical devices used against the (mostly people of color and economic underclass) Criminalized Americans are working very well to make digestible (palatable for publics) speech and action (oppression, violence, torture, destruction of future, dehumanization) that in any other circumstance would be called out as completely unacceptable.

Importantly, while the WWII dehumanizing rhetoric against Japanese Americans is widely *seen* and *recognized* by scholars today, the dehumanizing rhetoric against Criminalized Americans is today deeply *unseen* and *unrecognized* by both scholars and the public. While research demonstrates that under current laws and definitions of 'crime' and 'criminal' almost all Americans would have to go through all the penal system steps to ultimately serve a lengthy prison sentence, only the targeted few do so (Coyle, 2018a). That the re-framing of Japanese Americans as "Japanese" and the re-framing of their kidnapping to concentration camps as a "relocation" to "pioneer communities" reflect propaganda and not reality is considered a matter of historical record. By contrast, that propaganda (not reality) drives the re-framing of Criminalized Americans still evades wide notice. Currently, moral entrepreneurs, progressive or conservative, and the entire public – save a few abolitionists – employ the same 'crime' and 'criminal' language.

Comparing the constructions of Japanese Americans and Criminalized Americans shows that the rhetorical work in both is arranged according to an underlying logic that depends on the frames of *war* (WWII and War on Crime), *protection* (Japanese Americans as 'Japanese' with all the danger/threat/fear entailed and Criminalized Americans as 'criminals' with all the danger/threat/fear entailed) and *aid* (on the one hand, Japanese Americans serving their country by "volunteering" to "relocate" to "pioneer communities" and the rest of the Americans protected from the 'Japanese', and on the other hand, Criminalized Americans given opportunity to 'atone' and 'reform' in 'Correctional' institutions and the general public being given a 'public safety' program).

In the cases of both Japanese Americans and Criminalized Americans, the absurd discrepancy between language and reality is helpful in exposing the activity of rhetoric and propaganda. In the first, 'evacuation' is used to describe the acts of intentional exclusion and forced removal from free society; 'relocation' to describe incarceration; 'non-aliens' to describe US citizens of Japanese ancestry; 'may be excluded' to describe being evicted from one's home; 'assembly centers' and 'relocation centers' to describe detention spaces; and 'pioneer communities' to describe concentration camps. In the second, 'crime' describes a miniscule amount of the daily transgression of law that is occurring. The word 'criminals' describes those whose transgressive acts are targeted for their transformation into Criminalized Americans. 'Correction' describes incarceration while 'accountability' describes being chosen to be made an example of. Additionally, 'public safety' describes the failure to address in any way the vast majority of interpersonal and structural harms performed daily. Finally, 'justice system' describes the systematic enactment of a selection process for the intentional exclusion and forced removal from free society of a few (disproportionately people of color and those belonging to the economic underclass).

In the cases of both Japanese Americans and Criminalized Americans, what is accomplished with such government rhetoric is the strategic and deliberate erasure of a dehumanization process: their abduction and incarceration, the lie that they understand and see their fate as underscoring justice and righteousness, and that what is done to them is defensible in the name of a supposedly accomplished public safety program.

The extensive labor to criminalize and enemify is done not only by those 'transporting', 'incarcerating' or in its more Orwellian form, 'helping' these *others* in our society. Instead, as Everett C. Hughes properly called it (1962), it is the *dirty work* of us all. For most of us, even if we do not lawyer, police or guard for our living, in so far as we once supported the view that Japanese Americans were, or currently endorse the view that Criminalized Americans are, lesser than *us* or an *out group* to our *in group*, we are doing the *dirty work* without which their fate would not be possible. As Hughes writes, "those pariahs who do the dirty work of society are really acting as agents for the rest of us" (Ibid, p. 7). It may be painful to sit with, but that makes it no less true: we are together doing this *dirty work*.

Ultimately, Criminalized Americans need the same recognition afforded to Japanese Americans: acknowledgement of the dehumanizing rhetoric created to produce consent production, cessation of criminalizing system targeting (penal abolition) and an apology along with reparations.

Notes

1 Kidnapping and internment camp placement of Japanese Americans occurred beyond the US mainland Pacific coast during the WWII timeline (e.g., the internment camps of Hawaii), as did such general type of activities occur under the guise of responding to the crisis faced by European Jews, Greek Orthodox and other populations (e.g., the Oswego, New York "refugee camps"). However, while equally grotesque, these other internments differ deeply in character from that of the Pacific coast actions against Japanese Americans that were an *en mass* incarceration of Japanese Americans.
2 Available here: https://www.youtube.com/watch?v=esVege1S0OE
3 The reader should pay close attention to the ceaseless reference of these US citizens as "Japanese," both in these quotes and others.
4 Again, who are being referenced here are not Japanese citizens fishing and farming in Japan, but US citizens fishing and farming in the US.
5 Film scenes show all of this happening on the west coast of the US.
6 All data collection occurred between October and December of 2019.
7 https://www.fbi.gov/about/mission
8 https://www.bop.gov/about/agency/agency_pillars.jsp
9 Ibid.
10 https://www.ice.gov/about
11 Ibid.
12 https://www.ice.gov/news/releases/hsi-computer-forensic-analyst-honored-tampa-bay-hispanic-hero#wcm-survey-target-id

References

Alexander, Michelle. 2012. *The New Jim Crow: Mass Incarceration in the Age of Colorblindness*. New York: The New Press.

Arrigo, Bruce A. 2001. "Transcarceration: A Constitutive Ethnography of Mentally Ill "Offenders"." *The Prison Journal* 81:2, 162–186.

Baysha, Olga. 2020. "Dehumanizing Political Others: A Discursive-Material Perspective." *Critical Discourse Studies* 17:3, 292–307.

Bernays, Edward L. 1928. *Propaganda*. New York: H. Liveright.

Brewer, Susan A. 2009. *Why America Fights: Patriotism and War Propaganda from the Philippines to Iraq*. New York: Oxford University Press.

Carpentier, Nico. 2017. *The Discursive-Material Knot: Cyprus in Conflict and Community Media Participation*. New York: Peter Lang.

Commission on Wartime Relocation and Internment of Civilians. 1982. *Personal Justice Denied*. Washington: GPO, as cited in Lee 2007.

Coyle, Michael J. 2013. *Talking Criminal Justice: Language and the Just Society*. London: Routledge.

Coyle, Michael J. 2018a. "Transgression and Standard Theories: Contributions Toward Penal Abolition." *Critical Criminology* 26:3, 325–339.

Coyle, Michael J. 2018b. "Who Is Mired in Utopia? The Logics of Criminal Justice and Penal Abolition." *Social Justice* 45:4, 79–115.

Coyle, Michael J. Forthcoming. *Seeing Crime: Penal Abolition as the End of Utopian Criminal Justice*. Berkeley: University of California Press.

Daniels, Roger. 1981. *Concentration Camps, North America: Japanese in the United States and Canada During World War II*. Malabor: Robert E. Krieger Publishing.

Dower, John W. 1986. *War without Mercy: Race and Power in the Pacific War*. New York: Pantheon Books.

Epps, Douglas and Rich Furman. 2016. "The 'Alien Other': A Culture of Dehumanizing Immigrants in the United States." *Social Work & Society* 14:2, 1–14.

Feeley, Francis McCollum. 1995. *A Strategy of Dominance: The History of an American Concentration Camp, Pomona, California*. New York: Brandywine Press.

Hughes, Everett C. 1962. "Good People and Dirty Work." *Social Problems* 10:1, 3–11.

Hulsman, Louk. 1997. *Themes and Concepts in an Abolitionist Approach to Criminal Justice*. http://hulsmanfoundation.org/wp-content/uploads/2014/07/abolitionistapproach.pdf (accessed October 15, 2016).

Kappeler, Victor E., Gary Potter, and Mark Blumberg. 2005. *The Mythology of Crime* (4th Ed.). Long Grove: Waveland Press.

Lee, Fred I. 2007. "The Japanese Internment and the Racial State of Exception." *Theory & Event* 10:1. doi:10.1353/tae.2007.0043 (accessed February 2, 2020).

Mathiesen, Thomas. 2015. *Politics of Abolition Revisited*. Philadelphia: Routledge.

National Japanese American Citizens League. 2013. "Power of Words Handbook: A Guide to Language about Japanese Americans in World War II." https://jacl.org/wordpress/wp-content/uploads/2015/08/Power-of-Words-Rev.-Term.-Handbook.pdf (accessed February 8, 2020).

Navarro, Anthony V. 2010. "A Critical Comparison between Japanese and American Propaganda during World War II." https://msu.edu/~navarro6/srop.html (accessed February 5, 2020).

Nishiura Weglyn, Michi. 1996. *Years of Infamy: The Untold Story of America's Concentration Camps*. Seattle: University of Washington Press.

Orwell, George. 1946. "Politics and the English Language." *Horizon* 13:76, 252–265.

Reeves, Richard. 2015. *Infamy: The Shocking Story of the Japanese American Internment in World War II.* New York: Henry Holt and Company.

Renteln, Allison Dundes. 1995. "A Psychohistorical Analysis of the Japanese American Internment." *Human Rights Quarterly* 17:4, 623–627.

Rock, Adam. 2014. "The American Way: The Influence of Race on the Treatment of Prisoners of War During World War Two" Dissertation. https://stars.library.ucf.edu/etd/4740/ (accessed January 30, 2020).

Simon, Jonathan. 2007. *Governing through Crime: How the War on Crime Transformed American Democracy and Created a Culture of Fear.* New York: Oxford University Press.

18

RAP'S SIGNIFICANCE TO THE FORMATION OF THE BRITISH ABOLITIONIST MOVEMENT

Marc Jacobs

Introduction

Despite the significance of Radical Alternatives to Prison (RAP) in establishing an abolitionist movement in Britain during the 1970s, it has received only limited commentary. That which does exist is written by academic activists, most prominent of which are Mick Ryan and Joe Sim who were involved with the organisation during its existence. Individually and collaboratively Ryan and Sim have written a small number of publications evaluating the activities and fortunes of RAP. Ryan's accounts derive from his commitment to ensure the existence and contribution RAP made to the formation of a British abolitionist movement is not ignored and forgotten. As he explains, "I do not want commentaries on penal change in Britain during this period to become (wrongly) a history of critical silence" (Ryan, 2003, p. 69). In keeping with Ryan's sentiment, this chapter will restate the contribution made by RAP in helping galvanise a British abolitionist movement during the 1970s and 1980s. It will be argued that second-wave abolitionism that exists today, as an activist and academic movement, is more sophisticated as a result of the campaigns, activities and refinements to the political and intellectual arguments that RAP engaged with.

To be clear, the argument made in this chapter as to the pivotal role RAP played in crystallising a British abolitionist movement in the 1970s has less to do with any tangible successes the group had with the campaigns it conducted. RAP's contribution relates to it wrestling with and refining its abolitionist politics and intellectualism, the lineage of which can be traced to the abolitionist movement and academia that exists today. As is still the case, the abolitionist movement in the 1970s comprised of activists and academics whereby the two identities merged. Ryan, for example, was a lecturer at a polytechnic as well as being very much involved with RAP. The synergy between activism and academia was mutually beneficial. The involvement of academics enriched discussions in RAP regarding strategy and ethos, while academics benefitted by gaining impetus and grounding to their scholarship.

The exchange of sociological academic thinking and activism produced "a criminology from below" (Sim, 2013, p. 3), which shaped and influenced the scholarship of academics in Britain. Similarly, Belknap (2015) expounds the importance of activist criminology whereby criminologists dedicate themselves to working to alleviate oppression and strive towards engendering social justice. Academics have a moral duty to dislodge the hegemony of the crime control industry by building alliances with activists and campaign groups and in so doing, this, in turn, informs academic scholarship and teaching.

The activities in which RAP, with the support of academic activists, was involved and the questions it raised energised a climate in which critical questions concerning prison were taken up by other newly formed radical penal activist groups. Fuelled by a backdrop of crisis within prisons the prisoners' rights activist group, Preservation of the Rights of Prisoners (PROP), formed in 1972, so too Women in Prison (WIP) in 1983. Both groups were co-founded by people who were or had been imprisoned along with concerned academics. Mike Fitzgerald was publicity officer at PROP while also developing an academic career. Pat Carlen had already established herself as an academic. Her research for *Women's Imprisonment* (1983) motivated her to co-found WIP with Chris Tchaikovsky who had served a custodial sentence (Tombs, 2010). Out of the milieu of anti-prison politics and activism, Ryan, Sim, and Tony Ward were instrumental in setting up INQUEST in 1981 to investigate deaths in custody and support affected families (Ryan, 1996).

The struggles regarding strategy and politics that RAP wrestled, still beset the abolitionist movement today. The primary dilemma concerned the extent to which RAP should advance alternatives to prison, as compared to campaigning for the abolition of, not just prison but the entire 'justice' system. Moreover, for some, '*radical alternatives*' meant not alternatives to prison so much as achieving an *alternative social order* to that of being based on capitalism. RAP's attempts to wrestle with deep-seated dilemmas regarding its politics and purpose aided the development of a more refined and nuanced abolitionist critique and praxis during the 1970s and 1980s and consequently provides valuable lessons for second-wave abolitionists so they can more ably bring about a future without the need for prisons.

Activists, radicals and academics

The motivation to establish RAP, which formed in October 1970, was the belief that prison continually failed to achieve its stated objectives. RAP disputed the officially stated purpose of prison which claimed to be for, "the training and treatment of convicted prisoners ... to encourage and assist them to lead a good and useful life" (Home Office, 1964, p. 4). Instead RAP argued that "there is no evidence that the experience of prison either reforms or deters; but there is plenty of evidence that it destroys" (RAP, 1971, p. 13). That people in prison received correctional and rehabilitative 'treatment' in humane conditions so that they could be safely returned to society as healed individuals was regarded as a fallacy, which produced a smokescreen that legitimised prisons.

The existing penal lobby, represented by The Howard League for Penal Reform and the National Association for the Care and Resettlement of Offenders (NACRO), failed to make the case that rehabilitation within prison was impossible, let alone question prison's wider ideological function. RAP argued that The Howard League was complicit in perpetuating a flawed institution by lobbying for prison reform rather than radical change. RAP was critical of the penal lobby groups for being too liberal and closely allied with central state institutions (Ryan, 1978).

Unlike the well-connected middle-class humanitarians who characterised the membership of the Howard League, RAP consisted of former members of the Prison Reform Council, who had come to realise the futility of campaigning for reform. RAP's members consisted of people in prison or had been imprisoned, their relatives, and anti-nuclear activists, some of whom had been jailed for civil disobedience and political activists. RAP also attracted social workers and "young radicals working at the sharp end of the criminal justice system" (Ryan and Ward, 1992, p. 322). Radical probation officers were drawn to RAP as casework shifted towards sociological approaches that took account of the offender's wider social conditions (Ryan, 1976, p. 75). This resulted in a political commitment to bring about social change which involved questioning whether it was acceptable to be "like a first aid worker treating symptoms while the disease itself, an unequal society ... go(es) unchecked" (Ryan, 1978, p. 123).

As a result of their discussions with people held in a maximum-security wing, Cohen and Taylor wrote *Psychological Survival* (1972). The book revealed the conditions and experiences of people held on long-term sentences in a maximum-security wing, giving them a voice and showing them to be quite different from the dangerous monsters the authorities claimed them to be. Cohen and Taylor's experience of the obstacles put in their way by the prison authorities and eventual forced termination of contact with the men held in the maximum-security wing led them to write *Prison Secrets* (1976) which was published by RAP. In *Prison Secrets* (1976) they argued that the secrecy concerning prisons insulated them from public scrutiny and allowed the state to deny any problems that existed.

Both texts countered the dominant narrative about prisons spun by the authorities under a veil of tightly controlled information and censorship. Sim, Scraton and Gordon (1987, p. 11) remark that by offering insight into the lives of those imprisoned, and thereby producing a competing narrative to that of officialdom, *Psychological Survival* (1972) provided an impetus for critical research on prisons. Ryan's (1983) *The Politics of Penal Reform* is an early example of a sociologically informed critical analysis of the crisis affecting prison during the post-war decades. It sought to offer an antidote to the more administrative texts on prisons that existed at the time. Whereas Fitzgerald and Sim's *British Prisons* (1979) represented one of the first abolitionist inspired critical textbooks on prisons.

Given the sociological concerns of the academics identified it is no surprise that they were also involved with the National Deviancy Conferences (NDC). The NDC were scathing of positivism which informed the correctionalist ethos that underpinned penal and social welfare. There was a shared affinity with the concerns of RAP which, as with the NDC, sought to focus on a sociological analysis thereby discrediting the therapeutic model of punishment. The NDC, "provided a forum, as well as support ... to radical groups such as ... RAP" (Cohen, 1988, p. 234). The shared concern with sociological and critical issues between the NDC and RAP would have contributed to helping cement abolitionist arguments.

Both the NDC and RAP were beset by a struggle to maintain accord between moderates with more liberal concerns and radicals who subscribed to a Marxist analysis that sought to bring about comprehensive changes to the social order. Within RAP this tension manifested between those who sought practical alternatives that were untainted by the harm, brutalisation and stigmatisation experienced as a result of imprisonment and those who regarded devising alternatives as tantamount to being complicit with what was regarded as a flawed system. The division between moderates and radicals and the drift towards greater political militancy led to a crisis and almost collapse of RAP in 1975.

Marxism and penal abolition

In *The Case for Radical Alternatives to Prison* (1971) RAP highlighted the fantasy that rehabilitation can ever be achieved in prison. RAP sought to expose rehabilitation as a charade that disguised a system that brutalises, dehumanises and degrades people held in prison. Rather than suggest prison reforms RAP sought to offer alternatives that would lead to the ultimate goal of prisons being abolished. While acknowledging that, "there can be no blanket alternative to prison" (RAP, 1971, p. 14), RAP set out a number of alternatives to prison where people who violate the law receive a non-custodial sentence served in their local community and be managed by local people. Such alternatives avoided the negative features of the existing system, namely being highly centralised, professionalised and formulated around coercive correctionalism. Instead, "new alternatives should offer life enhancing rather than life destroying opportunities" (Cohen, 1980, p. 2).

RAP's foray into creating an experiment that might crystallise into something that could prove alternatives were possible was the Newham Alternatives Project (NAP) (Dronfield, 1980). The 1972 Criminal Justice Act created deferred sentences that allowed final decisions on sentence to be postponed providing those sentenced the opportunity to change. "The Newham Alternatives Project hoped to be a significant factor in those changed circumstances, a centre offering support and advice which would help offenders 'get themselves together' and pull out of the downward spiral to prison" (Ryan, 1978, p. 127). The project was run by helpers who provided a "friendly place in the locality where referrals could go for support and advice as and when they needed it" (Ryan, 1978, p. 128). A key principle underpinning the project was that participation was voluntary. NAP therefore offered a more informal model, based on mutual co-operation, trust and dialogue in contrast to that of the formal system of punishment, which operated on a very different ethos. However, NAP amplified the internal divisions which existed within RAP between the moderate pragmatists and the radicals.

Since its formation RAP was affected by internal tensions between those who subscribed to a loosely Marxist critique of the social order and more moderate members who saw merit in suggesting alternatives to imprisonment. The dilemma was whether to be involved in practical solutions, which ran the risk of being incorporated into the existing system, or be more radical by revealing the true function of the criminal law and 'justice' system, and strive towards a fairer and more equal social order. On this matter one activist is quoted by Ryan (1978, pp. 140–141) as explaining that,

> For a long time now there has been some division of opinion in RAP about concrete 'alternatives', i.e. whether we should encourage people to start projects themselves and try to support them, or whether this was not simply our proper role. Perhaps … [NAP] epitomises this difference … although my own work is entirely political it has seemed to me that individuals or groups of individuals with RAP's blessing might well do such work, but that it was tangential to RAP's main purpose and should never occupy much of our energies.

There were critics from within RAP of NAP, who accused it of doing little to destabilise the existing system. "The only real justification for operating alternatives within the existing political order was if the offender/victim was helped to understand his oppression" (Ryan, 1978, p. 141). Not only did NAP not do this but "there is very little evidence that NAP managed much in the way of political education" (Ryan, 1978, p. 142).

The tension also became apparent when community sentences were created by the 1972 Criminal Justice Act. It might have been thought that community sentences would be something that RAP would welcome given that they offered an alternative to imprisonment. RAP had theoretical and political objections. Theoretically RAP felt that community sentences contained incompatible penal objectives. Community sentences could not both punish *and* rehabilitate. In relation to political objections, community sentences were regarded as a means by which to perpetuate social control and oppression in a class divided society.

Such criticisms revealed the Marxist sentiments of radicals within RAP who sought to expose the true function of prison. It was argued that being imprisoned had "long since lost any pretensions of leading their inmates towards a good and moral life and have stood for the past century as stark symbols of basic social control and repression" (RAP Newsletter, March 1975 cited in Ryan, 1978, pp. 119–120). Prison was regarded as one part of the machinery of repression. The origin of the entire system of control, it was argued, is the selective attribution of the status of crime to forms of behaviour. Behaviour that causes harm is endemic throughout all classes, yet it is the lower classes who most frequently succumb to being officially processed through the criminal justice system. The poor are easily portrayed as 'criminals' even though some forms of "'crimes' do not warrant the name" (RAP, 1971, p. 13), whereas the powerful escape scrutiny. As explained in *Alternatives to Holloway* (RAP, 1972, p. 32),

> Underlying the plans for a New Holloway (and for other new and bigger prisons) is the unquestioned acceptance of the whole super-structure of the law, the courts and the police, the definitions of who is 'criminal', in a word, of 'Justice'. The whole process of labelling a person as a 'criminal', a process of which prison is a small but important part, is taken for granted. It is very important to see that the definition of certain sorts of acquisitiveness and violence as 'criminal', and acceptance of other sorts of acquisitiveness and violence as commendable, reflects and perpetuates the vested interests and inequalities of power, wealth and status which have characterised British society from the time of the despotic barons, through landowners to industrialists today. The law, its substance and its application, are rooted in the inequalities of the past.

Community sentences, it was argued, added to the extension of class control via new more liberal means, which deflected attention away from the problems associated with prison. As explained in an edition of RAP's Newsletter (March 1975, cited in Ryan, 1978, p. 120),

> The 'humanity' and 'niceness' [of community sentences] … should not confuse the basic issues. That if we have a repressive society, it is best to have the control that is exercised out in front in the nastiness of the prison system rather than performing similar functions more effectively and wrapped up in cotton wool of community service.

Marxist beliefs, which placed the 'criminal justice system' within a broader political and social context, were present in RAP's campaign against the detention of juveniles. In its pamphlet *Children Out of Trouble* (1974), RAP explained that the mystification of class control is based on economic disadvantage and marginalisation. Violations of the law by juveniles were regarded as a response to inequality in wealth and power. Indeed, RAP sought to demonstrate that people who violate the law were victims of their lower class position. In *The Case for Radical Alternatives to Prison* RAP (1971, p. 10) suggested that there exists a high correlation between bad housing and delinquency and that in one study 92% of those arrested came from the working class. "So in addition to the poorest housing, the worst schools, the least attractive work and the most sparse social facilities, the working class is also the main recipient of the penal process" (RAP, 1971, p. 10). Official explanations did not attribute crime to the economic and social inequalities the poor experience, instead this explanation was supplanted by creating the illusion of democracy and pathologising members of the lower classes who readily become the target of the 'justice system'.

For these reasons, as Cohen (1998, p. 103) explains,

> the object of abolition is not just (!) prisons, not just (!) punishment, but the whole apparatus of criminal justice and the very concept of crime itself. The vision is a society without punishment, where human inflicted pain is reduced to the minimum.

Radicals within RAP were derided for their utopianism which without a more substantive plan would never be achieved. Cohen analyses the dilemma as needing to resolve three concerns. These were an "obligation to honest intellectual inquiry", "a political commitment to social justice" and third "(and potentially conflicting with both) … the demands for short-term humanitarian help" (Cohen, 1998, p. 122). For the Marxists in RAP, the first two requirements were met. Here they were able to produce an emancipatory knowledge that challenged hegemonic political interests by exposing the values upon which they are based and aim to change the status quo. However, the third requirement risked producing a reforming rather than abolitionist measures something radicals found more difficult to come to terms with. Advancing alternatives to prison within the prevailing economic and social structure risked being co-opted and legitimising the things that needed to be transformed. The difficulty with resolving the tension that existed between abolitionism and reformism led to a crisis in RAP during the mid-1970s. It is to this crisis that we now turn.

Alienation and division

The commitment to a Marxist analysis of the wider framework of control led to the loss of members with more moderate concerns, which resulted in RAP becoming more isolated. As Ryan (1978, pp. 144–145) comments, RAP "developed from a highly heterogeneous group to a smaller radical group between 1970 and 1974" and that this may have been "an almost inevitable development, as RAP's political edge became more radical so those members with a purely humanitarian interest were forced out since they suddenly realised that they were on the wrong bus".

On a number of campaigns RAP had developed an alliance with other penal activist and reform groups. However, this always became uncoupled by RAP's radicalism. RAP welcomed PROPs formation in 1972. As with RAP, PROP acknowledged that people in prison were victims of social inequality and powerlessness, a position that was exacerbated by being imprisoned, ostensibly so welfare professionals could 'treat them'. Consequently, PROP included a determination to "bring about the eventual abolition of all prisons" in its 'Statement of Intent' (cited in Fitzgerald, 1977, p. 137). However, PROP was essentially concerned to campaign for the rights of those imprisoned, thereby improving prison conditions and the experiences of people in prison. So, "however laudable PROP's reformist efforts might be … there could be nothing more than a modest cooperation between the two groups because PROP's efforts were not thought of as being connected in any way with RAP's over-riding concern, abolition" (Ryan, 1978, p. 114).

In relation to a campaign against control units RAP "began very much on the inside track" (Ryan, 1976, p. 78) as the liberal penal reform groups also opposed their use. Control units were introduced as a solution to problems posed by those who were regarded as repeatedly troublesome. While the existence of control units was not denied the crippling nature of the regime only came to light due to an investigation by journalists who reported it in the *Sunday Times*. RAP formed an alliance with NACRO, the Howard League and PROP via the Control Units Action Group. However, the Howard League and NACRO after disagreements with RAP split from campaigning jointly. This could hardly be a surprise given an edition of the *RAP Newsletter* it pointed out that in relation to control units there was "no shortage of alternatives as offered by NACRO but these could often be seen as reformist, using methods of social control" (cited in Ryan, 1976, p. 78).

In relation to the campaigns concerning women in prison, the Howard League shared some concerns with RAP. However, as was the case regarding control units, there was little hope of sustaining an alliance for long as,

> considerable stress was placed upon the idea that [RAP's] campaign was not only to be interpreted widely in the sense that it was about the role of women in society in general, but that, more crucially, it was about 'the social inequalities of opportunity and of power' that exist to determine exactly what should be regarded as criminal, and how these inequalities discriminate against the disadvantaged and the poor in favour of the powerful and the wealthy.
>
> *(Ryan, 1978, p. 107)*

Such a radical and wide-sweeping approach was too unpalatable for the Howard League.

As we saw in relation to the discussion concerning NAP, opinion was divided within RAP as to whether members should be involved with establishing practical projects offering alternatives to the formal justice system or pursue a political campaign against the penal system and status quo more generally. By becoming increasingly radical RAP risked having any policy relevance at all. In relation to reforms either suggested by itself or other penal lobby groups RAP's radical position meant that it, "did not believe that the prison system could be undermined from within, reforms were either humane and neutral or simply conservative, reinforcing the system under the banner of progress" (Ryan, 1978, p. 140).

The limited successes and discomfort among moderates within RAP with the radical politics contributed to a crisis within the organisation. However, a lifeline was provided by the publication of Mathiesen's *The Politics of Abolition* (1974).

Resuscitation then demise

The wait for the revolution that would result in the collapse of the prison system was made more bearable thanks to the publication of Mathiesen's *The Politics of Abolition* (1974). This text allowed hard-liners to navigate a course that avoided proposing reforms that might be co-opted rather than de-legitimise prison. Mathiesen distinguished between positive and negative reforms. Positive reforms resulted in changes to prisons which legitimised them by improving conditions, whereas negative reforms undermined their existence.

> RAP's failure to make the distinction between positive and negative reforms [before this time], its inability or unwillingness to realise that not all reforms support the prison system limited its activities to a very narrow base .... Paralysis was averted once RAP realised that by pressing for negative reforms the crisis [in prisons] could be precipitated by action.
>
> *(Ryan, 1978, pp. 139–140)*

It was therefore hoped this would lead to prisons eventual collapse.

During the 1980s RAP became "more theoretically sophisticated and politically astute" (Sim, 1994, p. 268). In the face of an expanding justice and penal system and continuing crisis within prisons, Ward argued that RAP needed to "gain support for reforms of the penal system which while making it more humane will also *show up its inherent limitations and contradictions*" (emphasis in original, cited in Sim, 1994, p. 269). Issues such as the use of drugs to control people in prison, solitary confinement, the system of security classification, secrecy and censorship were matters in which RAP might achieve its goals of radical change. These issues fitted with the strategy of identifying areas that amounted to negative reforms. However, it became evident that distinctions between positive and negative reforms were far less clear since a reform may contain both elements.

During the 1980s RAP shifted from its Marxist analysis by engaging with Foucault's post-structuralism and feminism. As Ryan and Ward (1992, p. 326) write,

> no longer did the world appear to be neatly divided between the 'powerful' and the 'powerless', nor were 'crimes of the powerful' the sole prerogative of the ruling class, once the concept was extended to take account of the power of men over women, of white people over black and of adults over children.

It was increasingly realised that the initial Marxist theoretical position which argued power was monopolised by a ruling elite was, as Foucault and the feminists demonstrated, dispersed and possessed, by different groups who imposed themselves on others. As Ryan and Ward (1992, p. 326) go on to say it was looking at the various locations of power,

> that those of us who came into the penal lobby with a fairly traditional Marxist framework began to question whether privileging productive relations as the site on which all oppression hinged was simply inadequate, and to turn toward the post-structuralist analyses of Foucault and others for an alternative.

While engagement with issues raised by feminists, such as Box-Grainger (1982), in relation to sexual violence and rape provided RAP reason to continue, a tension existed whereby RAP either had to soften its commitment to prison abolition or abolition needed to be "pushed back into a remote, post-patriarchal future" (Ryan and Ward, 1992, p. 327). As demonstrated by the Sex Offences Group, an organisation set up within RAP, which argued for a policy of exemplary or retributive punishment "as an appropriate response to *some* offences" (cited in Sim, 1994, p. 271). The group made 10 proposals to deal with sentencing and imprisonment of rapists, conceding that while custodial sentences may be appropriate that it "can only be effective if it is used against a backdrop of real equality of opportunity for women – an equality that offers women economic independence, political, ideological and sexual determination" (cited in Sim, 1994, p. 271).

RAP's engagement with feminist issues raised some awkward questions, which required it to concede that prison could not be abolished entirely in the medium term, if at all. Although the consequence of having to navigate the issues raised by feminists arguably blunted RAP's abolitionist agenda, RAP's most successful campaign concerned the problems faced by imprisoned women and objections to rebuilding Holloway Prison. The focus on women's imprisonment, though ultimately failing to prevent Holloway being rebuilt, contributed to the formation of Women in Prison in 1983 as well as helping stimulate research on female victimisation and punishment (Carlen, 1983).

Ryan and Ward (1992, p. 327) claim that during the 1980s RAP was successful in bringing about a consensus between itself, the liberal penal lobby and Labour Party. This consensus concerned agreement on several issues. Yet this success along with the presence of WIP, INQUEST and raising various issues which were adopted by the Howard League for Penal Reform and the Prison Reform Trust, RAP found itself without a distinctive role. Its members dissipated or became involved with other groups so that by 1988 RAP evaporated.

Conclusion praxis and social change

RAP formed as part of the wider counter-cultural movement which questioned the state's exercise of control. RAP's members possessed a mix of liberal and left-wing political sensibilities, which resulted in internal disagreements about its purpose, strategies and politics. It succumbed to a radicalisation of its politics and purpose in the 1970s which almost brought the organisation to an early end. Despite having "a hard-line position RAP was involved from the beginning in a series of campaigns around specific issues" (Sim, 1994, p. 266). By propagating alternatives to prison RAP encouraged "thought experiments about a future society" (Cohen, 1998, p. 110) which challenged the existing system of control. Being based on bottom-up activism it provided a "criminology from below" (Sim, 2013, p. 3) that destabilised the hegemony of the prison and pushed the liberal penal lobby onto more radical terrain.

The dividends derived from the synergy between activists and academics were mutually beneficial. Academics produced critical scholarship on prisons, authoring some of RAP's publications. Examples include Cohen and Taylor's *Prison Secrets* (1978), Cohen's (1979a) *Crime and Punishment* and Fitzgerald's (1975) *Control Units and the Shape of Things to Come*. They also wrote and edited articles published in RAP's journal, *The Abolitionist*. These academically informed publications contributed to a strategy of building a movement towards the abolition of prison. As Ward (1982, cited in Sim, 1994, p. 269–270) comments, "RAP's fundamental purpose is, through research and propaganda to educate the public about the true nature, as we see it, of imprisonment and the law". The reach of abolitionist arguments was extended by the academic literature written by Carlen, Cohen, Taylor, Fitzgerald, Ryan, Ward and Sim which filtered into the National Deviancy Conferences and impacted upon criminological scholarship and teaching.

Academic activists therefore aided the radical penal lobby by helping develop its sociological and theoretical arguments and inform strategies. They also elevated and gave greater impetus to the voices of those silenced by the 'justice system'. Furthermore, academic activists helped RAP to better understand and refine its analysis of the political economy in which prisons form a pivotal element. As a result, academic activists helped RAP's theoretical and intellectual evolution. Through their endeavours as activist-academics involved with RAP, their writing and teaching, and also, as in the case of Cohen, contributing to more widely read publications (see, for example, Cohen, 1974, 1979b) were engaged in a form of public criminology long before the term was coined by Loader and Sparks (2010). This *abolitionist public criminology* was and continues to be achieved by mobilising national and international grassroots activists, community groups, social movements, students and academics to engender "insurgent knowledges" (Sudbury, 2009, p. 27).

Although RAP dissipated it is the contention of this chapter that it helped galvanise the conditions in which other radical penal groups such as PROP, WIP and INQUEST emerged. Furthermore, the commentaries produced by the academic activists, along with their involvement with the radical penal lobby groups in the 1970s and 1980s, provide an intellectual heritage, which today has gained new traction via the work of second-wave abolitionist activists and academics. A proposition made in this chapter is that this traction has been given greater significance as a result of the engagement of academic activists who have kept abolitionist debates alive, even during a period when it was regarded as unfashionable (Sim, 1994).

When asked about the relationship between the abolitionist critique and the radicalisation of criminology Ryan replied, "the sheer weight of that critique was massive and at an intellectual and academic level, criminology was never the same again" (cited in Roberts, 2007, p. 24). Similarly, Sim argues that "it has had an impact ideologically. It challenged the idea of what crime is, you can see it working its way into new strands of criminology, like social harm" (cited in Roberts, 2007, p. 36). Additionally, such abolitionist concerns and questions have begun to seep into the university curricula (Barraclough, 2010; Brown and Schept, 2017; Chartrand and Piché, 2019).

A key aim of this chapter was to point to the significance of RAP in helping to facilitate a British abolitionist movement. Through a discussion of some of the campaigns, activism and alliances RAP made, it has been argued that the involvement of academic activists was not only important in helping shape RAP but also to cultivate a climate that was critical of prisons in which other radical penal lobby groups emerged. The reason for identifying and re-asserting the corpus of writing produced by academic activists in this chapter is to respond to Ryan (2003, p. 69) and Sim's (1994) concern not to allow the formation and distinctiveness of the British abolitionist movement to be snuffed out. By recounting RAP's existence, it is argued that the vitality and richness of second-wave abolitionist campaigning, activism, teaching and scholarship benefits from the foundations and lessons learnt by the first-wave British abolitionists who were involved with RAP. This appreciation is instructive in helping second-wave abolitionists understand the politics of penality and help navigate the dilemmas and tensions of working towards an alternative social order where there is no need for prisons.

References

Barraclough, L. (2010). Reflections on Teaching Prison Abolition. *Radical Teacher*, 88, 42–52.

Belknap, J. (2015) Activist Criminology: Criminologists' Responsibility to Advocate for Social and Legal Justice. *Criminology*, 53(1), 1–22. https://doi.org/10.1111/1745-9125.12063

Box-Grainger, J. (1982) *Sentencing Rapists*. London: RAP.

Brown, M., & Schept, J. (2017). New Abolition, Criminology and a Critical Carceral Studies. *Punishment & Society*, 19(4), 440–462. https://doi.org/10.1177/1462474516666281

Carlen, P. (1983) *Women's Imprisonment: A Study in Social Control*. Oxford: Blackwell.

Chartrand, V. & Piché, J. (2019) Abolition and Pedagogy: Reflections on Teaching a Course on Alternatives to Punishment, State Repression and Social Control. *Contemporary Justice Review*, 22(1), 23–42. DOI: 10.1080/10282580.2019.1576129

Cohen, S. (1974) Human Warehouses: The Future of Our Prisons? *New Society*, 30(632), 407–411.

Cohen, S. (1979a) *Crime and Punishment*. London: RAP.

Cohen, S. (1979b) Community Control: The New Utopia. *New Society*, (15 March), 609–611.

Cohen, S. (1980) Introduction to Dronfield, L. *Outside Chance: The story of the Newham Alternatives Project* (pp. 2–6). London: Radical Alternatives to Prison.

Cohen, S. (1988) Footprints in the sand: a further report on criminology and the sociology of deviance in Britain. In M. Fitzgerald, G. Mc Lennan, and J. Pawson (eds) *Crime & Society: Readings in History and Theory* (pp. 220–247). London: Routledge

Cohen, S. (1998) Intellectual Scepticism and Political Commitment: The Case of Radical Criminology. In P. Walton, and J. Young (eds) *The New Criminology Revisited* (pp. 98–129). Basingstoke, Hants: Palgrave.

Cohen, S. and Taylor, L. (1972) *Psychological Survival. The Experience of Long Term Imprisonment.* Harmondsworth, Middx: Penguin Books.

Cohen, S. and Taylor, L. (1976) *Prison Secrets.* London: Radical Alternatives to Prison & the National Council for Civil Liberties.

Dronfield, L. (1980) *Outside Chance: The Story of the Newham Alternatives Project.* London: Radical Alternatives to Prison.

Fitzgerald, M. (1975) *Control Units and the Shape of Things to Come.* London: RAP.

Fitzgerald, M. (1977) *Prisoners in Revolt.* Middlesex: Penguin Books.

Fitzgerald, M. and Sim, J. (1979) *British Prisons.* Oxford: Basil Blackwell

Home Office (1964) *The Prison Rules 1964.* London: HMSO.

Loader, I. and Sparks, R. (2010) *Public Criminology?* London: Routledge.

Mathiesen, T. (1974) *The Politics of Abolition.* London: Martin Robertson.

RAP (1971) *The Case for Radical Alternatives to Prison.* London: Christian Action.

RAP (1972) *Alternatives to Holloway.* London: Christian Action.

RAP (1974) *Children Out of Trouble.* London: Christian Action.

Roberts, R. (2007) *What Happened to Abolitionism?* Unpublished MSc dissertation, London School of Economics.

Ryan, M. (1976) Radical Alternatives to Prison. *Political Quarterly*, 47(1), 71–81.

Ryan, M. (1978) *The Acceptable Pressure Group: Inequality in the Penal Lobby: A Case Study of the Howard League and RAP.* London: Saxon House.

Ryan, M. (1983) *The 1983 of Penal Reform.* Essex: Longman.

Ryan, M. (1996) *Lobbying From Below: INQUEST in Defence of Civil Liberties.* London: UCL Press

Ryan, M. (2003) *Penal Policy and Political Culture in England and Wales.* Winchester: Waterside Press.

Ryan, M. and Ward, T. (1992) From Positivism to Postmodernism: Some Theoretical and Strategic Reflections on the Evolution of the Penal Lobby in Britain. *International Journal of the Sociology of the Law*, 20, 321–335.

Sim, J. (1994) The Abolitionist Approach: A British Perspective. In A Duff, S. Marshall, R.E. Dobash and R.P. Dobash (eds.), *Penal Theory and Practice: Tradition and Innovation in Criminal Justice* (pp. 264–284). Manchester: Manchester University Press.

Sim, J. (2013) Abolitionism. In E. McLaughlin and J. Muncie (eds.), *The SAGE Dictionary of Criminology* (pp. 2–4). London: Sage.

Sim, J., Scraton, P. and Gordon, P. (1987) Introduction: Crime, the State and Critical Analysis. In P. Scraton (ed.), *Law Order and the Authoritarian State* (pp. 1–70). Milton Keynes: Open University Press.

Sudbury, J. (2009) Challenging Penal Dependency: Activist Scholars and the Antiprison Movement. In J. Sudbury and M. Okazawa-Rey (eds.), *Activist Scholarship: Antiracism, Feminism and Social Change* (pp. 17–36). Abingdon, Oxon: Routledge.

Tombs, J. (2010) Pat Carlen. In K. Hayward, S. Maruna and J. Mooney (eds.), *Fifty Key Thinkers in Criminology* (pp. 232–238). Abingdon, Oxon: Routledge.

19

THE STRUGGLE OVER THE OTTAWA-CARLETON DETENTION CENTRE

Challenging neutralization techniques, fighting state inertia

Aaron Doyle, Justin Piché, and Kelsey Sutton

Introduction

The Ottawa-Carleton Detention Centre (OCDC) was envisioned as a progressive "rehabilitation unit" when opened in 1972 (Oliver, 1985, p. 188). Instead, the jail became notorious for its inhumane conditions and the focus of intensive media scrutiny, a series of coroner's inquests into deaths in custody, numerous legal actions, and a government task force on crowding and poor conditions of confinement. Since 2012, the Criminalization and Punishment Education Project (CPEP) – a group of professors and university students, current and former prisoners, and their loved ones and other community members – has been actively advancing ways to lessen the use and harms of imprisonment at OCDC. Officials and politicians have attempted to deflect our critiques and co-opt alternatives we present. This chapter examines the tactics used by these proponents of incarceration to reproduce the status quo. We begin by reviewing the history of Ottawa's three jails,[1] the problems plaguing each, and the governmental response – in each case, building a bigger and 'better' jail. Next, we locate our work within the abolitionist tradition. We then explore CPEP's efforts to challenge problems at our local jail and examine the neutralization techniques (Mathiesen, 1990) used by government officials to stifle our efforts. We conclude with a brief discussion of factors that have helped CPEP continue to persist in the face of government tactics and other factors that might thwart change.

The more things change …

Before Canada was born as a white settler-colonial country in 1867, it was necessary to build a courthouse and a jail to obtain formal county status in Ontario, which was then the province of Upper Canada (Brown, 2006). This drove construction of Ottawa's first jail in the basement of the courthouse in 1842. For the next 20 years, the courthouse jail became synonymous with unhygienic conditions, with one observer noting that its cells were "damp, dark and unwholesome" (Meredith, 1861, as cited in Oliver, 1998, p. 350). By the late 1850s, crowding had become a fixture in Ottawa's first jail, as authorities responded to a perceived upsurge in 'crime', mostly sex work, drug use, and vagrancy. Government inspectors defined the place as "wretched and poisonous" and "the most abominable jail in the entire province" (Ottawa Citizen, 1862). The jail was subsequently deemed inadequate and a new one was constructed next to the courthouse (Ottawa Citizen, 1862).

Opening in 1862, the new Carleton County Gaol (CCG) was initially praised by local officials and the press. In their 1863 report, inspectors regarded the new jail as a significant upgrade and "probably the best in Canada" (Oliver, 1998, p. 351). However, the CCG soon became known for dehumanizing treatment of prisoners, and deprivations of basic necessities like food (Carleton County Gaol, 1880) and health care (Carleton County Gaol, 1885). Many prisoners became ill (Carleton County Gaol, n.d.) and some died (Ottawa Journal, 1896, 1908; Ottawa Citizen, 1944) in numbers well beyond those of the state executions on its grounds (Ottawa Journal, 1972). By the 1930s, there were calls to replace the jail (Ottawa Journal, 1937). One journalist remarked the jail was "built about 75 years ago to meet the needs of a much smaller population than it serves today … It is just not adequate for the Ottawa and Carleton of these times" (Ottawa Journal, 1937).

Such calls were acted on decades later when Alan Grossman was Ontario's Minister of Reform Institutions from 1963 to 1968. The provincial government enacted sweeping reforms, including taking over county jails and replacing many with bigger institutions. The CCG – "overcrowded", lacking "plumbing, recreational facilities" and characterized as "a depressing atmosphere" (Ottawa Journal, 1969) – was among the first replaced by Grossman, who believed "new detention centres" would "allow the ministry to institute rehabilitation programs and provide inmates with something to do with their time" (Oliver, 1985, p. 188).

In 1972, the Ottawa-Carleton Detention Centre (OCDC) opened as part of this wave of new "rehabilitation units". It was seen by the provincial government as creating "broad horizons for the introduction of intelligent and humane methods of meeting the needs of those who enter its door" (Oliver, 1985, p. 188). Praise from media across Canada ensued. A *Brandon Sun* newspaper article, entitled "Inmates may want to call this jail home", stated: "Officials at the new [OCDC] are hoping their $4-million jail with its country-club setting, colour coordinated dormitories, lounges and library will be the kind of place prisoners won't mind calling home" (Brandon Sun, 1972). Locally, news coverage projected certainty that OCDC would result in meaningful change. An *Ottawa Journal* story remarked: "Nestled among the trees … [OCDC] resembles a high school in design … it will afford its projected 164 inmates a remarkable degree of freedom, respect and privacy" (Makow, 1972).

Yet, in the following decades, OCDC, and other provincial jails built of the period, have fallen dramatically short of that progressive vision (see Benslimane et al., 2020). Today, the jail is very crowded, chaotic, freezing in winter and boiling in summer, and marked by pervasive filth such as blood, urine, and faeces on the walls, poor air quality, flooding in cells, inadequate laundry, lack of personal hygiene products, and the spread of terrible infections. Around two-thirds of the prisoners in the 585-bed capacity jail on any given day are on remand awaiting court dates, mostly for non-violent offences, due to a massive explosion in the remand population in Ontario in recent decades (Doyle and McKendy, 2019). A quarter to a half of prisoners are living with mental health issues like schizophrenia or bipolar disorder. Prisoners entering the jail are often poor or homeless and/or racialized. As with American prisons, which are part of a broader racialized apparatus of control (Davis, 2003), in Canada prisons are settler-colonial institutions that extend the historic spatialized control, notably of Indigenous peoples through reserves and residential schools (Martel et al., 2011), along with Black people who were historically subject to slavery, segregation and criminalization (Maynard, 2017).

OCDC prisoners often tell us they are treated like dogs. Lack of access to proper medical, mental health and dental care, programming, educational and recreational opportunities, and re-entry supports are consistently cited (Speight et al., 2019a). This situation persists despite a 2004 court ruling that OCDC's conditions did not meet United Nations minimum standards, with Judge Denis Power arguing that the jail brought the administration of justice into disrepute and awarding a prisoner three days credit for each day served there (O'Neill, 2004). Among recent high-profile OCDC atrocities: Christina Jahn – living with mental health issues and diagnosed with cancer – spent over 200 days in solitary, leading to a human rights settlement (*Jahn v. Ontario*, 2013); Julie Bilotta gave birth to her son Gionni Lee on the floor of a segregation cell in September 2012 without proper medical attention as her pleas for help were ignored – a baby that died a year later from respiratory problems that began in the first days of his life (Fiander, 2016); the brutal beating of Jean Paul Rhéaume – who had a developmental disability – as he was "handcuffed, shackled and pinned face down on the concrete floor" as "one or more guards stomped on his head until he lay in a pool of blood", which was subsequently covered up by staff (Ontario Ombudsperson, 2013); media revelations that prisoners were being forced to sleep in shower areas due to crowding; and a series of deaths by suicide, including those of Cleve "Cas" Geddes, Justin St. Amour, and Yousef Hussein within a ten-month period in 2016 and 2017 (Seymour, 2017).

It is in this context that authorities announced, in May 2017, that they were again going to address persistent problems by replacing the existing 585-bed jail with an "innovative" new and bigger 725-bed jail. If built, the "Ottawa Correctional Complex" will cost up to $1 billion to design, build, finance, and maintain during a 30-year public-private-partnership (Piché and Doyle, 2018). Reviewing this history can create a sense of pessimism and inevitability, but other outcomes are possible.

Theorizing change and inertia

Modern prisons are perpetually subject to reform (Foucault, 1977). They have proved intractable and attained a deep hegemony. However, although the prison may be stone, its future is not written in stone – instead, incarceration and its edifices are shaped by diverse competing forces and may be targets of struggle (Goodman et al., 2015). The idea of the prison is entrenched in our lives from birth and the notion that human caging is the right response to 'crime' is common sense for many (Davis, 2003). However, given its human and financial costs, and richly documented failures, the reproduction of the prison idea takes ideological work. Prison abolitionists thus face an ideological struggle, not only with imprisonment's place in common sense, but also with those who respond to our challenges by actively defending incarceration (Piché, 2014).

Defenders of the prison exist within and outside the state. The state itself is far from monolithic (Jessop, 1990) and is instead a collection of relatively autonomous institutions and actors, with competing political parties trading power, and often-fraught relationships between politicians, civil servants, and community-based organizations. This can open-up opportunities to advance radical alternatives in rare instances or result in further consolidation of penal power in others. Even so, the prison in general remains a formidable bulwark of the state, which remains the master and arch-defender of confinement.

Thomas Mathiesen (1974) helped found and sustain the Norwegian Association of Penal Reform (known as the KROM in Norway), which has worked towards prison abolition for decades. From this experience, Mathiesen (1990) produced an account of the "neutralization techniques" used by defenders of the prison to combat challengers. For Mathiesen (1990, p. 137), these "techniques vary from the more or less open dismissal of ideas which are in conflict with prevailing system interests to techniques which more subtly and unnoticeably deleted them from the agenda". Mathiesen (1980, p. 288) also suggested that the state may "define in" more co-operative actors that might upset the status quo, while "defining out" more threatening actors. As we will discuss, "defining in" and "defining out" presents a particular challenge to abolitionist organizations, as it may fracture alliances with more moderate organizations aimed at shared short-term goals to reduce the use and pains of imprisonment.

Examining the dynamic interplay between the neutralization techniques described by Mathiesen and responses by activist organizations to counter them, Carlton and Russell (2015, p. 5) suggest the former "are not a one-way process" as "prison authorities do not merely suppress or 'strangle' activist strategies". Facing what Myra Marx Ferree (2004, p. 141) would call "soft repression" – understood as "the collective mobilization of power, albeit in nonviolent forms and often highly informal ways, to limit and exclude ideas and identities from the public forum" – Carlton and Russell (2015, p. 5) note that "activists adapt and respond to changing conditions", which "can actually produce new forms of resistance".

While overturning common sense beliefs that support the prison is certainly part of the work abolitionists necessarily engage in, the contemporary world is replete with the persistence of situations in the absence of persuasive ideological support for them. This means to impact change, other barriers beyond those that are simply ideological must also be considered. Some barriers to change are "built in" to the situation, ranging from massive institutional and bureaucratic inertia, to toothless accountability mechanisms that maintain a sheen of democratic responsiveness, but limit substantial policy reversals. Other neutralizing factors include constraints faced by community groups like CPEP, who lack resources available to the state and experience personal costs of volunteer activism such as burnout and turnover in campaigns sometimes lasting years. With these broad points in mind, we turn to a specific account of our organizing efforts and some of the challenges we have encountered.

Encounters with neutralization techniques and factors

With a long-term goal of abolition by attrition (Knopp et al., 1976), CPEP works to document the brutalities of incarceration, and push towards reducing imprisonment and diminishing the pains of human caging as interim goals, with a focus on OCDC. Since 2012, we have proposed diversion (e.g. bail reforms, transformative justice, etc.) and decarceration measures (e.g. temporary absences, etc.) to shrink the jail population as steps towards abolition (Doyle et al., 2016a). We have also battled to improve jail conditions through "non-reformist reforms" (Doyle et al., 2016b) compatible with the long-term goal of abolition (Mathiesen, 1974). These included an on-site kitchen to replace the privatized system whereby frozen meals prepared off-site are reheated, referred to by prisoners as "dog bowls" (CPEP, 2016). CPEP has also pushed for things like a new free phone system and alternatives to imprisonment to keep prisoners connected to, and in, their communities to the extent presently possible (Benslimane et al., 2019).

Over eight years, we have tried many approaches. We have had many public and private meetings with prisoners and their loved ones, community allies, OCDC and jail system officials, politicians, and other actors. We have put on numerous public panels and organized three large public forums, each with hundreds in attendance, along with a series of community arts events and film screenings promoting prisoner justice. We have staged numerous demonstrations and vigils, filed many Freedom of Information requests, made short videos and distributed them on social media, published many newspaper opinion pieces, and done dozens of media interviews. In December 2018, we established a hotline operating on weekday afternoons that prisoners can call to address issues at the jail and make connections to facilitate community re-entry. In our first year, the hotline took 3,402 calls (Benslimane et al., 2020).

We have also worked with many community groups, for example, Mothers Offering Mutual Support (a group of mothers of prisoners), the Canadian Somali Mothers Association, the Elizabeth Fry Society, and the Defence Counsel

Association and other lawyers. In trying to bring about social change, one learns a lot about the forces and techniques that work to reproduce the status quo. We focus on a few examples below.[2]

Being "defined in" and "defined out"

Our first major initiative was a lengthy public forum in autumn 2013. Over 250 people attended and former prisoners detailed the horrors of OCDC as television news cameras rolled, beginning an extensive set of negative media coverage of the jail's conditions (e.g. Ottawa Citizen, 2013). Shortly afterwards the provincial government established Community Advisory Boards (CABs) for OCDC and nine other provincial jails. These were positioned as "independent bodies (that would) strengthen links between the community and provincial institutions" and "increase transparency and accountability" (MCSCS, 2014). OCDC's CAB consists of volunteer community members appointed by the province who can enter and inspect the jail any time, meet with management monthly, and produce annual reports. While efforts to establish CABs were already underway when we began organizing, their creation served as one response by the province to public demands for action.

The CAB has produced critical annual reports consistent with our observations of problems at the jail (e.g. OCDC CAB, 2017) and has successfully lobbied to resolve individual cases of prisoner mistreatment. However, the CAB remains constrained. One problem is that CAB members have to take oaths of confidentiality, which limits their ability to make problems at the jail public. CAB members are thus "defined in". CAB members are volunteers with limited time as nearly all have full-time paid employment elsewhere. The ministry also controls if and when the CAB's annual reports are made public. The last annual report made public was based on observations from 2016 and was released after a delay of more than six months. None of their annual reports have been made public by the government since. The limitations of the CAB are revealed by the situation in which CPEP members have been tempted to volunteer for it, partly because it would give us the authority to go into the jail and meet with prisoners at will. However, we have declined because the oath of confidentiality would stifle our efforts to push for change.

The creation of the CABs also meant that, in early 2019, when we raised issues from callers to our hotline with government officials, a letter from the jail's superintendent brushed us off, stating:

> The OCDC maintains positive relationships with the community through its work with the Community Advisory Board (CAB) … Members of the CAB can tour the institution and speak to inmates. Any concerns identified through these discussions are brought forward to my attention … I trust the above information, which outlines the various processes that are available for inmates, addresses your concerns.
>
> *(Speight et al., 2019b, pp. 21–23)*

The implication was that, unlike the CAB, we were not an approved official process and thus could be ignored. Essentially, we had been what Mathiesen (1980) calls "defined out", made possible through the creation of the CAB, the provincial government's preferred, official version of "community input". Other efforts to "define-out" CPEP's work following the launch of the JAIL hotline were made by several OCDC staff and members of their union who claimed on Twitter that our reports and related op-eds were based on false information provided by manipulative prisoners. Others went as far as to harass and dox some of us as a means of discrediting CPEP's work.

The OCDC task force and defining-in

While we succeeded in raising public awareness in our first four years of organizing, the current and former prisoners we heard from reported few changes within the jail itself. The inertia had us feeling at the time that we would be very pleased if we could just move the needle even slightly, with short-term aims like just getting the jail to wash prisoners' blankets once a month and sterilize shared nail clippers. However, after we spent years working on OCDC issues, what brought things to a public crisis finally were accounts emerging in spring 2016 that the jail was so crowded that prisoners were sleeping in a shower area. The provincial government was heavily criticized and in a rapid chain of events the jail superintendent was fired. Even then-Premier Kathleen Wynne, Ontario's political head, was called to account by the media and stated that things had to change. Then-Minister Naqvi, touted by many as leadership material, faced a political future suddenly in peril.

The ministry adopted another behind-the-scenes tactic at this time to defuse criticisms of crowding at the jail by quickly and quietly transferring large numbers of OCDC prisoners to other jails in different parts of the province outside the media spotlight. Naqvi's more highly public response, however, was creation of a task force on OCDC that was "to develop an action plan to address overcrowding and capacity issues … and to identify long-term solutions to improve the health and safety of all inmates and staff" (OCDC Task Force, 2016). A representative of MOMS, with whom CPEP had been working closely for years, was asked to join the task force. We continued to consult frequently with her, warning of the perils of collaborating with the state, even lending her Mathiesen's (1990) book. CPEP also made two written submissions to the task force (Doyle et al., 2016a, b) knowing she would actively put our recommendations on the agenda.

This task force led to some basic improvements we had pushed for, such as more regular access to yard time, more recreational opportunities and equipment, access by more community volunteers, and the introduction of more bail beds as an alternative to pre-trial detention. However, many of the more serious changes recommended by task force were defined as "long term goals" and thus not acted on. The ministry had to report a year later on progress towards the task forces' goals, but "long term goals" had timelines beyond the reporting period, so were pushed into the indefinite future, outside the scope of accountability mechanisms – a good example of "postponement" (Mathiesen, 1990, p. 38).

Agreement and inaction

While we have navigated being "defined in" and "defined out" over the years, we also noticed other communications tactics. For instance, as if echoing our calls for the decriminalization of drug use and of people living with mental health issues, former 'corrections' minister Naqvi would make assertions very consistent with our positions. For instance, in one media interview he stated, "If someone has serious mental health or addiction challenges, is sending them to a correctional institution, is that the right place?" (Seymour, 2016). However, in practice, little action was connected with such statements. Mathiesen (1990, p. 38) referred to this as puncturing, "whereby the practical significance of the new idea is diminished, while a front of understanding, interest, and perhaps even enthusiasm for the idea is maintained" (ibid).

The announcement of a new, bigger jail and the fallout

When the 2016 task force action plan was released, we were hopeful about the prospect of change given Minister Naqvi's rhetoric, including a statement that building a new jail would "fail taxpayers" and

> by building more jails, you are essentially building more capacity, and five years from now you'll be at square one. You haven't really addressed the real problem. What we need to focus on is to reduce the demand for jails ... That's where real transformation takes place.
>
> *(Seymour, 2016)*

Indeed, no one on the task force recommended building a new facility. However, there was an unexpected turn in May 2017 when Marie-France Lalonde – the newly appointed 'corrections' minister – announced that the government would be replacing the 585-bed OCDC with a new and bigger 725-bed jail. In the process, the province took the idea of putting in place "alternatives" to confinement like bail beds and said they would continue with those "alternatives", while also building a bigger jail. This exercise in "net-widening" (Cohen 1985) – that is, bringing more people under state control, whether behind or beyond bars – illustrates Mathiesen's technique of "puncturing", whereby a proposed measure is supported, but subverted in practice and gutted of meaningful change. Mathiesen (1990) also described the technique of making reference "to instructions, orders, [and] demands from the outside in general" (ibid, p. 37) to justify the intensification of existing arrangements. In this case, the provincial government cited projected population growth in Eastern Ontario and anticipated the need for more jail beds if current criminalization trends hold (e.g. Lalonde, 2018). We later learnt from material on an architectural firm's website that plans for a new jail were already underway a year earlier (Parkin, 2016), even as Naqvi was telling the public when he was 'corrections' minister that, "I think we are failing our taxpayers, if that's the solution we think is appropriate" (Seymour, 2016).

The announcement of the new and bigger jail led to considerable tensions in our close working relationship with the MOMS group, which had been "defined in" for the OCDC Task Force. They came out publicly in favour of the new jail, albeit one that they argued should not be any bigger than the existing jail. The MOMS cited the decaying physical infrastructure and bought-in to promises of new services that would allegedly be made possible by a new jail.

The provincial government also absorbed our critiques of the privatized jail food system to justify building a new and bigger jail. In a video we distributed on social media, we argued the food system was inadequate, wasteful, expensive, and represented a threat to security for prisoners and staff (CPEP, 2016). The provincial government turned around and argued we needed a new jail to add an on-site kitchen that would provide nutritious meals to prisoners, which they argued was not possible at the current jail due to space restrictions, as if diminishing OCDC's population and repurposing existing jail space was impossible.

The provincial government also used this issue to neutralize Larry Seguin, one key critic, by defining him in. Having written critical opinion pieces about the jail from inside it, recounting how the site was so crowded he had been forced to sleep in a shower area, Seguin was contacted by Minister Lalonde to setup a meeting and media photo opportunity. At that mediatized meeting, the formerly critical prisoner came out in favour of the new jail, swayed in part by the promise on an on-site kitchen (Seguin, 2017). The fact that the current jail itself had once had an onsite kitchen, which could have been restored, was not discussed.

Other critics have also been "defined in". For example, a long-time reporter who wrote the most damning stories about the jail in recent years was named a justice of the peace in 2017. As a result, he switched occupations, taking on tasks including overseeing bail hearings, and was off the jail news beat for good. Today, a variety of journalists without specialized knowledge on imprisonment cover the jail. Two other important allies who worked for community organizations and were critical of the government also later took up staff positions in the government. We have no evidence that any of these moves were deliberate government efforts to stifle criticism, but they certainly had that effect.

Inertia through ministerial shuffling

There are numerous other factors that have created inertia where OCDC is concerned. One is repeated turnover of key political players. Over the last eight years, CPEP has dealt with four provincial 'corrections' ministers under the Liberals and two more ministers under the Conservatives. Thus, controversies attached to previous ministers blow over and new ministers require time "to get up to speed" before taking action. Ministers are often shuffled out before any meaningful or sustainable changes are put in place. Changes in the ruling party create further "postponement" (Mathiesen, 1990), partly due to changes in policy direction. More broadly and simply than this, our jail and the apparatus that surround it have a massive amount of bureaucratic and institutional inertia that places the onus constantly on a challenger group such as ourselves to force change.

Epilogue and conclusion

CPEP's community organizing to reduce the use and harms of imprisonment in the short-term, while working towards abolition in the long-term, continues as does our fight against the new jail. The day following the election of a Conservative Government of Ontario in June 2018, our campaign shifted its focus to new Premier Doug Ford, spending each of the next 99 days sharing concrete ways the new administration could enhance community well-being and safety without building a new and bigger jail in Ottawa (CPEP, 2018). It is around this time that a notice for an information session on the new Ottawa jail disappeared from the Ministry of Community Safety and Correctional Services' website and things went quiet about any further steps towards building a bigger jail in our city.

As deep cuts to education and social services were being rolled out in year one of the new provincial government's mandate, we used an extended Facebook and Twitter campaign and further op-ed writing to question how upwards of $1 billion slated for a new jail could be better spent and criticizing the idea that an alleged cost-conscious government was moving forward with a billion-dollar boondoggle (Piché, 2018). A public information session about the project never took place and there was little mention of the project for months. In fact, the provincial budget released in April 2019 made no mention of it (Ministry of Finance, 2019). As of February 2020, there has been little movement on the new jail plans other than to say it is coming at some point down the road (Infrastructure Ontario, 2019).

What are we to make of this? Our best guess is that some combination of financial austerity concerns and fear of local political fallout, partly generated by groups like us, has pushed the timeline for the project well into the future, leaving this public fight over the future of (alternatives to) imprisonment for another day. However, we remain vigilant as we wait and see. Research on social movements suggests that success is often difficult to assess, especially in the short-term (Meyer, 2003). Even if we have been temporarily successful in helping stave off a new and bigger jail, looking at the cyclical history of Ottawa jails suggests it is only a matter of time before the idea actively resurfaces. Our experience also shows us that Mathiesen's (1990) analysis of techniques of neutralization remains very apt, and that abolitionist groups need to be alive to the problems of "defining in" and "defining out", but also that we can work through these problems. The ideology of imprisonment is a key source of inertia, but not the only source.

Through our long struggle, CPEP has also run-up against constraints at the organizational level. Over the eight years we have operated, we have had many dedicated members, a number of who gave a great deal individually for a year or two and then moved on, due to a combination of other developments in their lives, burnout, or, in some cases, re-incarceration. Until recently, where we secured some external and university funding to help operate the JAIL hotline (see Benslimane et al., 2020), we have mostly operated on a minimal funding model with limited expenses, receiving small donations from key organizers and limited sums for particular items we could cover as institutional expenses. One key to sustained capacity for our small organization is the involvement of university professors and a stream of young, idealistic, and energetic students. Teaching classes with experiential learning components has dovetailed with CPEP's work, as has supervision of many graduate students involved in the group. We have also been able to access some university resources, such as space for meetings. Another central component has been a core of passionately committed members with lived experience of incarceration or of having loved ones incarcerated. Some of those with lived experience are now students pursuing undergraduate or graduate degrees. Our group composition including current and former prisoners, researchers, and others with expertise on prison issues, helps facilitate regular news media access.

A university-based group like ours has some capacity advantages in the long struggle we face, but building greater and deeper relationships with people working for social justice where areas of mutual concern exist is key to deliver meaningful change (Piché, 2016). For instance, CPEP's recent work with other groups to shrink the use of imprisonment through attrition on campaigns, including "Contain COVID-19, Not People" with the Toronto Prisoners' Rights Project (HRT, 2020), have translated into diversion and decarceration proposals gaining serious traction. This is evident in OCDC's population having lowered to 400 prisoners, well below its capacity of 585 beds, only a few weeks into the public health crisis taking hold in Ontario (Helmer, 2020). Thus, when facing neutralization techniques and dead-ends, abolitionists must persevere and continue to organize so that they are positioned to capitalize on "turning points" when they emerge (Mathiesen, 2008, p. 62) and increase demands for social change when the impossible suddenly becomes possible.

Notes

1 We would like to acknowledge the assistance of Aislinn Gallivan with the historical research that supports this chapter.

2 See Maadarani (2020) for a more detailed account of neutralization techniques deployed to maintain the status quo at the Ottawa-Carleton Detention Centre that goes beyond conditions of confinement CPEP has campaigned on that we briefly address in this paper by also exploring access to justice issues, inadequate mental and physical health care, and the continued use of solitary confinement.

References

Benslimane, S., Piché, J., Speight S., Dobson, L. and Doyle, A. (2019) *Will You Accept the Charges?* Ottawa, Criminalization and Punishment Education Project.

Benslimane, S., Speight, S., Piché, J. and Doyle, A. (2020) 'The Jail Accountability & Information Line: Early Reflections on Praxis', *Journal of Law & Social Policy*, vol. 33, pp. 111–133.

Brandon Sun (1972) 'Inmates May Want to Call This Jail Home', 27 September.

Brown, R. (2006) *Behind Bars: Inside Ontario's Heritage Gaols*, Toronto, Natural Heritage Books.

Carleton County Gaol (n.d.) 'Prisoner Records'.

Carleton County Gaol (1880) 'Prisoner Records', 31 August.

Carleton County Gaol (1885) 'Prisoner Records', 2 October.

Carlton B. and Russell E. (2015) '"A Gender for Change": Cycles of Women Penal Reform and Reconfigurations of Anti-Prison Resistance in Victoria, Australia', *Penal Field*, vol. XII. Available at https://journals.openedition.org/champpenal/9103 (Accessed 30 March 2020).

Cohen, Stanley (1985) *Visions of Social Control: Crime, Punishment and Classification*, Cambridge, Polity Press.

Criminalization and Punishment Education Project [CPEP] (2016) 'End Food Privatization at Ottawa's Jail', *YouTube*, Ottawa, 13 May.

Criminalization and Punishment Education Project [CPEP] (2018) '99 Alternatives to Jail Expansion in Ottawa', *Tracking the Politics of Criminalization and Punishment in Canada*, 19 September.

Davis, A.Y. (2003) *Are Prisons Obsolete?* New York, Seven Stories Press.

Doyle, A. and McKendy, L. (2019) 'Risk Aversion and the Remand Population Explosion in Ontario', in Hannem, S., Sanders, C., Schneider, C., Doyle, A. and Christensen T. (eds.) *Security and Risk Technologies in Criminal Justice*, Toronto, Canadian Scholars' Press, pp. 199–224.

Doyle, A., McKendy L. and Piché J. (2016a) *Strategies to Reduce Crowding at the Innes Road Jail*, Criminalization and Punishment Education Project report submitted to the Ottawa-Carleton Detention Centre Task Force, 5 May.

Doyle, A., McKendy L. and Piché J. (2016b) *Strategies to Improve Conditions at the Innes Road Jail*, Criminalization and Punishment Education Project report submitted to the Ottawa-Carleton Detention Centre Task Force, 16 May.

Ferree, M.M. (2004) 'Soft Repression: Ridicule, Stigma, and Silencing in Gender-Based Movements', *Research in Social Movements, Conflicts and Change*, vol. 25, pp. 85–101.

Fiander, S. (2016) *Pregnancy, Birth, and Mothering Behind Bars: A Case Study of One Woman's Journey through the Ontario Criminal Justice and Jail Systems* (unpublished MA thesis), Brantford, Wilfrid Laurier University.

Foucault, M. (1977) *Discipline and Punish: The Birth of the Prisons* (trans. A Sheridan), London, Penguin.

Goodman, P., Page, J. and Phelps, M. (2015) 'The Long Struggle: An Agonistic Perspective on Penal Development', *Theoretical Criminology*, vol. 19, no. 3, pp. 315–335.

Harm Reduction Toronto [HRT] (2020) *Contain COVID-19, Not People*. Available at https://harmreductionto.ca/contain-covid-19-not-people (Accessed 30 March 2020).

Helmer, A. (2020) 'Physicians Warn Inmates Like "sitting ducks" in Call to Depopulate Jails', *Ottawa Citizen*, 24 March.

Infrastructure Ontario (2019) *2019 Market Update: Alternative Financing and Procurement Projects*, Toronto, Government of Ontario.

Jahn v. Ontario (2013) "Public Interest Remedies", *Human Rights Tribunal of Ontario.*

Jessop, B. (1990) *State Theory*, Cambridge, Polity Press.

Knopp, F.H. (ed.) (2005[1976]) *Instead of Prisons: A Handbook for Abolitionists*, Oakland, Critical Resistance.

Lalonde, M.-F. (2018) 'Participants in the Friday April 20 Meeting Regarding Correctional Transformation and the New Ottawa Correctional Facility', Toronto, Ministry of Community Safety and Correctional Services, 26 April.

Maadarani, M. (2020) *Inside the Black Box of Jail: Barriers to Change at the Ottawa-Carleton Detention Centre* (unpublished master's thesis), Ottawa, University of Ottawa.

Makow, H. (1972) 'New Carleton Jail – A Prisoner's Dream?' *Ottawa Journal*, 23 February.

Martel, J., Brassard, R. and Jaccoud, M. (2011) 'When Two Worlds Collide: Aboriginal Risk Management in Canadian Corrections', *British Journal of Criminology*, vol. 51, no. 2, pp. 235–255.

Mathiesen, T. (1974) *The Politics of Abolition*, London, Martin Robertson & Company.

Mathiesen, T. (1980) *Law, Society and Political Action: Towards a Strategy under Late Capitalism*, New York, Academic Press.

Mathiesen, T. (1990) *Prisons on Trial*, London, Sage.

Mathiesen, T. (2008) 'The Abolitionist Stance', *Journal of Prisoners on Prisons*, vol. 17, no. 2, pp. 58–63.

Maynard, R. (2017) *Policing Black Lives: State Violence in Canada from Slavery to Present*, Halifax, Fernwood.

Meyer, D. (2003) 'How Social Movements Matter', *Contexts*, August.

Ministry of Community Safety and Correctional Services [MCSCS] (2014) *Community Advisory Boards*, Toronto.

Ministry of Finance (2019) 2019 *Ontario Budget: Ontario's Plan to Protect What Matters Most*, Toronto.

Oliver, P. (1985) *Unlikely Tory: The Life and Politics of Allan Grossman*, Toronto, L. & O. Dennys.

Oliver, P. (1998) *Terror to Evil-Doers*, Toronto, University of Toronto Press.

O'Neill, J. (2004) 'Corrections Ministry, Jail System go on Trial', *Ottawa Citizen*, 30 October.

Ontario Ombudsperson (2013) *The Code: Investigation into the Ministry of Community Safety and Correctional Services' Response to Allegations of Excessive Use of Force against Inmates*, Toronto.

Ottawa-Carleton Detention Centre [OCDC] Community Advisory Board [CAB] (2017) *Annual Report 2016*, Toronto, Ministry of Community Safety and Correctional Services.

Ottawa-Carleton Detention Centre [OCDC] Task Force (2016) *Action Plan*, Toronto, Ministry of Community Safety and Correctional Services.

Ottawa Citizen (1862) 'The Ottawa Jail', 12 July.

Ottawa Citizen (1944) 'Thomas O'Keefe Dies in Carleton Jail', 29 July.

Ottawa Citizen (2013) 'Conditions at the Ottawa Carleton Detention Centre Must Be Fixed', 2 December.

Ottawa Journal (1896) 'How J.R. Moir Died', 21 January.

Ottawa Journal (1908) 'Death from Suffocation', 28 January.

Ottawa Journal (1937) 'Hulls New Jail to Set an Example', 11 June.

Ottawa Journal (1969) 'New Jail Drive Gets Backing', 3 January.

Ottawa Journal (1972) 'Three Died on Ottawa Gallows', 11 November.

Parkin Architects Limited (2016) 'Parkin Awarded Functional Program for Adult Detention Centres', Ottawa, 1 March.

Piché, J. (2014) 'A Contradictory and Finishing State: Explaining Recent Prison Capacity Expansion in Canada's Provinces and Territories', *Penal Field*, vol. XII. Available at https://journals.openedition.org/champpenal/8797 (Accessed 30 March 2020).

Piché, J. (2016) 'Assessing the Boundaries of Public Criminology: On What Does (Not) Count', *Social Justice*, vol. 42, no. 2, pp. 70–90.

Piché, J. (2018) 'Premier's Support for New Jail Costly, Ineffective', *Ottawa Citizen*, 19 September.

Piché, J. and Doyle A. (2018) 'There Are Many Alternatives to a Bigger Jail', *Ottawa Citizen*, 5 May.

Seguin, L. (2017) 'From Shower Cell Inmate to Believer', *Ottawa Sun*, 9 July.

Seymour, A. (2016) 'Building a New Jail Would Fail Taxpayers, Naqvi Says', *Ottawa Citizen*, 11 April.

Seymour, A. (2017) 'Ottawa Man Taken Off Suicide Watch in Jail Less Than a Day Before Killing Himself', *Ottawa Citizen*, 27 March.

Speight, S., Benslimane, S., Piché, J. and Doyle, A. (2019a) *Jail Accountability & Information Line: Quarterly Advocacy Report #3*, Ottawa, Criminalization and Punishment Education Project.

Speight, S., Benslimane, S., Piché, J. and Doyle, A. (2019b) *Jail Accountability & Information Line: Monthly Report #1*, Ottawa, Criminalization and Punishment Education Project.

PART IV
Resisting carceral logic

20

SOMETHING FROM HERE

Emanuel "Eoz"

Stereotype of only routine treatments
He is not really defined by an activity, he defends himself serenely
A little more on this side, a little less to get out there
Such a long wait that can be summed up in one day.
To someone else.
Achievements that annoy, losses that rejoice
Nosy kind of arousing doubts
How much can a mind poison?
Every one treading his own thread.
And what a mess comes along with so much crossing
Those who carry scissors, do not clash with those who untangle threads
There is a connection even in the most absurd
Otherworldly expectations
It's your look, it's your smile
The one that saves me
Lost in white smoke.

21

DISENTHRALL

Emmanuel X

In 1960, Eleanor Roosevelt said, "No one can make you feel inferior without your consent".

Free us from bondage; give us liberty or give us battle.

Solemnity-solitary and confinement where the walls hold silent screams. Lives are lost in vain. A society that craves liberty. Some individuals crave liberty more than the air they breathe.

Vital. Nothing is more precious than freedom. Favorable to or in accord with concepts of maximum individual freedom possible. The elements of incarceration are a tangible force. Cripple you mentally. Dismantle you emotionally. Desolate you physically and leave you scrambling. Spiritually broken.

I witnessed religious individuals lose faith in their God … and subsequently losing faith in their selves. Scattered; searching for ideals or anything to grasp on tight from the tugging of insanity – from the tugging of delusion that desperately attempts to still the core of their identity. Broken. Submerged into ruins losing all sense of hope and direction. Stolen. Stripped away from our opportunity to share the full experience of humanity. To thrive in society. To give and contribute to our communities. To experience nature – the nourishment of our kids and to provide for and watch our families grow.

My experience of incarceration feels like family members are in quarantine. A system has been created into a penal colony as if we're a virus; a deadly plague stripped from civilization. Isolated in confinement; as if we're infected with a deadly disease that gnaws our identities until we become nothing more than a number. A statistic. A scientific experiment to contest theories against theories …. and in the process masterminds make billions off of the martyrs.

Democracy is ignored. The element of humanity is trampled. Chronic suffering. Incarceration closing in and squeeze tight until individuals' sanity starts to burst one by one. How long would it take before civilization hears the muffled screams of a stolen society? Some are forever lost as if they were an abandoned nation. Still I can feel those expired individuals inside of me. It's melancholy … roaring loudly. They're lost spirits. Their muffled screams vibrate my core.

I've been incarcerated for nearly a decade. And been held in solitary confinement – in a cell smaller than an average bathroom with no TV, radio or window for five years. Yet I continue to survive the years of penal hardship. Shackled and handcuffed every time I move. Forced to live within myself as if "self" was a cell. My self-made cell becoming the core of my strength.

My endurance has mustered resilience and a deep craving to contribute to humanity as a whole. I've found inside of myself universal consciousness. But what about the unfortunate? The ones that are not able to muster the strength to bare the weight of suppression and incarceration?

Throughout my incarceration I witnessed and experienced years of corporal punishment. Our authorities-crooks watching over and abusing alleged crooks. Crooks watching over and abusing the innocent. There's no balance.

The infliction of pain leaving behind scars physically, mentally and emotionally. A land where love and compassion is famine-frozen tears. The collateral damage. The casualties of society hurts. The muffled screams of an abandoned nation shall soon be heard.

A broken civilization

The neighborhood I grew up in as a child I seen at least 85% of my male childhood peers become incarcerated. I see them all the time in the prison Society. For a time I thought it was by coincidence. That's until I learned of a hidden heritage. That we are threated and looked upon as a maroon Society. The hunted.

The history of the Saramaka people of Surinam in South America began around 1685 when African and Native slaves broke free and escaped. In order to survive they united and formed a maroon Society; a rebel against slavery. Back then "maroon" was considered: fugitive slaves. In the 17th and 18th centuries "maroon" was any of a group of blacks descended from fugitive slaves living in the West Indies and Guiana. For eight generations Dutch armed forces opposed them and tried to dismantle their community. But they never gave up the fight against freedom.

For the Saramakans? Liberty came in 1761 when opposition abandoned their wars for peace. But here in modern times we're still living in slavery. The new maroons.

Abraham Lincoln introduced the 13th Amendment on January 1, 1863 – the Emancipation Proclamation to end slavery. Freeing the slave in those territories still in rebellion against the Union.

The 13th Amendment to the US Constitution abolishes slavery throughout the United States in 1865 (except) as punishment for a crime. Fourteen states' constitutions still allow slavery as a punishment for a crime as part of a compromise to pass the amendment in Congress.

After the Civil War when slavery was abolished a mass-amount of former slaves were arrested for minor crimes and held in bondage as part of a "convict-leasing program". The men and women were paid nothing while they worked for private companies including United States Steel Corporation.

It seems as if the Emancipation Proclamation changed slavery from a private-owned business into a corporation … slave labor morphed into a universal franchise.

History shows a chronological record of events. British-America back in the 1600s on both Northern and Southern American continents, Europeans enslaved Africans and Native Americans in order to multiply their profits in the fastest possible time, which resulted in laws and policies being tailored that were genocidal to Africans and Indians. The English looked upon the two races as inferior and only exited to make a profit. Today this is called racism. The two identities of the past and the present almost seem parallel. Racism masked behind the disguise of a penal system.

Since labor was in short supply in British America the earliest colonists enslaved Indians. Then it was Africans. In the English law unending bondage did not exist. The first form was called "indenture" which lasted for seven years. No matter what color you were "indenture servants" could be mistreated while in service just the same as an incarcerated individual. Their personal life and their time extended by scheming masters the same as it goes on in the penal system. All three races (Africans, Caucasians and Indians) were abused under this system.

In modern times a prosecutorial culture is to win by all means necessary. Ethics are expelled. The penal system should be purged. But instead its judicial system prompts barbarian battles in its arena as if it was a theater-giving victory not to the just, but to those who present the most dramatic presentation in order to captivate and deceive the majority. Even if it fosters intentional misconduct by prosecutors … they're given a round of applause.

The first Africans introduced into the Jamestown's economy was in 1619. They became indentured servants. Upon their release they became successful in the United States in Virginia. But in the 1630s the indenture rules started to change for the worse. It then became legal to hold Africans or Indians for over the maximum of seven years. The laws became tailored to hold an indentured servant for life. Now it has morphed into full blown slavery. The same way the penal system can hold an individual for "life".

The change started on the English-ruled Island of Barbados. The governor announced that Africans and Indians should serve for life. In 1636 only Caucasians received contracts of indenture. The first North American that was legally enslaved and sentenced to work until he died was in 1636 a Massachusetts Indian. Ten years later, governor John Winthrop decided it was favorable to exchange Indian slaves for Africans.

Why?

Because Africans were thousands of miles away from home. This idea of keeping slaves distant from their homes and families was crucial to having them under strict control. British merchants took Indians enslaved on the mainland and shipped them to the West Indies. This was the only secure and safe way to enslave Native Americans. Bondage was only secure when its prey had no safe place to turn to: no community to support them, and no family nearby to console or defend them.

This perspective helps us understand the elements of incarceration. The modern day slavery that uses our families hard earned money (tax payers' dollars) to sponsor our enslavement and to tear families apart.

For what?

For profit! And racism has been part of the ingredients of centuries. Consider the innocent. Those who have been trailed down, tried and convicted; only for the penal system to acknowledge an individual innocence 15–20 years later. A habit that has become repetitiously apologetic only after lives have been destroyed. An error that has been embedded in the penal culture. Lives have been severed. No amount of apologies or money could ever fix this judicial mistake or pay for what has been stolen from us.

Is it a crime? Is democracy demolished or is it a simple mistake that continues to shatter the lives of millions? If incarceration is slavery than abolishment is worth fighting for. Consider the frequency of flagrant prosecutorial misconduct. Consider that this conduct immutably goes unpunished even when it's the basis for reversal of convictions. Prosecutors are nearly 100% immune to punishment for intentional wrong doing. Because of this fundamental principle alone, the judicial system contributes to its corruption.

The battle between right and wrong must be ignited, and our citizens are the torch of justice.

This is a revolution. A movement that has engrossed society. This is the generation of integrity.

The United States is a country that's home to 5% of the world's population. Yet it holds approximately 22% of the world's prisoners. I live in a country that imprisons more of its population than any other country in the world. And I have lived in the state of Louisiana my entire life. A state that held the title as the incarceration capital of the world.

I witnessed the effects repetitiously – and still do to this day. And yet, willing to be the living testimony of a martyr. They say "time" heals all things. The psychological wounds that heal only leave behind large sensitive scabs, to remind you of its presence as if pain was a pioneer. Or a plague that spreads throughout the world. Families suffer. Adolescence forsaken.

I'm forced to try to raise my son from a cell thousands of miles away separated by razor wire fences equipped with motion-detectors, watch-tower and armed guards with assault rifles. And still I'm met with more opposition ... the persons that make it even harder for individuals to communicate or provide for their families. More chaos. It's a constant pain that throbs in my brain and heart.

What about the perspectives of the young sons and daughters of those who have been snared into the penal colony? They're sentenced with us. The penal system causes years of collateral damage that can never fully heal. What has been took could never be given back. What has been lost could never be found. Collateral damage a life time.

Some families of my peers are broken. Mothers and fathers; sons and daughters; brothers and sisters, dislodged into ruins. Torn apart. The impact causes the lives of innocent citizens to shatter, erode or descend into poverty.

The convicted along with their families are disobliged by these circumstances. Spirits are broken. Souls are scorched and minds are lost in the black hole. Lives are taken. They've taken their own lives or their lives are taken by the hands of opposition that strives to suppress them.

Barbarism

For centuries we have recorded history of suppression. Over time we will either become a more civilized humanity or continue to enslave humankind as if they are uncivilized animals or beasts. How can we create a firm legacy as a nation if we continue to frame our citizens in captivity? How can we continue to devastate our communities with servitude and oppression?

Metaphorically speaking the penal system is constructed as a mechanical rug that's being used to sweep scattered tools underneath, wherein these tools should be polished and utilized for its purpose to fix and contribute to society as a whole, which has a far greater value and profit to its nation, than to be piled under the rug or put on a shelf to rust and cause erosion.

The image of "incarceration" is "incorporation". A business that monopolized slavery. The strength of each notion depends not on capital alone, but on its citizens as well. We're dealing with a case and situation that demands prompt action and remedy. The need, demand and requirement are to provide opportunities for each community instead of discreet segregation.

Our kids should be surrounded by invigorators and not a penal system that desperately tries to lure them in.

The core of our future lies in the hands of our youth. Instead of their country invigorating them, they are being primed for destruction. Cops profiling and harassing our adolescents as their role models and parents are being enslaved. And we watch them subconsciously walk into the same snares that continue to destroy the generation before them.

The audacity was mustered to call them barbarous and a threat to the society. The same society where the school system for the minority is inadequate to even stabilize 25% of its attendees. Education is one of the #1 ingredients to success. Their foundation has gone astray, anticipating them to take the blame, invoking failure and destruction. We live in a society that scorns our youth because of a constructed mechanical system that sabotages their identities and their opportunities are introduced to erosion.

As a society it's our duty to till the land; to raise our kids and watch their dreams blossom into reality. Or allow reality to pull our future into slavery as if it was by coincidence and not by design. Doomed if they become a product of their environment. Our future is doomed if we as a whole continue to allow our citizens and children to lack opportunity and support and subsequently become wrapped in the penal system that's cultivated for our destruction and for destroying our future.

We as a nation are an army. We could battle for liberation with a sword of justice. Or we could allow the word slavery to be reconstructed into "penal system". Or substituted and masked by the modern word incarceration. But we as an army decide to face reality head on and take full responsibility as a nation and stand up to this plague that has been tormenting families for centuries. We as an army have the power to introduce this distorted penal system to annihilation.

The power of liberation is not in a single individual but in a society as a whole. Power is nothing without a demand. As Alice Walker says, "The most common way people give up their power is by thinking they don't have any".

22

CONTESTING THE COLLATERAL DAMAGES OF IMPRISONMENT FROM BELOW

Valeria Vegh Weis and Julieta Sosa

Understanding abolitionism as a social movement directly engaged in resisting and contesting the penal logic, policies, and practices, this study explores the possibilities to build grassroots counter-carceral strategies in a specifically dramatic context: re-entry. It is then when people are confronted with a neoliberal job market that systematically rejects those with criminal records and when the lack of sufficient welfare policies makes it evident that the criminalizing system is aimed at inoculating people and not rehabilitating them.

The study explores a brand-new Argentinean grassroots initiative aimed at overcoming one of the hardest collateral consequences of punishment, i.e., unemployment. In what can be described as "a path of social justice against and beyond the carceral state" (Brown and Schept, 2017), a group of people who have been subjected to the criminalizing system decided to form cooperatives in different fields in order to create collective working opportunities by and for themselves.

This is a scholar-activist written piece, by Valeria Vegh Weis, a female critical criminologist, and Julieta Sosa, a female activist who is at the forefront of the described grassroots initiative. The combination of theoretical knowledge and activist experience has the potential to dig into the connection between theory and the real problems that people who experienced incarceration suffer when they pretend to "dismantle, change and build". As Saleh-Hanna states: "It is an underlying philosophy in the abolitionist methodological realm that, to portray criminal experiences, it is best to hear about them from the sources" (2008, p. 448).

The study first exposes the socio-economic situation in Argentina and the particular conditions of the prison system. Second, the piece introduces the Southern Criminology approach to frame the particularities of the Argentinean situation, while uncovering the two main criminologist developments contesting carceral logic in the region. Third, the research presents the case study relying on observant participation and on the voices of the protagonists.

Neoliberal agenda, poverty, and the less eligibility principle in Argentina

Material conditions in the global south expose harsher difficulties in comparison to the global north. In Argentina in particular, the neoliberal agenda carried out by the government from 2015 to 2019 increased the number of people living in poverty (CELS, 2019). The most recent statistics expose that a third of the population was living below the poverty line by 2018 (INDEC, 2019, p. 3). This means that about 33% of the population did not have the minimum resources to satisfy their basic nutrition needs (p. 11). The reality might be even worse because official statistics are not reliable. Indeed, the United Nations Economic, Social and Cultural Rights Committee criticized the national statistics system and called the government to align its methodology with the one used by international organizations (Comité de Derechos Económicos, Sociales y Culturales de las Naciones Unidas, 2018, par. 11). To confront this lack of reliable official data, social organizations published their own statistics. In April 2019, they registered more than 7,000 homeless people residing in the capital city, Buenos Aires, compared to just 4,000 people living on the street one year prior. Women, mothers with children and LGBTQ+ population are those in the worst situation (CELS, 2019). In addition to these staggering statistics, almost 50% of the employed population nationwide is currently in an informal job, without access to social security and union representation (UCA, 2019).

Why are the poverty and employment statistics so crucial in properly analyzing imprisonment conditions and life after release? This might be well explained by recovering the notion of less eligibility which accounts for the modification in the conditions of punishment in each historical period. Rusche and Kirchheimer suggest that to serve as a deterrent, punishment must offer worse conditions than those that the labor market offers to the worst-off stratum of the working class (2009, p. 4). In other words, in order for the state to use encarceration to intimidate, prisons must be known for offering conditions which would be considered even worse than the worst conditions experienced outside. If non-convicted poor people are starving on the streets and the prison offers food and shelter with reasonable conditions, deterrence disappears and poor people may not be just willing, but potentially even eager to be incarcerated (see, e.g., Metraux and Culhane, 2004; Kushel et al., 2005). Going further, social policies might also be considered in relation to the criminalizing system. Social policies of the welfare system deal with the working-class already struggling to keep themselves at the poverty line or higher if they are lucky, while the justice system provides even worse conditions as a way of deterring criminal activity (Vegh Weis, 2018).

To imagine that Argentinian prisons are less desirable than living without the basic means of survival is a gut-wrenching thought. The most recent statistics show that prior to incarceration 70% of the 85,283 prisoners did not have a full-time job, 84% did not have secondary education, only 6% had access to higher or university education, and prison resources were so scarce that 76% did not receive any job training while serving their term (SNEEP, 2017, par. 9, 10 and 14). In April 2019, and as a result of the dire situation, the Ministry of Justice declared a state of emergency for the prison system (PPN, 2019).

Toward a southern perspective

Southern Criminology understands that criminological research should include the experiences and perspective of the global south to foster broader analysis on criminological issues and the democratization of knowledge worldwide (Carrington et al., 2018, p. 10). In specific relation to Latin American, Southern Criminology might help to clarify that this region has not been just a recipient of European knowledge, but also a vital actor and producer of autonomous knowledge (Härter and Vegh Weis, 2018). Notably, acknowledging that criminology is becoming more and more fragmented as a result of the development of new theories (Bosworth and Hoyle, 2011, p. 3), Southern Criminology is not considered as a new theory but as a perspective that can enrich the existing approaches (Carrington et al., 2018, p. 10).

The distinction North-South traditionally refers to the division between Western Europe and North America on the one side and Latin-America, Africa, Asia, and Australia, on the other (Carrington et al., 2018, p. 10). However, this might be too simplistic considering that Australia, e.g., is located in the geographical South but it is, at the same time, a main actor in the development of criminological knowledge on a global scale. Under this logic, South does not seem to refer just to a geographical division but to power regimes that are particularly traversed by language hierarchies (see Faraldo-Cabana, 2018). Most of the literature developed in the Latin-American criminological scene is written in Spanish or Portuguese and there are very few translations of this work into English. On the other hand, and probably as a consequence of the remaining colonial logic, Latin-American students and scholars regularly consume literature written by and for populations in Europe or the US.

Then, we could understand South, first, as a geographic metaphor that involves the former colonies that remain as low-income or middle-income countries without a key place in world politics and that, therefore, lack a central role in the global production of knowledge. Second, we could also understand South as a geographic metaphor of those places within each region, country, city or location that are less developed and have a lower impact on decision-making processes at the socio-economic and political levels, all of which makes them less relevant in terms of knowledge production. Third, we could also understand South as a demographic metaphor of those whose voices are not usually heard and whose problematics, experiences, and perspectives do not appear in mainstream theories (Vegh Weis, 2020a). Therefore, a Southern Criminology should not just spread the voices from the geographical South, but also foster a perspective that questions colonialism, economic inequality, racism, class oppression and the gender gap. This is relevant as many exponents from the South are not necessarily critical. As Mignolo (2017) explains, most of the former colonies have been decolonized in the sense that the control of the government is now under local authorities, but the old logic remains, i.e.: "the native elites did exactly what the colonizers were doing but in the name of national sovereignty [while leaving] intact the political theory and political economy (e.g., Capitalism and the modern-bourgeois Western state-form of governance)". This phenomenon is reflected in the production of knowledge with a good part of the southern theoretical production emulating the Northern paradigms.

The following question is then, what have been the Southern critical voices saying in relation to the contestation of the carceral state? In Argentina and probably Latin-America as a whole, the debate has been mostly focused on the development of a local critical criminology in the 1970s and 1980s and, most recently, on the enforcement of comprehensive reforms based on penal guarantees (*garantismo penal*) to confront punitive efforts. Both approaches are, in their core, aligned with the claims of penal abolitionism understood as an "insistent and insurgent argument to abandon criminal justice' logic and practice" (Coyle and Schept 2017) and its acknowledgment that "law breaking is a ubiquitous human behavior that elicits selective responses contingent on historical forces and social order regimes" (Coyle and Schept 2017). Indeed, the local critical criminology from the 1970s and 1980s was oriented to contest hegemonic and punitive approaches from the North. Rosa del Olmo, Roberto Bergalli, Lola Aniyar de Castro, and Raul Zaffaroni were among the main representatives from this school. Particularly interesting is the Manifesto de Criminólogos Críticos (Critical Criminologists Manifesto) written and disseminated in Mexico in 1981 under the coordination of the Universidad de Zulia, where they state:

> The social realities in Latin-American, even if diverse, respond to a uniform logic that was dictated by the politics that divide the word between central and peripheric nations, even though the latter – including the Latin-American ones- have intrinsically not only the material possibilities, but also the individual capacities that could allow them to become an homogenous force to give value to the regional interests.
>
> *(quoted in Aniyar de Castro and Codino, 2013, p. 273)*

Particularly in relation to the carceral logic, they stated: "The criminal law has served as an instrument to deepen social differences and the criminal legal science has justified the official punitive intervention to aide minoritarian privileges" (p. 272). Finally, concerning the colonial logic that still perdures in the southern academic world, the Manifesto claims: "The legitimation of the unequal criminal law for Latin-America has been corroborated by the subaltern role that has been performed by the traditional criminology" (p. 272).

Currently, the most critical voices are more aligned to the so-called garantismo penal or derecho penal mínimo (Zaffaroni, 1988, 2011) which does not necessarily disagree with abolitionist claims. As Zaffaroni explains: "Abolitionism exposes to us that the punitive power is irrational because it does not sort out the conflicts … thus, it is not more than an instrument for social verticalization" (2012, p. viii). However, the particular feature of the *garantismo penal* is that it proposes that we must use the constitutional guarantees that the liberal criminal law offer to contain the punitive power. Following this logic, he adds that the *garantismo penal* should thank abolitionism for the grand challenge: never legitimate the punitive power (p. xiii). Most recent initiatives aligned with the abolitionist praxis were a ministerial program that introduced civil medical, psychological, and social care in prisons for people with mental health issues, uncoupling these services from correctional officers (Vegh Weis, 2015). Other recent experiments involve non-punitive approaches in cases of gender-based violence. These positions claim that if the feminist movement is trying to change the structural nature of violence and demand radical transformations, it cannot do so through punitive solutions that are only individually based, enhance violence and do not question or challenge the system as a whole (Arduino, 2017). Lastly, it is worth mentioning that the long struggle to decriminalize abortion and the personal use of cannabis, thus alleviating some the challenges faced by the most at-risk populations, is still underway in Argentina. Abortion is currently considered illegal according to the criminal code for both women and medical staff involved in the practice, but regularly occurring demonstrations have been applying pressure on the Parliament to legalize the procedure. With regard to cannabis, the Supreme Court issued a ruling which states that when consumption takes place within the private sphere, it falls outside the scope of criminal law while further efforts to legalize its consumption are in motion.

Overall, from a Southern perspective, contesting carceral logic demands the unearthing of the relationships between the carceral state, abolition, racial capitalism, settler colonialism, white supremacy, and patriarchy. This includes paying specific attention to the selective performance in terms of class, race, gender, and ethnicity that the criminal law and the criminalizing system perpetuate in addition to the imperialist power relations that continue to shape Latin-American criminal policy (Vegh Weis 2018, 2020b).

A case study of resistance from below: CTEP and SUPLA

Prior passages made it clear that a Southern perspective on criminology and resistance demands the acknowledgement of socio-economic characteristics that reign in this part of the globe, the unemployment rates, the extension of informal jobs, the state of emergency of the prison system, and also the epistemic imperialism that continues to obstruct the potentially enriching dialogs between the

North and the South. Furthermore, as in most parts of the world, the population targeted by social and criminal selectivity does not have a voice in the public arena (Scott, 2016). The particularity of the Argentinean situation is that not only imprisoned people are being silenced, but also half of the employed population who have precarious jobs and do not have the right to be unionized. Both phenomena are undeniably interrelated considering that after the degrading prison experience and the criminal records that come along with it, the best-case scenario for former prisoners is accessing these informal job opportunities that will still deny them a voice in the matter and limit their rights. In other words, the carceral logic continues even after prison, extending the effects of criminal selectivity to the outdoor space.

The same way that, from an abolitionist perspective, it is not possible to believe that solutions to social harms will come from the criminalizing system, it is not possible either to look for alternatives to post-carceral stigmatization and unemployment in the bureaucratic offices that are inserted in the carceral logic. Thus, the search for grassroots resistance options to deconstruct and build other possible paths resulted in the creation of the Central de Trabajadores de la Economía Popular (CTEP, i.e., the Center of Workers of the Popular Economy). CTEP is a national union made up of those workers who could not be part of the existing unions because they perform informal activities, which on a whole are referred to as the "popular economy". In the words of two leaders of the CTEP: "The popular economy is the economy of those excluded because it is the result of those activities that emerged from the inability of the labor market to offer dignifying and well-remunerated jobs" (Grabois and Pérsico, 2015). In short, CTEP – a union for the informal workers – was created as a way to allow them to raise their voices and work collectively.

At some point, it became clear that, within the challenging situation of the informal workers, there was a subset that was experiencing even more deteriorative situations: people in prison. This was the breaking point that allowed for the creation of the Sindicato Unido de Trabajadores Privados de la Libertad (SUPLA, i.e., United Union of Incarcerated Workers), the first union of incarcerated people in the country that has been functioning in the prison Complejo Penitenciario Federal de Devoto since 2012. Cristian Reyes, one of the founding members, recalls:

> The idea of creating a union came up one afternoon while we were sharing a "mate" [Argentinean tea] in the prison university center ... we realized that almost nobody was working, nobody was receiving a salary ... It was then that we decided to create a union and register it at the Ministry of Labour to expose that 1,700/1,800 incarcerated peers were demanding a job with a decent salary, as the Constitution promises, because if not it would be as if we were in slavery. At that moment, there were only 200 to 250 people working in prison, and those workers had been chosen arbitrarily by the prison officers.

Cristian also clarifies how these efforts have to be made *in spite of* the carceral system, where prison officers and the administration continuously attempt to discourage them:

> We need training and knowledge to be functional in society, we need diplomas, but most of the formerly incarcerated people lack that. The prison is a depository of poor people and the education system is as discretional and selective as prison.

Currently, SUPLA has 800 members and it is a legitimate actor that dialogs with the prison board and other institutions. Moreover, the union obtained jobs for almost all the incarcerated people in the prison. It put an end to informal employment, and it achieved the increase in assigned working hours to reach the 200 hours of employment that guarantee a minimum wage. However, none of these precious achievements diminish the ongoing conviction of the organization members to address the futility of prison as a tool for rehabilitation. Moreover, the socio-economic composition of the people behind bars (and, therefore, part of SUPLA) makes it clear that "the fact that criminalized and penalized individuals are characteristically poor and racialized or otherwise marginalized is interpreted as a performative contradiction of a system pretending to serve as a moral compass" (Mathiesen, 2006, pp. 55–65).

Besides the needs that come with imprisonment, there was another unresolved problem. What happens in the "outside" when former prisoners are released into the "free" world, but collateral consequences of punishment remain an obstacle when attempting to obtain a formal job and make a decent living? As previously mentioned, the same criminalizing system that destroys lives through carceral logic does not provide any remedy in life on the other side of the bars. People go back to the same broken socio-economic environment that they were living in before imprisonment, not to mention the same lack of support from the government. As Verónica Pelozo, wife of a former prisoner and co-founder of *Cooperativa Hombres y Mujeres Libres*, states: "The illusion for me, a person not familiarized with the carceral logic, was that after release everything was going to be okay and that we will manage, but no, it is super tough". Christian Escanes, who served time for 11 years, adds: "there is nothing for the former detainees at the point of thinking 'how rough freedom is!'". He continues:

> in most of the cases you are one person when you get into [the prison] but the person that gets out is a very different one, a more violent one, without opportunities and with the stigma that comes with the criminal record that cannot be erased for ten years.
>
> *(Canal Abierto, 2017)*

In the same vein, Brunela and Clara (2014) claim:

> Rehabilitation is the idea that the prisoners can improve their ties with society. The problem is that the strategy to achieve this is being behind bars, isolated … [afterward] the idea is that prisoners are rehabilitated and become ready to return to society. The curiosity is that this presupposes that people have not been part of society for a while, as if the prison were a hole in the earth. However, the prison is an institution that exists in our society …

Moreover, the parole board and welfare offices might offer some help on the basis of their individual inclinations and despite the lack of resources, but it takes them eight months to one year to handle a request. As Waicki, a former prisoner, clarifies:

> those are the most complicated months … months during which you have to eat, have a dignifying salary … because it is difficult to go back to freedom and have the will to buy things and not be able to do it because you get the worst possible jobs and you get paid almost nothing.

Waicki and many others learned first-hand how rehabilitation (does not) work in practice and that this is not a problem in the system, but actually how the system was designed to work.

Confronting this scenario and instead of pointlessly challenging this situation individually, the prisoners-centered organization Atrapamuros and other formerly incarcerated people decided to create cooperatives within the CTEP to look for job opportunities after release. In the beginning, four already formed cooperatives joined together: Los Topos formed in 2015 to work in the development of drinking water projects, including once financed by the United Nations and the National Secretariat of Habitat; Riff formed in 2014 to offer serigraphy and ironwork; Las Termitas which involves woodwork production; and the textile Cooperativa Hombres y Mujeres Libres created in 2013. Verónica Pelozo recalls about the creation of this cooperative:

> [My partner] told me "What am I going to do?" … there were no possibilities to receive labor training in the prison, so he suggested that I should do some job training paid with the money he was receiving for his work in prison to "hurry things up". Then, I did a serigraphy course and I bought a printer. The idea was that after release we could work with it … When we were out in 2013, someone gave him a sewing machine, that was everything in the first moment: an old machine.

With the growing number of formerly incarcerated people joining the CTEP, a special secretariat aimed at dealing with the specific needs of this group was created in 2017: the Secretaría de Ex Detenidos/as y Familiares (SEDyF, i.e., the Committee of Former Detainees and Relatives). The presentation of the Secretary claimed:

> To face the unfairness of the system that does not allow us, former detainees, to get a dignifying job and that leaves women in an even worse situation … we organize ourselves … and we build a solution based on the popular economy.
>
> *(CTEP, 2017)*

One of the founder members of the SEDyF remembers:

> The meetings started at the beginning of 2017 … we were a group with no clear ideas apart from sorting out problems, day after day … nobody before had organized the formerly incarcerated people in a union so we did not have prior recipes to learn from. We started to gather every other week, we register the cooperatives … We acknowledge that prisoners' problems do not have a good reception in society so we thought that before releasing the SEDyF we should go to radio and TV programs because we wanted to shout aloud that there would be no solution to the lack of security and stability if we could not ensure that the people released from prison have job opportunities and that the many laws already in existence do not protect them ….

Together they achieved several goals, particularly a resolution issued by the Instituto Nacional de Asociativismo y Economía Social (INAES, i.e., the National Institute of Associativism and Social Economy) that declares the governmental interest for the cooperatives and that stipulates advantages to create new cooperatives. The SEDyF also signed an agreement of cooperation with the Ministry of Justice to ensure that the job training in three prisons will be provided by the cooperative members. Overall, 400 people are currently working in the cooperatives.

Notably, these outcomes were not granted by a system aimed at perpetuating the exclusion of those who experienced imprisonment. On the contrary, they were achieved through the collective organization. As one of the Secretary members states: "These outcomes are the result of the struggle and the organization that we have been pursuing for years so that the state recognizes us and supports the people so that they do not go back to prison" (SEDyF, 2018). The demonstrations run by the Secretary to achieve these goals usually consist of "mobilization and productive exhibition" which means that they organize demonstrations where they expose the products they make to clarify that they do not want caritative help but rather recognition for their work. Moreover, for them, it is clear that "what we are doing should be done by the state", as Lupo, member of the cooperative Las Termitas, affirms. Also, José, another cooperative member, states:

> We are replacing the role of the state, yet what we are doing is invisible. When people go to the parole office, they are directed to "call the cooperatives" as if we have the resources or the funding to do their work; our work is all effort-based and it is even more effective than theirs.
>
> *SEDyF (2017)*

reiterates in the same logic:

> we are the ones who have been working on the topic of imprisonment and the systematic violation of human rights in our country; we are the ones who have been supporting our fellows that have been suffering from inequalities within the system and the first ones to suffer the economic adjustments made by the powerful ones; we are the ones that believe that we must debate what they are trying to cover. We believe that the only way to escape this system that excludes and imprisons is through collective organization within the popular economy.

As it becomes clear, the SEDyF is built on the conviction that prison is there to serve a social order where former prisoners are not welcomed. In Argentina's case, the state that promises certain guarantees is the same that violates these promises at every possible level. The only way out of this predicament is to move toward self-organization, which would force the state to provide the necessary public policy to minimize the harms produced by imprisonment. Aside from ensuring a basic income, the SEDyF has also made progress by serving as a space where people can confront another negative effect of imprisonment, isolation. They are a collective where people involved have the opportunity to raise their voices and start on a life path that doesn't lead back to prison, which is a very common outcome for former prisoners. Nacho, from the cooperative Los Topos, says:

> the system limits you in one way or the other. It tells you "do not learn, do not study, stay as you are", "if you are a 'negro'[1] from a popular neighborhood, a slum, a squatter settlement, stay at home". We are the ones that have to change this.

Lupo also highlights the collaborative approach that leads the activities in the cooperatives: "The demands are not individual anymore, we are not an isolated person confronting the system with a broken bottle to get something to eat, now we are together to think collective demands". Moreover, the joint claims surpass the issues strictly related to the cooperative work and involve the discussion of broader topics concerning the prison system and the collateral consequences of punishment. Through these discussions, the members make their first steps as activists: "We became political actors, we are not alone in a cell anymore, because we transcended the prison walls in the idea of changing something", Lupo says. They fought the deteriorative and isolating effects of prison by politically understanding their experience, the functioning of the criminalizing system and its selective clients, and what they had to confront once outside prison. Noemí Santana, member of the SEDyF, President of the textile cooperative Hope and mother of one child that was killed by the police and another one who is serving a nine-year-long sentence, explains: "We try not to allow the pain to immerse us in hate, but to instead use that pain to build new things via organization and via the life experience of each member of the SEDyF" (Canal Abierto, 2017). For example, the person of the SEDyF who was in charge of mothers with children that were confined to house arrest was extremely concerned about the situation of these women. Then, another member of the SEDyF suggested that it might be good to go to the houses to provide some food to these women. This was an innovative approach that helped the person in charge and also helped the detainees, many of whom had never been visited before. Moreover, the existence of the Secretary encourages its members to acknowledge that they too can take part in the security debates that tend to rely on imprisonment as the only possible solution, instead of promoting non-punitive inclusive public policy. Lupo says:

> when the lack of security and stability once again becomes a topic in mainstream media, we have a lot to say … We do not hide the identity of former prisoners: we say that we have been in jail and that we have to create our own jobs in order to make a living since there is a severe lack of public policies.

All the efforts made by SEDyF still carry endless challenges. The work of the cooperatives is unstable, compensation is low and there are even legal obstacles. One of those obstacles is that, according to the statute that regulates cooperatives, it is not possible to be a member of the council if you have been convicted of any crime. The legal regime that states that prison serves as place for rehabilitation is also the creator of obstacles that impact even the self-organized labor opportunities available to people who have experienced confinement. Luis Magallanes, a member of Los Topos, says: "This is one of the many restrictions that we have to face when we try to get a dignifying job". The SEDyF prepared a bill to change this norm but it could not make into the Senate. The struggle continues and overcoming these challenges will necessarily encompass getting out of the carceral logic.

Conclusion

The chapter exposes the importance of contesting carceral logic from below and engaging in emancipatory politics and praxis within the specificities of the southern socio-economic context. To do so, the study dealt with the particularities of the unfair resource distribution in Argentina and how this affects the situation of formerly incarcerated people looking for employment opportunities. The study dives into the work of several cooperatives that are run by people who have served time in prison and that function within the CTEP – a national union of informally employed workers. The self-managed cooperatives appear as an emancipatory experience that can help to develop a counter-carceral logic for the period after release, when people are in the most precarious situation (of vulnerability). In the same way that the criminalizing system has been proven broken by abolitionist critiques, the carceral logic for the post-imprisonment period is not working either (at least for the purpose of rehabilitation that it claims to pursue). Learning how to behave in a free world while being behind bars is the correlate of trying to be re-inserted into society with criminal records tied to your name, playing the role of an invisible weight burdening every aspect of an already complicated existence. The carceral logic leaves people stigmatized and mostly alone in a society that, on the basis of mainstream media and government of crime, believes that they are the porters of the worst existing social harms.

Confronting this situation, the case study illustrated how organization was the path chosen by those who have experienced prison to overcome individual strategies through a collective agenda aimed at challenging the obstacles of post-imprisonment. Moreover, the study highlighted how the collective organization does not only ensure a decent income, but also fosters a collective identity that reduces the collateral damage of confinement and prevents further criminalization. Police and other authorities would continue to hunt these previously convicted persons, but now these individuals have a collective to refer to and the political understanding about how the criminalizing system works: not in their favor. In short, and as the leitmotiv of the SEDyF claims, "through the collective organization, we will never go back to prison!".

Note

1 In Argentina, the term "negro" does not necessarily refer to a person of African descent. Indeed, the Black-Argentinean population is scarce. Instead, the term *negro* refers to people from disadvantaged neighborhoods and low socio-economic status with often darker skin and hair who tend to be discriminated when seeking jobs or inclusion in mainstream social spaces, over-policed and over-criminalized.

References

Aniyar de Castro, L. and Codino, R. (2013) *Manual de Criminología Sociopolítica*, Buenos Aires, Ediar.

Arduino, I. (2017) 'A 'A Cordera ni probation, a las mujeres ni justicia', *Cosecha Roja*, 8 November [Online]. Available at http://cosecharoja.org/cordera-ni-probation-las-mujeres-ni-justicia/ (accessed 24 March 2020).

Bosworth, M. and Hoyle, C. (2011) *What Is Criminology?* New York, Oxford University Press.

Brown, M.and Schept, J. (2017) 'New abolition, criminology and a critical carceral studies', *Punishment and Society*, vol. 19, no. 4, pp. 440–462.

Brunela and Clara (2014) 'Sin gorra ni cachiporra: Repensando el rol de la cárcel en la sociedad. Reflexiones sobre las ideas de resocialización y reinserción', *Viento Colectivo Cultural,* 1 May [Online]. Available at https://otroviento.blogspot.com/2013/11/sin-gorra-ni-cachiporra-repensando-el.html (accessed 24 March 2020).

Canal Abierto (2017) 'Ex detenidos y familiares militantes por una libertad digna', 6 November [Online]. Available at: https://canalabierto.com.ar/2017/11/06/ex-detenidos-y-familiares-militantes-por-una-libertad-digna/ (accessed 24 March 2020).

Carrington, K., Hogg, R. and Sozzo, M. (2018) 'Criminología del Sur', *Delito y Sociedad*, vol. 27, pp. 9–33.

CELS (2019) 'Segundo censo popular de personas en situación de calle en la CABA', 11 July [Online] Available at https://www.cels.org.ar/web/2019/07/segundo-censo-popular-de-personas-en-situacion-de-calle-en-la-caba/ (accessed 24 March 2020).

Comité de Derechos Económicos, Sociales y Culturales de las Naciones Unidas (2018) 'Observaciones finales sobre el cuarto informe periódico de Argentina', E/C.12/ARG/CO/4, Oct. 12.

Coyle, M. J. and Schept, J. (2017) 'Penal abolition and the state: Colonial, racial and gender violences', *Contemporary Justice Review. Issues in Criminal, Social, and Restorative Justice*, vol. 20, no. 4, pp. 399–403.

CTEP (2017), 'La CTEP lanza su secretaria de ex- detenidos/as y familiares', June 13 [Online] Available at http://ctepargentina.org/la-ctep-lanza-secretaria-ex-detenidosas-familiares/ (accessed 24 March 2020).

Faraldo-Cabana, P. (2018) 'Research excellence and anglophone dominance: The case of law, criminology and social science', in Carrington, K., Hogg, R. Scott J. and Sozzo, M. (eds.), *The Palgrave Handbook of Criminology and the Global South*, London, Palgrave, pp. 163–182.

Grabois J. and Pérsico, E. (2015.) *Trabajo y Organización de la Economía Popular*, Buenos Aires, CTEP – Asociación Civil de los Trabajadores de la Economía Popular.

Härter, K. and Vegh Weis, V. (2018) Transnationales Strafrecht in transatlantischer Perspektive (1870–1945). Ein Dialog zwischen dem globalen Norden und dem globalen Süden, *Max Planck Institute for Europan Legal History* [Online] Available at https://www.rg.mpg.de/forschung/transnational-criminal-law-in-transatlantic-perspective (accessed 24 March 2020).

INDEC (2019) 'Incidencia de la pobreza y la indigencia en 31 aglomerados urbanos Segundo semestre de 2018', *INDEC*, vol. 3, no. 59, pp. 1–16.

Kushel, M. and Hahn, J., Evans, J., Bangsberg, D. and Moss, A. (2005) 'Revolving doors: Imprisonment among the homeless and marginally housed population', *American Journal of Public Health*, vol. 95, pp. 1747–1752.

Mathiesen, T. (2006) *Prison on Trial*, Winchester, Waterside Press.

Metraux, S. and Culhane, D. (2004) 'Homeless shelter use and reincarceration following prison release', *Criminology & Public Policy*, vol. 3, no. 2, pp. 139–160.

Mignolo, W. (2017) 'Interview', *E-International Relations*, 21 January [Online] Available at https://www.e-ir.info/2017/01/21/interview-walter-mignolopart-2-key-concepts/ (accessed 24 March 2020).

PPN (2019) 'Emergencia carcelaria', 5 April [Online] Available at https://www.ppn.gov.ar/institucional/noticias/2167-emergencia-carcelaria (accessed 24 March 2020).

Rusche, G. and Kirchheimer, O. (2009) *Punishment and Social Structure*, New Brunswick-London, Transaction Publishers.

Saleh-Hanna, V. (2008) 'Penal abolitionist theories and ideologies. In *Colonial Systems of Control: Criminal Justice in Nigeria*, Ottawa, Ontario, University of Ottawa Press, pp. 417–456. https://muse.jhu.edu/book/4441

Scott, D. (2016) 'Hearing the voice of the Estranged other: Abolitionist ethical hermeneutics', *Kriminologisches Journal*, August. pp. 184–201.

SEDyF (2017) 'Nuestra Salida en Construcción' [Online] Available at https://eltermometroweb.com/2017/05/29/nuestra-salida-construccion-campana-la-reincidencia/ and https://notasperiodismopopular.com.ar/2017/06/01/nuestra-salida-construccion-campana-dificultades-salir-carcel/ (accessed 24 March 2020).

SEDyF (2018) 'Logramos el reconocimiento de las cooperativas de liberados', 6 February

SNEEP (2017), SNEEP 2017 [Online] Available at https://www.argentina.gob.ar/justicia/afianzar/sneep2017 (accessed 24 March 2020).

UCA (2019) 'Documento de trabajo heterogeneidad y fragmentación del mercado de trabajo (2010–2018)', Apr.

Vegh Weis, V. (2015) 'Salud y cárcel: el derecho a la salud en ámbitos de encierro', *Revista Institucional de la Defensa Pública de la Ciudad Autónoma de Buenos Aires*, vol. 5, no. 7 pp. 57–94.

Vegh Weis, V. (2018) *Marxism and Criminology: A History of Criminal Selectivity*, London, Haymarket Books.

Vegh Weis, V. (2020a) 'It is time! Towards a southern convict criminology', in Ross, J, Ian and Vianllo, F. (eds.) *The Future of Convict Criminology*, London: Routledge.

Vegh Weis, V. (2020b) 'Policing in times of global governace. The counter-terrorism law as a platform for the suppression of native-Argentineans' social protest by the Gendarmerie', in Klára, K and Nagy, V. (eds.), *New Perspectives in Post-transitional Policing Studies*, Neatherlands, Eleven.

Zaffaroni, R. (1988) *Criminología. Aproximación desde un margen*, Bogotá, Temis.

Zaffaroni, R. (2011) *Las palabras de los muertos*, Buenos Aires, Ediar.

Zaffaroni, R. (2012) *El abolicionismo penal en América Latina Imaginación no punitiva y militancia*, Buenos Aires, Editores del Puerto.

23

LAND, RACE AND STATE

Situating the carceral state and the mass imprisonment of Māori in Aotearoa within the settler-colonial landscape

Verena Tan

On Friday 20 April 2018, Julia Whaipooti, a Māori Ngāti Porou lawyer, addressed the United Nations Permanent Forum for Indigenous Issues about the proposed "mega-prison" to be built in Waikeria, Waikato, Aotearoa (New Zealand). The facility was planned to be three times larger than any prison in New Zealand, housing 3000 prison beds, compared to the current capacity of 806 beds. Calling out the systemic racism within the justice system and mass incarceration of Māori, Whaipooti (2018) stated:

[S]tatistics show that at least half the prison will be filled with Māori ... The prison is also on confiscated Māori land, land that was taken from Māori under the Public Works Act for the benefit of the public. We see no benefit in land being taken for us to build institutions that harm us ... The burden of imprisonment is carried disproportionately by Māori, we are 15% of New Zealand's population, but we make up over 50% of our male prison population, 60% of our female population and 70% of our youth justice facilities.

In recent years, settler societies such as the United States, Canada, Australia and New Zealand are incarcerating Indigenous populations at an increasingly rapid pace (see Chartrand, 2018). Relocation, containment and isolation are techniques used by settler colonial states against Indigenous populations to remove them from land and diminish resistance against the exercise of state sovereignty and colonial exploitation of resources (Coulthard, 2014; Estes, 2016). Whaipooti's statement speaks directly to the ongoing oppression of Māori people in Aotearoa through settler colonialism and the continued removal of Māori from land by settler governments. Since the signing of the Treaty of Waitangi, also known as *Te Tiriti o Waitangi*, Māori have had their *Tino Rangatiratanga* (sovereignty and self-determination) diminished and usurped by the *Pākehā* (settler) government. The government has stolen land, disrupted *iwi* (people, nation) and infringed upon and destroyed the ability of *iwi* to care for the health and well-being of its people.

This chapter examines how the prison industrial complex and the carceral state are embedded within settler colonialism, heteropatriarchy and global imperialism's ongoing project of colonial expansion. Rather than isolating the prison industrial complex as a product of carceral logic born from the state, this chapter explores how settler colonial and heteropatriarchal logics established and maintain the settler state, thus providing the framework and structure for mass incarceration and prison expansion. Throughout the chapter, I examine how settler colonial aims, such as land usurpation and resource extraction, are achieved through the incarceration of Indigenous peoples as part of a broader project of colonialism and global imperialism.

This chapter first provides a definition of settler colonialism and discusses how, as a framework for examining the carceral state, settler colonialism intersects with racial capitalism. The chapter then establishes how the prison industrial complex relies on the increased criminalisation and disposability of marginalised populations in order to justify its expansion and deny the systemic and institutionalised racism upon which it is founded. I assert, throughout the chapter, that tough on crime policies are neoliberal strategies that are used to justify, contain and dispose of populations that the state has largely marginalised and abandoned. Arguing that the prison industrial complex is founded upon principles of containment, relocation and imperial expansion, I propose that its development and ongoing existence relies on the continuing dispossession of Indigenous peoples. To explain, I focus on Māori in Aotearoa, New Zealand, and demonstrate how the prison industrial complex functions in New Zealand to dispossess Māori populations from their land and incarcerate them at significantly higher rates than their non-Indigenous counterparts.

By establishing a framework of settler-colonialism that has historically focussed on eliminating Indigenous peoples through direct genocidal techniques, this chapter demonstrates how, in contemporary times, settler colonialism continues to operate through carceral logic to regulate, contain, and eliminate Indigenous peoples. Identifying Indigenous women as the fastest rising prison population, this chapter highlights the gendered nature of mass incarceration and the heteropatriarchal drive of the settler state. It explores how the separation of Indigenous women from their families and communities is an intervention of the settler state to diminish the political role of Indigenous women as leaders and life givers. By understanding the way that the carceral state is structured through settler colonialism, heteropatriarchy and global imperialism, this chapter aims to contribute to the development of abolitionist alternatives that respond to settler colonial logics and challenge not only the carceral state, but ongoing Indigenous regulation/elimination and land dispossession.

Land, race and the state

Settler colonialism has always relied on racial regimes to produce and maintain the settler state (Wolfe, 2006, p. 387). The colonial nation building project required, and continues to require, Indigenous land and racialised labour forces in order to produce capital and secure settler supremacy. Indeed, Glen Coulthard argues that settler colonialism "is not a 'thing', but rather the sum effect of the diversity of interlocking oppressive social relations that constitute it" (2014, p. 15). Its effects occur "*in relation to or in concert with* axes of exploitation and domination configured along racial, gender and state lines" (Coulthard, 2014, p. 14). Similarly, Clarno explains that settler colonialism operates through racial projects to dehumanise the "native" population, justify legal dispossession and form racialised hierarchies (2017, p. 5).

At the heart of settler colonialism is "land, race and the state" (Clarno, 2017, p. 5). The state itself requires the racialisation and the subsequent categorisation and exploitation of Indigenous peoples and the labour of Black and racialised people. For example, the Doctrine of Discovery – an international law principle put forward by Spain, Portugal and England in the 15th century – hierarchically organised people based on perceived race, religion and "civility" (Miller et al., 2010; Reid, 2010). The Doctrine, which deemed Indigenous land *terra nullius* (land that is legally deemed to be unoccupied or uninhabited), racialised Indigenous peoples and categorised them as lawless, inferior, savage and in need of "salvation". This colonial logic was used to justify colonisation and the usurpation of Indigenous land (Lindberg, 2010, pp. 92–93). Settler states then relied upon exploited labour through Black enslavement and racialised indentured servants to "develop" and privatise the land for settlement.

Through a myriad of processes that dispossess Indigenous peoples of their land, including exploitation, abandonment by the state and genocide, settler colonialism works alongside the capitalist strategy of marginalisation to stratify class along racial lines. Put a different way, through settler colonialism, land is taken from Indigenous populations for settlement and resource extraction, while the development and deployment of racial capitalism functions to exploit racialised labour in service of resource extraction and colonial expansion. Both logics work together to develop the nation, provide capital reward for the settler state and provide resources for the white capitalist elite. The logics of settler colonialism and racial capitalism create(d) the conditions that enable(d) a settler state, and a thriving prison industrial complex, to be built on stolen Indigenous land.

As the Waikeria Prison illustrates, the land that prisons are built on is stolen Indigenous land, either taken through force during colonial settlement or by continuing dispossession through legal processes of the settler state. The Waikeria Prison, established in 1911, is currently situated on land of Raukawa *iwi* (people or nation), that was confiscated under the Public Works Act 1981 in the early 20th century, for the purposes of a reformatory farm (Eparaima, 2017). The prison is located within the Wharepūhunga rohe, a region of cultural and ancestral significance to the Raukawa people, and there are number of sites of cultural significance located within land (Eparaima, 2017). In the area are four Raukawa *Marae* (sacred meeting sites), three of which are within 6 km of the prison. The state is only able to propose an expanded mega-prison because land was taken from the Indigenous people in the area, the Raukawa *iwi*, and the people forced from the land are then housed within the facility through the expanding Māori prison population.

Disposable populations

While denying the systemic and institutionalised racism upon which it is founded, the prison industrial complex relies on the increased criminalisation of particular populations in order to justify its expansion. The political justification for prison expansion is often proposed, paradoxically, as a result of the "need" to manage the exponential increase in incarcerated people. For example, from November 1999 to March 2019, the prison population in New Zealand increased from 2647 to 10645, increasing the rate of incarceration from 135 people per 100,000 to 214 per 100,000 (Department of Corrections NZ, 1999; Department of Corrections NZ, 2018). During that time, Māori have consistently constituted approximately 50.0% of the prison population (Department of Corrections NZ, 1999; Department of Corrections NZ, 2018). It is this increase in the prison population that was the main justification for the expansion of the Waikeria Prison.

People who are criminalised and detained in prisons are often barred from access to other life pathways and neglected and excluded by the state (Meiners, 2015, p. 122). Populations previously used by the capitalist state for labour are subsequently labelled as disposable, in need of management and available for incarceration. This idea is rooted in the neoliberal principle of "free market fundamentalism", which relies on the increase of privatised services and the deterioration and disappearance of social welfare initiatives. Free market fundamentalism increases wealth disparities and marginalises populations, making them susceptible to poverty and rendering them as surplus and disposable (Clarno, 2017, p. 11; Giroux, 2009, p. 5, Kelley, 2000). When social welfare services are cut and/or under-resourced, individuals are burdened with the sole responsibility for their economic and social situation. The responsibility for social inequality is then deflected away from the state and displaced onto the people and populations from which the state extracts land and labour. Indeed, market fundamentalism, as a product of the neoliberal extension of racial capitalism, operates on distinctly racial lines and leads to the disposability and social death of populations of racialised poor around the world (Giroux, 2009, p. 24). Coupled with the ongoing settler colonial logic to "eliminate the native", the carceral state creates vast populations of racialised and Indigenous peoples at its disposal to target for criminalisation.

This "organised abandonment", which has been well documented by prison abolitionist Ruth Gilmore, is achieved through economic impoverishment and systemic discrimination that justifies an increased securitisation against these surplus populations (Gilmore, 2007, p. 178; Maynard, 2017, pp. 71–2). Neo-liberal strategies of governance have led to the decrease in state responsibility for social welfare and social outcomes, placing the responsibility and blame onto individuals for their poverty, criminalisation and disadvantage (Gilmore, 2007, p. 7).

As responsibility for criminalised behaviours becomes pinned on individual and community failure, rather than on the colonial processes that develop and maintain the state, these marginalised and expendable populations are then policed with impunity (Brown and Bloom, 2009, pp. 152–3). Indigenous, Black and racialised communities that live in poverty become blamed for their life conditions and their criminalisation becomes a natural extension of their suffering. When their labour and presence on the land is no longer necessary or economically beneficial to the state and the nation building process, then their elimination and disposal through incarceration and privatised prisons become a profitable venture.

In New Zealand, when the Treaty of Waitangi was signed in 1840, Māori believed it would protect and respect *Tino Rangatiritanga*, which loosely translates to sovereignty or self-determination (Hitchcock, 2018). Māori believed that the autonomy they had in relation to their land, resources and life would remain intact. However, continual breaches of the treaty through theft, land confiscation and the transferal of resources to settlers and the Crown resulted in long-term economic destruction for Māori (Te Puni Kōkiri, 2007, p. 9; Hitchcock, 2018). This economic marginalisation and exclusion through land dispossession has directly translated into the current economic framework through which the criminalisation of these populations operates. Paralleling the overrepresentation of Māori in prisons, Māori have the highest unemployment rate at 10.8%, compared to the rest of the country at 4.9% (Ministry of Business, Innovation & Employment, 2017). In other words, Māori represent approximately 16.5% of the New Zealand population, yet they represent 28.5% of the unemployed in New Zealand (New Zealand Government, 2017). In particular, Māori youth have an unemployment rate of 20.4%, and almost a third of Māori youth are not currently practising employment, training or education (New Zealand Government, 2017). At the same time, Māori youth come into contact with the justice system at a rate of 225 per 100,000, compared to a rate of 32 per 100,000 for European New Zealanders (Ministry of Justice, 2019; New Zealand Government, 2017). Exclusion from employment and participation in the economy is a significant way that Māori are pushed into conditions that lead to their criminalisation and being labelled surplus and disposable.

There is money in prisons

The political and economic benefits of prison expansion have been widely acknowledged by prison abolition activists and scholars (Goldberg and Evans, 1998; Davis, 2000). These activists and scholars explore how political investments in the privatisation of prisons and the exploitation of prison labour are connected to increased profits for private multinational companies and government budgets (Goldberg and Evans, 1998, pp. 6–7). These connections show how tough on crime policies work to expand the prison industrial complex at the expense of racialised and marginalised people (see Davis, 2003; Gilmore, 2007; Alexander, 2012). Within the United States and Canada, certain sentencing rules, such as mandatory minimums, rapidly populate prisons and increase the demand for more institutions (Gilmore, 2007, p. 108; Thibault, 2016, p. 13). Similar policies in New Zealand and Australia, including the three strikes rule and restrictions on bail and parole, have resulted in a paralleled prison expansion throughout settler states (Lamusse et al., 2016, pp. 38–44; Whaipooti, 2018). Following the Global Financial Crisis, prison facilities became marketed as providing economic stimulation for communities and state investment in prisons revealed the increasing anxiety over economic threats and market collapse (Thibault, 2016, p. 48; Meiners, 2015, p. 120).

As demonstrated in the public support for the Waikeria Prison, prisons are marketed as creating jobs and social services for the community in New Zealand (Gilmore, 2007, p. 22; Lines-Mackenzie, 2018). The proposed expansion is a public-private partnership project and the successful contractor, Pacific Partnerships, stated that the build would be "boosting employment and business opportunities to the benefit of communities, our clients and the industry" (Pacific Partnerships, 2018). The town of Otorohanga in the surrounding Waikato region has been supportive of the build as it has been marketed to increase prison jobs for the community, including the building of housing and medical facilities for the town (Fox, 2017; Lines-Mackenzie, 2018). Rather than the state providing adequate housing, healthcare and employment support for the community, the government is choosing to build a prison and promote it as a means for the communities around it to access the aforementioned services. Once established, this mega-prison will become reliant on the continual production of disposable populations.

When closely examining the demand for prisons, what becomes clear is that this increase in privatised prison investment and increased securitisation of certain populations are not a result of increased criminal behaviour. Rather, the expanding prison industrial complex is a natural consequence of neoliberal strategies that marginalise and abandon populations, justifying their containment and disposal. Specifically, in settler states, prison expansion and privatisation continue to enable and justify the removal of Indigenous life from land.

Containment, relocation and imperial expansion

While the expansion of prisons and the increased dominance of a carceral regime is only a recent phenomenon, incarceration practices and criminalisation of populations has been occurring for many decades through racialised regimes and settler colonial logic. In the infamous attack on the settlement of Parihaka in 1881, the New Zealand government sent 1600 Armed Constables to use military force to remove and imprison Māori into penal slavery (Scott, 1975; People Against Prisons Aotearoa, 2017). The Māori living at Parihaka were asserting Māori land ownership in peaceful resistance to the colonial confiscation of their land across Aotearoa. In a clear continuation of colonial dispossession and carceral logic, the Armed Constabulary responsible for the mass incarceration at Parihaka were converted into the New Zealand Police in 1886, where they continue to this day to imprison Māori on mass (People Against Prisons Aotearoa, 2017).

The settler state has historically used criminalisation of Indigenous life as a tactic to control and eliminate threats to its sovereignty, such as the criminalisation of Indigenous populations and their cultural practices during the 19th and 20th centuries (Brown and Bloom, 2009, p. 153). For example, the removal of Indigenous children into residential schools, missions, boarding schools and other facilities during the 20th century was a state-driven move in New Zealand, Australia, Canada and the United States (Bringing Them Home, 1997; Giago, 2006; Truth and Reconciliation Commission, 2015). The removal and forced assimilation of Indigenous children was a tactic informed by carceral logic to facilitate the separation, relocation and containment of Indigenous children from their families and land.

In New Zealand, the forced assimilation of Māori through education first began through schools established by Anglican Missionaries, but soon progressed into official government policy that subsidised church boarding schools in order to assimilate Māori children as quickly as possible. Under the *Native Schools Act 1858*, the government set up a regime for "civilising the natives and pacifying the country", as well as creating Māori as a labouring underclass to serve settler interests (Walker, 2016, pp. 23–24). The prohibition and punishment of Māori culture and language was a key precursor to the punitive and carceral logic that guides how the state has evolved to incarcerate Māori in order to suppress Māori life.

Heteropatriarchy and the incarceration of Indigenous women

Indigenous women are one of, if not *the* fastest growing population within prison systems in New Zealand, Australia and Canada. Similar to the stealing and assimilation of Indigenous children, the exponential incarceration of Indigenous women is a clear example of the inherently heteropatriarchal nature of settler colonialism. The carceral regimes that disrupt and harm the connections that Indigenous children have with their families are also at use in the increased surveillance and state control over Indigenous women. Māori women are known as *te whare tangata* (the house of humanity), who play a vital role in their communities by providing life and taking care of the younger generations (Higgins and Meredith, 2011). By incarcerating Māori women, the settler state is actively severing the ties between communities and their future generations. Indeed, the incarceration of Māori women is intimately tied with settler colonial aims to assimilate Indigenous children and suppress Māori life.

The particular idea of motherhood upon which Indigenous women (and all racialised women) are judged, is constructed upon Western neoliberal values. This framework erases how the structure of the settler state relies on a white supremacist hierarchy and actively pushes Indigenous and racialised communities into poverty by removing social supports and entrenching intergenerational poverty. For example, state-regulated services, such as parole and child welfare have powers of policing and regulating the lives of Indigenous women through drug testing and the increased privatisation of testing equipment and services (Brown & Bloom, 2009, p. 162). The result is intensified scrutiny and criminalisation of Indigenous and racialised mothers that often results in incarceration, for "[t]he threat of loss of parental rights and the possibility of criminal charges have emerged as increasingly salient modes of state control in the lives of poor women" (Brown and Bloom, 2009, p. 162). Given that 60% of Māori in prison report having children, and Māori women represent 60% of incarcerated women in New Zealand, a significant proportion of Māori mothers are separated from their children due to incarceration (Te Puni Kōkiri, 2011, pp. 12, 16). The increased criminalisation and incarceration of Indigenous women in New Zealand and across the world demonstrate how the prison is an effective tool of the state to separate Indigenous children from their primary source of life and disrupt community connection and cohesion.

Ultimately, the way that the carceral regime operates upon the lives of Indigenous women reveals that race, gender and class intersect within a political economy that facilitates settler colonialism and its goal to eliminate Indigenous populations. Colonial tactics such as the relocation, containment and isolation of Indigenous children are used by settler states against Indigenous populations to disrupt family structures in the interest of ongoing land dispossession (Coulthard, 2014; Estes, 2016). The number of incarcerated Indigenous women in Canada has increased by 97% within ten years (Correctional Service Canada, 2014), 148% since 1991 in Australia (Walters and Longhurst, 2017) and 56% in just five years in New Zealand (Walters, 2018). The separation of Indigenous women from their communities, families and particularly children, parallels ongoing settler state interventions to diminish the political role of Indigenous women as well as their importance as reproducers of Indigenous life and survival (see Lumsden, 2016; Simpson, 2016). However, even outside the prison structure, Indigenous women are subject to intense surveillance and policing that effectively results in their captivity and elimination. Settler colonialism has not ceased but continues to act in concert with neoliberal tactics of containment, isolation and relocation to make way for capitalist expansion upon racial lines.

Conclusion

> It would be impossible to decolonise Aotearoa without abolishing prisons, but it would also be impossible to abolish prisons without decolonising Aotearoa.
>
> *(Lamusse et al., 2016, p. 34)*

In New Zealand, an abolitionist future must, first, reverse the elimination of Māori *tino rangatiratanga* (sovereignty and self-determination) and reinstate Māori systems that place decision-making and power back into the hands of *iwi* (people or nation). The abolitionist group No Pride in Prisons in New Zealand centralises decolonising Aotearoa and the fulfilment of *tino rangatiratanga* within their abolitionist demands (Lamusse et al., 2016, p. 10). Among their demands, they call for the reinstatement of *Tikanga Māori*, the first legal systems of Aotearoa, which prioritises relationships and kinship (Lamusse, et al., 2016, p. 35). *Tikanga*

Māori is fundamentally opposed to colonial legal systems that exert violence and harm onto Māori through the suppression and usurpation of *tino rangatiratanga*.

In countries like New Zealand, Australia, Canada and the United States, the colonising population continues to dominate the land and population through the creation of the settler state. These countries are not "post-colonial", as settler populations continue their attempts to exert control over land, governance and Indigenous populations. While the debate about the proposed Waikeria "mega-prison" in New Zealand appears to be a local issue of domestic politics, Whaipooti's recent address to the UN Forum reminds us that prison expansion, while occurring at a local level, is an inherently global phenomenon. The prison industrial complex assists and enables ongoing settler colonialism, as well as global expansion through the cultivation of capital, tactics of securitisation and militarisation, as well as the incarceration of bodies across borders. As mentioned, land, race and the state are all central to the expansion of the prison and its economic implications. Enabled by the acquisition of Indigenous land through state laws, and the demand for prison beds through the criminalisation and economic disposal of Māori, the prison acts as a political and economic strategy in New Zealand to reinforce the state and its expanding corporate interests. By abandoning Māori populations and leaving them as surplus and disposal and open to criminalisation, the prison industrial complex and its accompanying carceral logic offer an understanding of how settler states like New Zealand continue to dispossess and eliminate Indigenous populations through increased surveillance and containment.

It is essential to understand that the recent phenomenon of the prison industrial complex and carceral expansion is not new, but a reinvigorated manifestation of the racist, class-based and gendered regime that enabled settler state formation and the ongoing dispossession and elimination of Indigenous and other marginalised populations. These logics continue to act to expand state power and control, which is enhanced through a political climate of criminal sanctions and privatisation. Developing alongside one another, racial capitalism and settler colonialism function to usurp Indigenous land, abandon populations and increase securitisation in order to uphold bourgeois populations and white settler economic domination. These logics provide the conditions, not only for prison expansion but also for imperial expansion and the increasing militarisation against both local and international threats. Only once we understand the complex intersecting logics that enable local prison expansion that target Indigenous populations, particularly Indigenous women, can we begin to examine how we might respond to the prison industrial complex through a decolonial framework.

References

Alexander, M. (2012) *The New Jim Crow: Mass Incarceration in the Age of Colourblindness*, revised edition, New York, The New Press.

Brown, M. and Bloom, B. (2009) 'Colonialism and carceral motherhood', *Feminist Criminology*, vol 4, no. 2 pp. 151–169.

Chartrand, V. (2018) 'Broken system: Why is a quarter of Canada's prison population Indigenous?' *The Conversation* [Online]. Available at https://theconversation.com/broken-system-why-is-a-quarter-of-canadas-prison-population-indigenous-91562 (Accessed 16 July 2019).

Clarno, A. (2017) 'Introduction chapter: Racial capitalism and settler colonialism', in Clarno, A. (ed) *Neoliberal Apartheid: Palestine/Israel and South Africa after 1994.* Chicago: University of Chicago Press, pp. 1–23.

Commonwealth of Australia Human Rights and Equal Opportunity Commission. (1997) *Bringing Them Home, Report of the National Inquiry into the Separation of Aboriginal and Torres Strait Islander Children from Their Families* [Online]. Available at https://www.humanrights.gov.au/sites/default/files/content/pdf/social_justice/bringing_them_home_report.pdf. (Accessed 29 July 2019).

Correctional Service Canada. (2014) *Research Results – Aboriginal Offenders* [Online]. Available at https://www.csc-scc.gc.ca/publications/005007-3027-eng.shtml (Accessed 16 July 2019).

Coulthard, G. (2014) *Red Skin, White Masks: Rejecting the Colonial Politics of Recognition,* Minneapolis, University of Minnesota Press.

Davis, A. (2000) 'Critical resistance to the prison industrial complex', *Special Edition, Social Justice*, vol 27, no. 3, pp. 1–5.

Davis, A. (2003) *Are Prisons Obsolete?* Toronto, Publishers Group Canada.

Department of Corrections NZ. (1999) *Census of Prison Inmates* [Online]. Available at https://www.corrections.govt.nz/__data/assets/pdf_file/0011/667730/censusfulldoc.pdf (Accessed 16 July 2019).

Department of Corrections NZ. (2018) *Prison Statistics* [Online], Available at https://www.corrections.govt.nz/resources/research_and_statistics/quarterly_prison_statistics.html (Accessed 16 July 2019).

Eparaima, V. (2017) *Proposed Alteration to Designation for Waikeria Prison: Planning Report under Section 198D of the Resource Management Act 1991* [Online]. Available at https://www.otodc.govt.nz/assets/Uploads/Notified-Applications/Wakeria-Prison-Expansion/FINAL-Waikeria-s198D-Report-30-June-2017-.pdf (Accessed 16 July 2019).

Estes, N. (2016) 'Fighting for our lives: #NoDAPL in historical context', *The Red Nation* [Online]. Available at https://therednation.org/2016/09/18/fighting-for-our-lives-nodapl-in-context/ (Accessed 16 July 2019).

Fox, A. (2017) 'Prison extension would be massive for Waikato', *Waikato Business News*, 2 November 2017 [Online]. Available at http://wbn.co.nz/2017/11/02/prison-extension-massive-waikato/ (Accessed 1 November 2018).

Giago, Tim A. (2006) *Children Left Behind: Dark Legacy of Indian Mission Boarding Schools,* Santa Fe, New Mexico, Clear Light Pub.

Gilmore, R.W. (2007) *Golden Gulag: Prisons, Surplus, Crisis, and Opposition in Globalizing California*, Berkeley, University of California Press.

Giroux, H. A. (2009) *Youth in a Suspect Society: Democracy or Disposability?* New York, Palgrave Macmillan.

Goldberg, E. and Evans, L. (1998) *The Prison Industrial Complex and the Global Economy,* Berkeley, Agit Press.

Higgins, R. and Meredith, P. (2011) 'Te mana o te wāhine – Māori women', *Te Ara – the Encyclopedia of New Zealand.* Available at: http://www.TeAra.govt.nz/en/te-mana-o-te-wahine-maori-women/print (Accessed 13 March 2020)

Hitchcock, J. (2018) 'The Treaty of Waitangi granted us tino rangatiratanga – but what is it?' *The Spinoff,* 6 February 2018 [Online]. Available at: https://thespinoff.co.nz/atea/06-02-2018/the-treaty-of-waitangi-granted-us-tino-rangatiratanga-but-what-is-it/ (Accessed: 13 March 2020).

Kelley, R. (2000) 'Forward chapter', in Robinson, C. (ed) *Black Marxism: The Making of the Black Radical Tradition*, North Carolina, University of North Carolina Press, pp. xi--xxii.

Lamusse, T., Morgan, S. and Rākete, E. (2016) *Abolitionist Demands: Toward the End of Prisons in Aotearoa*, No Pride In Prisons Press [Online]. Available at https://papa.org.nz/assets/bca4acc165/Abolitionist-Demands.pdf (Accessed 16 July 2019).

Lindberg, T. (2010) 'The doctrine of discovery in Canada', in Miller, R. et al. (eds) *Discovering Indigenous Lands: The Doctrine of Discovery in the English Colonies*, Oxford: Oxford University Press, pp. 89–125.

Lines-Mackenzie, J. (2018) 'Otorohanga still hoping for Waikeria prison expansion', *Stuff*, 22 April 2018 [Online]. Available at https://www.stuff.co.nz/national/102859006/otorohanga-still-hoping-for-waikeria-prison-expansion (Accessed: 16 July 2019).

Lumsden, S. (2016) 'Reproductive justice, sovereignty, and incarceration: Prison abolition politics and California Indians', *American Indian Culture and Research Journal*, vol. 40, no. 1, pp. 33–46.

Maynard, R. (2017) *Policing Black Lives: State Violence in Canada*. Black Point, Nova Scotia, Fernwood Publishing.

Meiners, E. (2015) 'Trouble with the child in the carceral state,' *Social Justice Journal*, vol. 41, no. 3, pp, 120–144 [Online]. Available at: http://socialjusticejournal.org/archive/137_41_3/137_07_Meiners.pdf (Accessed 16 July 2019).

Miller, R.J., Ruru, J., Behrendt, L. and Lindberg, T. (2010) *Discovering Indigenous Lands: The Doctrine of Discovery in the English Colonies*, Oxford, Oxford University Press.

Ministry of Business, Innovation and Employment. (2017) *Māori in the Labour Market*, New Zealand Government [Online]. Available at file:///C:/Users/RCW430-CAF/Downloads/STYLE%20-%20Open%20University%20Harvard_citation_hlp%20(1).pdf (Accessed 16 July 2019).

Ministry of Justice. (2019) *Youth Justice Indicators Summary Report*, New Zealand Government [Online], Available at https://www.justice.govt.nz/assets/Documents/Publications/E4NOUP-Youth-Justice-Indicators-Summary-Report-August-2019.pdf (Accessed 16 July 2019).

Pacific Partnerships (2018) 'CIMIC Group companies win NZ$750M prison PPP', *Pacific Partnerships* [Online]. Available at https://www.pacificpartnerships.com.au/en/news-and-media/latest-news/cimic-group-companies-win-nz$750m-prison-ppp (Accessed 16 July 2019).

People Against Prisons Aotearoa. (2017) 'Prison abolition is a Māori issue: The whakapapa of prisons in Aotearoa', *Mana Magazine New Zealand*, June 2017.

Reid, J. (2010) 'The Doctrine of Discovery and Canadian law', *The Canadian Journal of Native Studies*, vol 20, no. 2, pp. 335–359.

Scott, D. (1975) *Ask That Mountain: The Story of Parihaka*, Auckland, Heinemann.

Simpson, A. (2016) 'The state is a man: Theresa Spence, Loretta Saunders and the gender of settler sovereignty', *Theory & Event*, vol. 19 no. 4. Available at Project MUSE, muse.jhu.edu/article/633280.

Te Puni Kōkiri, Ministry of Maori Development. (2007) *Historical Influences Māori and the Economy*. Available at: https://www.tpk.govt.nz/documents/download/102/tpk-histoicinfluence-2007-eng.pdf (Accessed: 13 March 2020).

Te Puni Kōkiri, Ministry of Maori Development. (2011). *A Study of the Children of Prisoners, Findings from Māori data June 2011*. Available at: https://www.tpk.govt.nz/en/a-matou-mohiotanga/criminal-justice/a-study-of-the-children-of-prisoners-findings-from (Accessed: 13 March 2010).

Thibault, K. (2016) *The Canadian Carceral State: Violent Colonial Logics of Indigenous Dispossession* unpublished Masters thesis, Queens University, Available at https://qspace.library.queensu.ca/bitstream/handle/1974/14203/Thibault_Katie_L_201604_MA.pdf?sequence=1 (Accessed: 16 July 2019).

Truth and Reconciliation Commission (2015) 'Honouring the truth, reconciling for the future, summary of the final report of the Truth and Reconciliation Commission of Canada' *Truth and Reconciliation Commission of Canada* [Online]. Available at http://nctr.ca/assets/reports/Final%20Reports/Executive_Summary_English_Web.pdf. (Accessed: 29 July 2019).

Walker, R. (2016). 'Reclaiming Māori education', in Hutchings, J. and Lee-Morgan, J. (eds) *Decolonisation in Aotearoa: Education, Research and Practice*, New Zealand, NZCER Press, pp. 19–38.

Walters, A. and Longhurst, S. (2017) 'Over-represented and overlooked: The crisis of aboriginal and Torres Strait Islander women's growing over-imprisonment', *Human Rights Law Centre and Change the Record Coalition* [Online]. Available at https://static1.squarespace.com/static/580025f66b8f5b2dabbe4291/t/59378aa91e5b6cbaaa281d22/1496812234196/OverRepresented_online.pdf (Accessed: 16 July 2019).

Walters, L. (2018) 'Huge rise in female prison population "a problem": Corrections boss', *Stuff* [Online]. Available at https://www.stuff.co.nz/national/politics/101882714/huge-rise-in-female-prison-population-a-problem--corrections-boss (Accessed: 16 July 2019).

Whaipooti, J. (2018) *Address to the UN Permanent Forum on Indigenous Issues*, Facebook video, added by Māori Delegation to the United Nations 2018 [Online]. Available at https://www.facebook.com/raurangatahi/videos/162619764402967/ (Accessed: 16 July 2019).

Wolfe, P. (2006) 'Settler colonialism and the elimination of the native', *Journal of Genocide Research*, vol. 8, no. 4, pp. 387–409.

24

EXTREME HAZARDS

Emanuel "Eoz"

Extreme hazards.

Much of what starts with a "no".

INDEX

Note: Page numbers followed by "n" refer to endnotes.

abolition democracy 37, 46–47
abuse: childhood trauma and 51, 53, 60; domestic and family 53, 59–60; of power 56–57, 59–60
activist 184, 194
affect 77, 80, 83, 86–87
affective methodologies 81
alternative justice 22–23
American dream 122–123
ankle shackles 19
anti-Black 41, 99n4, 100n12
architecture 85–86
archive 82–83
Argentina 185–188, 193, 195
at-risk youth 122, 124
austerity 79

Bauer, S. 55, 57
Bernays, E. 132, 136; *see also* propaganda
Bierie, D. 54–58
bigotry, gender-nonconforming 19
Bill of Rights 123–124
book 20–21
BOP *see* Bureau of Prisons
Bronzefield prison 84–85
Bureau of Prisons 141

Camden policing 9–10
Caputo-Levine, D. 52
carceral: anti- 51, 61; apparatus 22–23, 28–29; containment 25; control 23; feminism xx, 78; habitus 52–53, 55, 59–60; institution 25, 27; knowledge 23; logic 1–8, 10, 22, 24, 31–32, 187–190, 194–195; logic, critique of 5; other 23, 28–30, 32; space 23, 26, 32
"career criminals" 127
Carpentier, N. 135, 140–141; *see also* enemy
CCWP *see* Central California Women's Facility
Central California Women's Facility xviii
citizenship 121, 123–124
code of silence 60
collective 184, 189, 192–193, 195; collective care xvii-xviii, xxi
concentration camps 132–138, 143
conformity 133, 142; *see also* consent; manipulate
consent, engineering of 132–133, 135–136, 141–144; *see also* conformity; manipulate
control units 154
cooperatives 184, 191–195
correctional officers xxi, 57, 71, 73, 188; *see also* guards, prison
Corrections Corporation of America 55
courtroom 7, 74–76
COVID-19 xix, xxi, 6, 9, 170
CPEP *see* Criminalization and Punishment Education Project
crimes against humanity 124
criminalization 2, 8; criminalize 24, 140, 142; criminalized Americans 132–133,

135–136, 139–144; criminalizing system 132, 135–136, 140–142, 144
Criminalization and Punishment Education Project 160, 163–166, 168–170
critical criminology 187

Davis, A.Y. 37, 45–46
decarceral feminism *see* feminism
decolonize 28, 99, 187, 205–206
defined and defining in/defined and defining out 163, 165–169
denaturalize 25–28, 30–32
desegregation 41
deterrence 127, 129
dirty work 144; *see also* Hughes, E.C.
discomfort 83–84, 87
Douglass, F. 42–43
drug program 68–69
drug ticket 68

elimination 199, 201–202, 204; *see also* genocide
embodiment 41, 80–81, 84
emotion 80–81, 83–84, 86
enemify 140, 144
enemy 135, 138, 140–142; *see also* Carpentier, N.
escape: imaginary 20; temporary 21

Fanon, F. 91–93
FBI *see* Federal Bureau of Investigation
Federal Bureau of Investigation 141–142
feminism 155–156; carceral xx, 3, 78, 97; decarceral 78–79, 80, 86–87, 87n3; methodologies 77–87; movement 188; queer 50
Ferrajoli, L. 105–110
The Fire Inside xix, xxi
Floyd, G. xxii, 9
Foucauldianism 155–156
Foucault, M. 105–107, 110–112, 163
Free Battered Women xx

genocide 22, 25, 27, 29, 38, 41, 200
grassroots 184, 189
guards, prison xviii, xx, 7, 18, 50–60, 72, 162, 182; *see also* correctional officers

Harcourt, B. 111
heteropatriarchy i, 5, 8, 24, 28, 78, 199, 204–205
Hobbes, T. 36, 39–40, 47
Holloway Prison 77, 79–84, 86, 152, 155
Howard League for Penal Reform 149, 154, 156
Hughes, E.C. 144; *see also* dirty work
hypersexualization 6, 17–18

ICE *see* Immigration and Customs Enforcement
immigrant 134, 137, 142; illegal 2; law 25
Immigration and Customs Enforcement 141–142
imperialism 8, 24, 30, 136, 188, 199
INCITE! xx, 3
indenture 43–44, 180, 200
Indian agent 24
indigenous justice 31
INQUEST 148, 156–157
institutionalised racism 93–94, 98, 199, 201
institutionalization xxi, 121, 124
intersectional 78, 90, 96, 98–99

jailhouse smell 19
Jim Crow 36, 45, 75–76
justice institutions 74–76, 78

labelling 54, 98, 152
landscape 8, 20, 32, 67
lawlessness 37–38, 41
life sentence xviii, 3, 68, 71, 123, 128
Lipsitz, G. 41, 44, 47n3, 94
lynch terror 45

Madrid v. Gomez 57, 126, 128–129
Manichean 36, 40–41, 46
manipulate 133, 136; *see also* conformity; consent
Māori women 204–205
Marks, C. xvii
maroon 42, 179; abolitionists 46–47; community 43, 46; intellectuals 37; radical 46–47; slave insurrections 43; society 179; strategies 46; towns 46
Marxism 91, 150–153, 155–156
Mathiesen, T. 155, 160, 163–164, 166–167, 169–170
McCarthy, J. 136
memories 18, 119
mental health: 6, 8, 30; in prison 120–131, 162, 167, 188
#MeTooBehindBars xxi
M'Naghten rule 125
modernity 22–24, 27, 38, 105, 107, 110–111, 112n1, 113n2
mutual aid xxi

NACRO *see* National Association for the Care and Resettlement of Offenders
NAP *see* Newham Alternatives Project

National Association for the Care and Resettlement of Offenders 149, 154
National Deviancy Conference 150, 157
NDC *see* National Deviancy Conference
neutralize 24, 133, 137, 168; factors 164; techniques 8, 160, 163–164, 169–170, 170n2
Newham Alternatives Project 150–151, 154

OCDC *see* Ottawa-Carleton Detention Centre
Orwell, G. 133, 144
Ottawa-Carleton Detention Centre 160–162, 164–170, 170n2
outlaw nation 7, 36–38, 44, 46

Palestinian women prisoners xxi
parole hearing xx, 69
pathological 2–3, 51, 61, 81, 153
Pelican Bay Prison 54, 128
penal humanism 7, 105–112; *see also* punitive humanism
positionality 80–82
poverty 2, 7, 22, 26, 38, 50, 79, 87, 122, 124, 131, 182, 185, 201–202, 204
Preservation of the Rights of Prisoners 148, 153–154, 157
prison industrial complex xvii, xxi, 8, 123, 199–203, 206
prison research 80, 87n4
privilege 5, 19, 23, 27, 29, 37, 92, 187
profiteering 72, 121–122, 124, 127, 180–182, 202–203
PROP *see* Preservation of the Rights of Prisoners
propaganda 132–133, 137, 143, 157; *see also* Bernays, E.
prosecutorial misconduct 181
public criminology 157
public safety xxii, 4, 23, 132, 140–144
punitive humanism 106–111; *see* penal humanism

queer 3, 10, 47, 50–51, 81, 96, 99

racial capitalism xxii, 2, 5, 140, 188, 199–201, 206
Radical Alternatives to Prison 8, 147, 150, 152
radical solidarity xvii-xxii
RAP *see* Radical Alternatives to Prison
rational choice 109, 126–127
recidivism 6, 72, 87, 127
Reclaim Holloway 77, 84
reflexive methods 79–81
rehabilitation 8, 26, 31, 78, 109, 120–121, 123, 149–150, 160–161, 190–191, 194–195
relational justice 31
reparations 9–10, 40, 44, 47, 108, 129, 132, 134, 142, 144; *see also* restitution
residential schools 22, 24–27, 30, 162, 204
resistance from below 188–194
restitution 132; *see also* reparations
rhetorical techniques 136–142
Rikers Island 19, 53

San Francisco Women Against Rape xx
segregation 22, 24–25, 27, 30, 71, 162, 182
self-determination 23, 41, 47, 198, 202, 205
sensory 81, 85
settler colonialism 36–41, 43–44, 188, 198–200, 204–206
Shumate, C. xix
site visit 77–78, 80, 84–86
slow violence 94–95, 100n11
social harm 36, 86–87, 158, 189, 195
Southern Criminology 184, 186
Southern perspective 186–194
sovereign 39–40, 46
sovereign immunity 36, 39–41
sovereignty 27, 187, 198, 202, 204–206
Stand Watie 37–38, 46
subjectivation 105–107, 110–111, 112–113n1, 113n5
suicide 26, 59, 120, 125, 127, 162
surveillance xxi, 2, 4, 6, 9, 37, 46, 56–57, 60, 91, 109, 139–140, 204–206
Survived & Punished xx

targeted 24–25, 31, 36, 43, 140, 143–144, 189
therapeutic 4, 78–79, 150
Thorazine 125–126
tino Rangatiratanga see sovereignty

voting 45, 121, 124, 129

Waikeria Prison 200–201, 203
Walker, D. 37, 42–43, 46
war on drugs 3, 41, 74–76, 120–124
Wells-Barnett, I.B. 37, 45–46
white supremacy xx-xxii, 2, 4–5, 24, 28, 30, 44, 135, 140, 188
whiteness, possessive investment in 7, 36, 41, 44–46, 47n3
Wilson, J. 109–110
WIP *see* Women In Prison
Women In Prison 148, 156–157
women's imprisonment 78–79, 156